MW00584495

PILLARS OF WEALTH

Pillars of Wealth

How to
MAKE, SAVE, & INVEST
Your Money to
Achieve Financial
Freedom

DAVID GREENE

BiggerPockets®
PUBLISHING
Denver, Colorado

Praise for
PILLARS OF WEALTH

"No one has taught me more about building wealth than David Greene."

—Brandon Turner, best-selling author
of *The Book on Rental Property Investing*

"*Pillars of Wealth* provides holistic, big-picture financial advice that few other real estate books touch. It's an excellent resource for anyone looking to take a comprehensive approach to wealth building."

—Dave Meyer, host of the BiggerPockets *On the Market* podcast
and coauthor of the best-seller *Real Estate by the Numbers*

"Earn more, spend less, and invest the difference—there are no new fundamentals, and David Greene's *Pillars of Wealth* is a to-the-point, information-packed manual that reinforces the old-school traits that lead to success. It's the path I followed to build wealth. If you're ready to play solid defense (saving and budgeting), go all-out on offense (earning and expanding your skillset), and invest wisely (optimizing your returns), then this book is for you. If you embrace the advice in this book and focus on your three wealth-building pillars, you will succeed in building lasting wealth with a strong foundation."

—Scott Trench, CEO and President of BiggerPockets,
best-selling author of *Set for Life*

"*Pillars of Wealth* is a masterfully crafted, comprehensive guide that unveils the secrets to attaining true financial freedom. This book is a roadmap for those who aspire to build lasting wealth and create a secure future."

—**David Osborn**, *New York Times* **best-selling author**

"David Greene is living proof that the fundamentals he lays out in *Pillars of Wealth* can and do lead to success. Building wealth isn't easy, but with the three pillars (offense, defense, and investing) as your foundation, you'll find yourself on the path to financial liberation."

—**Pat Hiban**, *New York Times* **best-selling author**

"I would never have turned the corner on building wealth through real estate were it not for David Greene and the financial philosophies he so clearly outlines in *Pillars of Wealth*. I'm jealous (in the best way possible) of any investor that gets to fast-track their way to real estate riches by picking up a copy of this book."

—**Rob Abasolo**, **cohost of the** *BiggerPockets Real Estate Podcast*

This publication is protected under the U.S. Copyright Act of 1976 and all other applicable international, federal, state, and local laws, and all rights are reserved, including resale rights: You are not allowed to reproduce, transmit, or sell this book in part or in full without the written permission of the publisher.

Limit of Liability: Although the author and publisher have made reasonable efforts to ensure that the contents of this book were correct at press time, the author and publisher do not make, and hereby disclaim, any representations and warranties regarding the content of the book, whether express or implied, including implied warranties of merchantability or fitness for a particular purpose. You use the contents in this book at your own risk. Author and publisher hereby disclaim any liability to any other party for any loss, damage, or cost arising from or related to the accuracy or completeness of the contents of the book, including any errors or omissions in this book, regardless of the cause. Neither the author nor the publisher shall be held liable or responsible to any person or entity with respect to any loss or incidental, indirect, or consequential damages caused, or alleged to have been caused, directly or indirectly, by the contents contained herein. The contents of this book are informational in nature and are not legal or tax advice, and the authors and publishers are not engaged in the provision of legal, tax, or any other advice. You should seek your own advice from professional advisors, including lawyers and accountants, regarding the legal, tax, and financial implications of any real estate transaction you contemplate.

Pillars of Wealth: How to Make, Save, and Invest Your Money to Achieve Financial Freedom
David Greene

Published by BiggerPockets Publishing LLC, Denver, CO
Copyright © 2023 by David Greene
All rights reserved.

Publisher's Cataloging-in-Publication Data
Names: Greene, David, author.
Title: Pillars of wealth : how to make , save , and invest your money to achieve financial freedom / David Greene.
Description: Includes bibliographical references. | Denver, CO: BiggerPockets Publishing, LLC, 2023.
Identifiers: LCCN: 2023936542 | ISBN: 9781960178022 (hardcover) | 9781960178039 (ebook)
Subjects: LCSH Finance, Personal. | Investments. | BISAC BUSINESS & ECONOMICS / Real Estate / General | BUSINESS & ECONOMICS / Personal Finance / Investing | BUSINESS & ECONOMICS / Personal Finance / Money Management | BUSINESS & ECONOMICS / Personal Finance / Budgeting
Classification: LCC HG179 .G74 2023 | DDC 332.024--dc23

Printed on recycled paper in the United States of America
10 9 8 7 6 5 4 3 2 1

MIX
Paper from
responsible sources
FSC
www.fsc.org   FSC® C008955

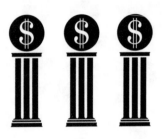

TABLE OF CONTENTS

Pillar I: Defense

Pillar II: Offense

Pillar III: Investing

Conclusion

INTRODUCTION

Why Read This Book?

You want to grow your wealth. It's okay to admit; we all do. Wealth comes in many forms, of course, from fitness to relationships to influence, but in this book, I'm referring to money. More money in your checking account, more assets on the schedule E of your tax return, and more income streams.

Does it feel weird to admit this? It shouldn't. Why is wanting more money something to be ashamed of? Is it because it's symbolic of being shallow, selfish, greedy, or any other negative emotion? We worry how we'll be perceived by others or we feel guilty for having these desires, so we keep it to ourselves.

Building wealth isn't a dirty idea. It does not mean you are selfish or greedy. In fact, in my experience, it's those who don't believe they can accumulate wealth who usually spread the negative stereotypes, like a defense mechanism from the pain of always wanting but never having. Those who don't believe in themselves become cynical and dismissive of others not afraid to go after their dreams.

Take fitness as an example. Everyone wants to look better, to be healthier and stronger and fitter, but you have to do the work on yourself. Who has achieved a certain level of fitness and then said, "You know, it's just so shallow and selfish of me to take care of myself?" Are they being shallow and selfish? No, of course not. Rather, most fitness fans are generous in sharing knowledge on meal prepping tips, nutrition, and workout routines so others can succeed too. Those who have excelled in a difficult area of life are rarely selfish with their knowledge.

Like anything else worth doing, fitness is a result of healthy habits. Attaining your desires doesn't just happen; it takes practice to create habits and get better at something. And we typically must make multiple attempts before we get better.

Wealth-building follows the same principles as fitness-building. Those who have accumulated wealth share information freely, and often encourage others to take the same journey. No one who has gained financial security says, "It's not worth it. It's better to be broke, scared, anxious, powerless, and bitter."

Now, financial freedom can be used to make others feel bad. We've all seen the videos of Ferraris or yachts filled with beautiful people drinking expensive champagne against beautiful backdrops. These images are used to sell to us. They're designed to make us want wealth *and* feel guilty for wanting it.

There are no marketing videos for all the charitable work done by those you don't even know are wealthy. The people who support orphanages, the vulnerable, the hungry. The ones who use their wealth to better humanity. How did they get wealthy? By putting their blood, sweat, and tears into changing themselves. They learned the secret of bringing value to people and getting even more back through reciprocity. Money just happens to be the medium in which value is exchanged in our society.

This Book's Purpose

This book is not to teach you a get-rich-quick scheme. Those never work. There is no long-term, sustainable path that follows any quick scheme. Not in fitness, not in relationships, not in wealth accumulation.

This book is a blueprint—a proven, simple formula for acquiring capital and investing it in real estate to grow it. You will learn about principles like the power of compounding interest and leverage, the only ways that anyone, anywhere, at any level can accumulate wealth, reach financial freedom, and become truly free to decide when, where, and how to spend their time, energy, and attention.

And this book is going to challenge you.

It will challenge your relationship with money (like using it to pursue comfort now by buying stuff instead of saving money to invest in your future).

It will challenge your beliefs about the world you live in, including expanding what you can achieve, the self-limiting beliefs holding you back, and that what you've been taught about money is frequently complete nonsense.

It will challenge the way you approach your work (bringing your best every day to grow the skills that can lead you to freedom from a job).

It will challenge the way you perceive your value (and how much you truly bring to society and your family).

It will challenge the way you believe others have amassed their wealth (which is often carefully and thoughtfully, not just handed to them).

It will challenge your habits (and encourage you to form better and healthier ones).

It will challenge your understanding of compounding (to grow not just your savings but also your interests, skills, equity creation, and more).

It will challenge your understanding of our current currency system (and how shaky and unreliable it is).

It will challenge your belief in yourself (and show you that you're capable of so much more than you can even dream).

My perspective on wealth-building isn't rooted in nebulous positive thinking or feel-good energy. It's rooted in patterns I've observed in my forty years of life. It's rooted in the principles that govern how wealth is built, which is related more to the laws of physics than to emotional manipulation. This is why I equate the wealth journey to the fitness journey. The challenge isn't in wishful thinking; it's in acquiring knowledge and then applying it regularly.

This book will guide you on your journey of accumulating wealth, including the principles that govern how it flows and to whom it flows. And that journey includes learning about real estate and the immense yet passive wealth it offers: Real estate has created more millionaires than any other asset class, which is why this book teaches you the power of real estate to build real wealth.

In addition, I'll share information to help you avoid the schemes of financial predators. Warren Buffett's rule of investing is don't lose money. To lose what you've built, especially to unscrupulous schemes, is not only financially but also emotionally debilitating. Imagine working hard to build your wealth only to lose it and have to start over from scratch. Would you do it all over again? Most wouldn't. Protecting the wealth you accumulate is equally as important as making the money, especially in the beginning of your journey when you've yet to develop the skills that make earning wealth easier.

There are so many people out there who want to take your money by pretending there are easy-peasy steps to build wealth. Every real estate guru, every real estate TV program, every real estate event that promises you'll earn wealth fast, easy, and without commitment is looking only to separate you from your money.

Consider the workout equipment sold on TV in the 1990s and 2000s. Do you remember the ThighMaster, Ab Lounge, or Shake Weight? Their premises were all the same. "Work out from the convenience of your own home! It's fast and easy! Simply use our product for ten minutes a day, and you'll get results in no time!" Cue to the smiling woman doing half sit-ups with zero sweat on her face, then cut to the image of six-pack abs. The message was clear: We have the hidden formula to avoid hard work, sweat, and pain. Give us your money and we'll provide the results.

I've yet to hear a success story from anyone who bought or used these machines. They mostly became dust collectors or makeshift clothes racks. Yet many units were sold. These companies found the formula to part a fool from their money: easy, fast, convenient!

Now, contrast this to CrossFit. The results are undeniable—I don't know anyone committed to attending CrossFit classes who doesn't eventually look significantly better than when they started. Why? Because CrossFit is physical hell. In fact, it's so difficult that CrossFit realized they had to create a culture of friendship and accountability to get people to stick with it. You have to be more concerned about the pain of missing class with others than the pain of attending it.

And guess what? It worked. An entire culture was born, and people became fitter. The lesson here is simple: If you want results, you must commit to something difficult and change your habits. In CrossFit, that includes workout habits and eating habits. In wealth-building, that includes earning habits and spending habits. If you want more wealth than you have now, change what you're doing.

So, I ask you, what about your relationship with money may be hurting you?

Your Relationship with Money

If money is...	Then you'll...
A source to make/buy friends	Spend it instead of investing it.
Exchanged for happiness	Have no control over your mood because it will depend on your financial situation.
A source of security	Have difficulty investing what you have saved.
A symbol of your value in the world	Artificially inflate your accumulation, essentially lying to yourself and others.
A way to keep score against others	Focus on earnings and pretax numbers.
An unfair and unjust tool the privileged use to hold others down	Avoid opportunities to make it, and resent others who have it.
An elusive unicorn	Never attract money.
Evil by nature and thus must be avoided	Steer clear of making connections with those who are good at wealth-building.
Confusing and beyond your capability to understand	Fall for get-rich-quick schemes and never develop the confidence to grow your money wisely.
Only a representation of value and something you can accumulate and use if you understand how it works	Love this book because you'll learn that money is only a tool, not a master.

Ultimately, money is energy. It is a means of exchange, yes, but it's also much more than that. It offers security, freedom, influence, and rewards. Do those sound like negative values? Sure, some people use money like a scorecard to let everyone know how well they're doing, but money used appropriately brings the freedom to engage in larger, grander pursuits. The fact that I am no longer tied to a traditional job gives me the freedom to write this book. This book will only sell as well as the information it contains, incentivizing me to write the best book possible to help you the most I possibly can.

In this case, making money on the sale of this book incentivizes me to be and do better. It encourages me to avoid being lazy and instead work on my writing. If the pursuit of money requires excellence, discipline, delayed gratification, and other virtues, what do we have to be ashamed of?

This book has a formula that anybody can follow. It contains information, or more accurately a perspective, that you likely haven't heard before. It may even directly contradict some of the things you've been taught about money, hard work, and capitalism.

No matter your starting place, I know you can increase your wealth. Oftentimes, it's those who start furthest back who discover superstar speed with momentum. I hope that a commitment to following this formula brings out the best version of you, and that it helps you bring more value to others, thus creating a virtuous cycle of wealth-building in your life. The most important step in creating more wealth is *raising our standards and expectations of ourselves*. To be better, be smarter, and be open to possibilities.

You are the only one who can decide the standards and expectations you want to set for yourself. You alone choose how much you can grow; you alone decide how you spend what you accumulate, how you spend your time, and what you focus on.

Everyone struggles with doubt, hopelessness, and insecurity at some point. These feelings convince us that we are powerless, a feather on the wind of fate. It's not true. Experiencing those emotions is normal. Expect and anticipate them, just don't believe them.

You stand at base camp deciding your financial life from this point forward. Reading this book and learning about passive income from real estate will lead you to financial independence; each step will move you closer to financial freedom and away from financial worries. This will be nothing short of a hero's journey. It will require all your skills, talents, and fortitude. Consider sharing your journey with others to increase your odds of building the right habits to free yourself from money worries. Just like with the CrossFit example, surround yourself with others who want the same thing as you— financial freedom. It's better to share this journey with others, to hold each other accountable, to lean on each other when things aren't going smoothly, and to cheer on each other when they are.

Chapter 1
THE GOAL

A cord of three strands is not easily broken.
—ECCLESIASTES 4:12

Why Work to Build Wealth through Real Estate?

You're reading this book because you want to build your wealth. Maybe you don't have any. Maybe you had some and lost it. Maybe you have some but want more. Does it really matter why?

According to *Forbes*, it does.

> Anyone who wants to get rich needs to know why they want to get rich. The "why" is often more important than the "how." After all, it is the "why" that will determine whether a person's motivations really are strong enough to drive them for the years and decades it might take to get rich.[1]

As I mentioned earlier, we all have our own motives for wanting to become wealthy. Some motives are noble, like having the time to do charity work and the money to help those who matter to us. Some

---

1   Rainer Zitelmann, "Scientific Study: Luxury Is Not What Motivates Rich People to Become Rich," *Forbes*, June 8, 2020, https://www.forbes.com/sites/rainerzitelmann/2020/06/08/scientific-study-luxury-is-not-what-motivates-rich-people-to-become-rich/.

are self-centered, like wanting to feel important over others. Your motives matter. They are your fuel, and not all fuel burns the same way or at the same rate.

This same *Forbes* article listed results from the author's book, *The Wealth Elite: A Groundbreaking Study of the Psychology of the Super Rich*:

In-depth interviews were conducted with forty-five superrich individuals, most of whom were self-made entrepreneurs with a net worth of $33 million to $1 billion. On a scale from 0 to 10, the interviewees were asked to explain what they associate with "money."

1. Security, namely that "I won't have any financial problems unless I make a massive mistake"
2. Freedom and independence
3. The opportunity to use money for new things, to invest
4. Being able to afford the finer things in life
5. Having money is personal confirmation that you got a lot of things right
6. With a large amount of money, and despite the envy the wealthy are sometimes confronted with, you receive greater recognition and have the opportunity to meet interesting people

In first place, by a wide margin, the interviewees rated "freedom and independence" as the aspect they most strongly associate with money. Only five interviewees selected a value below 7 for this aspect. ...Thus, it is the desire for freedom and independence, not the pursuit of luxury goods, that is the most important motivation for most rich people to become rich .[2]

Positive motivations like the freedom and independence to do what you want with your life are much stronger than negative ones, like seeking the approval of others.

---

2   Rainer Zitelmann, "Scientific Study: Luxury Is Not What Motivates Rich People to Become Rich," *Forbes*, June 8, 2020, https://www.forbes.com/sites/rainerzitelmann/2020/06/08/scientific-study-luxury-is-not-what-motivates-rich-people-to-become-rich/.

The right motivation also make sense outside of a discussion about wealth. It is what drove leaders like the Scottish knight Sir William Wallace, Revolutionary War hero George Washington, and religious prophets like Jesus and Muhammad. Even fictional characters like Maximus in the movie *Gladiator* (or any comic book superhero, for that matter) are motivated by positive reasons.

There are four foundational reasons to create wealth: freedom, purpose, security, and passion/fun. Focusing on these reasons will help provide you the right motivation to build wealth through real estate. On the other hand, if you want to make money only to impress others, you'll lose your drive—and the money will stop flowing because you've stopped being motivated. It's simply better to accumulate wealth for the right foundational reasons.

Freedom

Freedom is the most important reason; it comes in many forms and shows its value in many ways. Some people say that money is the root of all evil, but this misunderstanding comes from a misquoted Bible verse: "For the love of money is the root of all evil."[3] It means that loving money more than people causes pain and grief.

What if you seek wealth not for itself but as a value that brings you freedom?

There is the freedom from pain; specifically the pain that comes with poverty. Money helps you and your loved ones escape into better living situations. (I'll talk about this more later in Security.)

There's also the freedom from feeling stuck, like being able to leave a job you don't like, or worse, a job you despise or that is physically exhausting. Working a job that doesn't use your talents, abilities, and passions is a terrible way to live, especially when you have stress, anxiety, and discontentment in the workplace and in life.

The freedom to spend your time where and how you wish requires wealth. Being able to travel, work from remote locations, and have a well-balanced life are blessings. I would be miserable if I were forced back into working in an office or working for others. My abilities to speak, teach, write, and analyze properties are perfect for real estate, and I don't have to be in an office to do this. The teams I lead and

---

3 1 Timothy 6:10 (NIV)

relationships I build are much more fulfilling than simply clocking in and out every day. Financial independence motivates me to do the type of work I love.

Purpose

A strong sense of purpose, such as the ability to change your life or someone else's, is important when you're working toward financial independence. Because money is energy, it's one of the easiest and most flexible ways to impact the lives of those around you. From the Greater Good Science Center at the University of California, Berkeley: "Studies have uncovered evidence that humans are biologically wired for generosity. Acting generously activates the same reward pathway that is activated by sex and food, a correlation that may help to explain why giving and helping feel good."[4]

It is impossible to pay attention to someone else's needs when you feel like you're drowning in your own problems. As you grow your wealth, you'll find you not only have more means and resources to help others but that you also have more skills and knowledge. Why do I say this? Because those who accumulate wealth often are excellent problem solvers or have the desire to bring value to others. It's common to find the most successful folks guiding others and teaching them how to guide others in turn. This cycle helps many people in the beginning of their real estate journey toward wealth, and then they help others follow their journeys.

Security

In Abraham Maslow's hierarchy of needs, only our physiological needs for food and water are more important than our security and safety needs. If you don't feel safe, you can't enjoy life. For example: If you live in a dangerous neighborhood, it's hard to focus on much else than trying to stay safe. Money provides the opportunity to live easier and happier in a more secure area, and opens you up to think about new opportunities.

Wealth provides safety in other ways, like being able to buy health insurance or plenty of food. It allows you to not worry about how to pay

---

4   Summer Allen, "The Science of Generosity," Greater Good Science Center, May 2018, https://ggsc.berkeley.edu/images/uploads/GGSC-JTF_White_Paper-Generosity-FINAL.pdf.

your utilities or car payments, and especially not worry about paying your rent or mortgage. The constant fear of losing your home plays a significant role in your well-being. Research published in *Social Science & Medicine* found that people over age 50 who fell behind on rent were more likely to experience depression; renters living under the threat of eviction experienced poorer self-reported health outcomes, such as high blood pressure; and people threatened by eviction were more likely to have alcohol dependence.[5] In short, it's difficult to live a healthy, safe life without a strong sense of financial security.

Passion and Fun

Passion is what makes life fun! A 2009 study published in *Psychosomatic Medicine* revealed that those who experienced higher levels of fun and leisure time had a higher quality of life and better physical health.[6] This is why following your passion is important: When you spend your life working a job you don't like, or have no goals in mind, or can't see a light at the end of the tunnel, your quality of life is low.

Wealth also opens doors to activities that are fun. Beach vacations with zip-lining and jet-skiing, overseas trips, and sports like golf or marksmanship are pricey. Fun, but pricey. So is eating at fine restaurants and living in areas with beautiful weather. Those with wealth have opened doors that lead to a better quality of life.

How Wealth Is Measured

"Wealth" can be objectively defined by determining net worth and cash flow. These are simple ways to measure wealth, but what do these terms really mean?

Net Worth

This is the most common way to measure wealth. Your net worth is determined by taking the value of all your assets and subtracting

---

5   Hugo Vasquez-Vera et al., "The Threat of Home Eviction and Its Effects on Health through the Equity Lens: A Systematic Review," *Social Science & Medicine* 175 (February 1, 2017): 199–208, https://doi.org/10.1016/j.socscimed.2017.01.010.

6   Sarah D. Pressman et al., "Association of Enjoyable Leisure Activities with Psychological and Physical Well-Being." *Psychosomatic Medicine* 71, no. 7 (2009): 725–32. https://doi.org/10.1097/psy.0b013e3181ad7978.

the total amount of your liabilities. This means adding together the value of your assets like real estate, stocks, and capital, and then subtracting the amount of the debts you owe. Assets can be rental properties, your home, your car, your retirement account, and so on. Your debt includes mortgages, your car note, credit card debt, student loan debt, and so on.

The following items are the components of net worth.

- **Asset**. Anything you can sell that has a market value that's easy to measure.
- **Liability**. Debt you owe, often tied to assets used as security for the debt.
- **Equity**. The difference between the market value of your asset and the amount of debt you owe on it.

Example: You have a primary residence worth $250,000, with a mortgage balance of $175,000. That means you have $75,000 of equity in it. This is $75,000 toward your net worth.

Tracking your assets and liabilities on a spreadsheet is simple and extremely useful. The following is an example of a portfolio of real estate:

Asset	Value	Debt
44 Main Street (your home)	$250,000	$175,000
35 Jones Street (rental)	$150,000	$100,000
416 Pine Street (rental)	$75,000	$50,000
22 Fernley Road (rental)	$300,000	$200,000
765 Athens Drive (rental)	$125,000	$75,000
965 Stone Road (rental)	$200,000	$100,000
2017 Toyota Corolla (your car)	$10,000	$5,000
Total	$1,110,000	$705,000

In the above example, we can easily determine that the assets total $1,110,000 and the liabilities total $705,000. This gives a net worth of $405,000 (i.e., subtracting liabilities from assets). Adding the amount of capital you have in the bank would be all that's needed to complete the process. In most cases, it is faster, easier, and more efficient to build equity—that is, increase your net worth—via real estate by exchanging early equity in smaller properties for more equity in bigger deals or more income in different asset classes.

As you can see, net worth is simple to measure, especially with the help of a spreadsheet. Tracking the value of your assets and the amount of debt you owe on each asset is useful when combined with measuring cash flow.

The keys to building your net worth are:

- Buying appreciating assets.
- Exchanging them for better, bigger assets.
- Tracking your equity growth and its relationship to your net worth.
- Focusing on assets that can be easily exchanged or sold. For example, a business that depends on your involvement is difficult to sell and thus not a true asset.
- Considering ten ways to build passive wealth through real estate and how to then capitalize on them (explained in Chapter 12).

Cash Flow

Cash flow is the difference between what you make and what you spend. In real estate terms, it is the difference between the income a property produces and the expenses associated with it. If, at the end of the month, you have income left over after expenses, then you have a positive cash flow. Spreadsheets are useful to track the cash flow of your properties. Let's take the 22 Fernley Road rental property as an example:

Monthly Income/Expense	Amount
Rent	+$2,500
Mortgage	-$1,200
Property Taxes	-$310
Insurance	-$50
Property Management Fee	-$200
Maintenance	-$125
Capital Expenditures	-$125
Total Cash Flow	**$490**

In this example, the rental property produces $2,500 per month, with $2,010 in total expenses for the month. This means a monthly cash flow of $490 for the property, provided all expenses stay the same and you don't increase the rent. With your rental properties, you can add rows to track additional cash flow in, total expenses out, and the final amount accumulated.

Cash flow is an important metric in measuring wealth because it represents a recurring amount that will more or less be the same every month. This money can be saved or invested; with enough cash flow, you can substitute it for your W-2 income and quit the job you don't like. If you like your job, you can use cash flow to cover your living expenses and then save 100 percent of your income. At later stages of the wealth-building cycle, this income can be used to purchase extravagant items like nicer cars, trips, second homes, and jewelry.

Building streams of cash flow allows you to stop trading time for money and exit the rat race, a strategy that will become much clearer later in the book. These streams also allow you to earn more income than is typically possible when trading time for money, and it increases your rate of savings. Many fundamentals of prudent investing can be learned and developed through acquiring cash-flowing assets.

While real estate investing is the best known form of cash flow, you can also acquire it through the purchase of certain equities, investments into funds/syndications, and business opportunities, all of which will be covered in more detail later in the book.

The keys to building cash flow from real estate are:
- Learning to analyze properties from the perspective of the profit (cash flow) they may produce.
- Viewing real estate and other assets as income streams, as opposed to emotional objects.
- Comparing one asset class to another and looking for the highest cash-on-cash (CoC) return with the highest passive income (explained in Passive Income below).
- Learning the fundamentals of being a landlord and property manager in the early stages of your wealth-building journey to keep more of your income.
- Buying assets with income streams likely to grow each year.

Passive Income

Passive income is important to include when determining wealth because it is easy to build a large cash flow—or even net worth—but be handcuffed to the assets that built it. Not all assets are created equal; some will require more of your time, attention, and energy. Oftentimes, assets with the greatest cash flow also require the most work. It doesn't make sense to build your portfolio—the bedrock of your wealth—on a foundation that will prevent you from experiencing the freedom, fun, and security that your wealth is meant to provide.

I use what I call the "headache factor" to evaluate any potential investment opportunity. For instance, owning blue chip stocks is much less of a headache than owning a pool service company that requires your direct involvement and intervention. Even though buying or starting a small business may provide a higher CoC return, it comes at a price. The idea in building wealth is to buy investments, not trade one job for another. The ideal portfolio requires little of your time and attention and performs reliably without your involvement. Earning income through passive assets gives you back your time as you're increasing your wealth, which in turn supports your freedom.

You also get agency over where you must be—earning money through assets and investments doesn't require you to be in any particular location to manage them. This is so different from clocking in to work onsite, or overseeing a business or franchise.

Passive income can be measured by tracking how many hours a week you spend managing your portfolio; as you get older, you want assets that require less of your time and attention. If you find the passive income streams you've built require more than five hours of your time each week, you don't have passive income or a pure form of wealth. Understanding wealth for more than just its net worth or cash flow means you learn to build a portfolio geared toward passive income, not just massive income.

The keys to building passive wealth are:

- Looking for more than just the CoC return; also considering the work, time, and energy involved.
- Understanding that higher risk often comes with a higher return, while options with lower returns may come with less risk.
- Early in your journey when you have less cash flow, focusing on acquiring appreciating assets that may take more of your time

and attention but will increase in value. You can exchange them later for more passive income projects.

- To save money, learning how to be your own property manager. Later you can hire others to manage your assets to make your passive income streams even more passive.
- Learning to master leverage, eventually hiring others to manage your properties, allowing you to focus on higher revenue-generating activities.
- Learning tools like the 1031 like-kind exchange, return on equity, and cash-out refinances to buy passive income streams later in your journey.

These tools will be covered throughout the book in more detail.

The Three Pillars

This book is called *Pillars of Wealth* because financial independence is the result of having these three pillars as your foundation: defense, offense, and investing.

Defense

The first pillar is defense. In this context, I am referring to your ability to save what you've earned, a concept that is simple to understand but difficult to master. Sound defense also will create a hunger for later offense opportunities.

If your goal is to become wealthy, how important is defense? According to a *Forbes* article:

In the mid-1990s, two American researchers, Thomas J. Stanley and William D. Danko, surprised America with their book, *The Millionaire Next Door*, which quickly became a best-seller. They based their book on interviews they had conducted [with] 1,000 Americans with an average net wealth of $3.7 million.

- 50% of the millionaires had paid $399 or less for the most expensive suit they ever purchased and 75% had never paid more than $599.
- 50% of the surveyed millionaires had never spent more

than $140 on a pair of shoes and 75% had never spent more than $199.

- 50% of the millionaires had never in their lives spent more than $235 for a wristwatch and 75% had only ever paid less than $1,125.
- 50% of the millionaires never spent more than $29,000 for a motor vehicle and 95% had never spent more than $69,000.[7]

It was clear that those interviewees weren't interested in showing off or spending their wealth foolishly. Yet, the interviewers also found that the average American buyer—not a millionaire—"spent 78 percent of what the typical self-made millionaire did for his or her most expensive motor vehicle." That is not a defensive play.

Those who were interviewed were not motivated by what you might expect. They didn't spend money on glitzy, expensive items just because they could. They played defense with their money. Without defense, you cannot establish any reliable traction. Making more money only to spend it won't benefit you. To guide you on this journey, repeat this mantra: Every dollar you make is yours to keep.

Offense
The second pillar on your journey to wealth is to play offense, which is your ability to earn income. After you've mastered the fundamentals of defense, your next step is to add offense, or earn more income to net you more results. It's not just about saving money (defense), you must first earn it—and keep on earning it (and that's offense). One pillar without the other cannot build wealth.

To build your wealth, you typically acquire capital (that is, money) and then invest it. Pillar II in this book teaches you how to master offense.

Investing
Now for the third pillar: intelligent investing. There are many ways to invest your money, but as Andrew Carnegie said, "Ninety percent of all millionaires become so through owning real estate."

---

7   Rainer Zitelmann, "Scientific Study: Luxury Is Not What Motivates Rich People to Become Rich," *Forbes*, June 8, 2020, https://www.forbes.com/sites/rainerzitelmann/2020/06/08/scientific-study-luxury-is-not-what-motivates-rich-people-to-become-rich/.

This is how Barbara Corcoran says real estate investing snowballed her wealth:

> Buying real estate has made me rich—mostly through necessity, not by design. I bought my first itty-bitty studio after scraping together a few bucks because I needed to live somewhere anyway. A few years later, the studio doubled in value, giving me enough cash to plunk down 50 percent on a one-bedroom apartment. That soon rolled into a two-bedroom, then a three-bedroom, and finally landed me in my ten-room penthouse on Fifth Avenue in New York City. Buying that tiny studio was the most important decision I made because it got me in the game.[8]

Corcoran has built a real estate empire and is a regular investor on the TV show *Shark Tank*. Some of her simple but powerful facts about real estate are:

- Scrape together enough of a down payment to get started.
- Use loans to buy real estate.
- Real estate appreciates at above average rates compared to other investment options.
- Exchange one property for a bigger and better property.
- Use the idea of a "snowball rolling downhill."
- The longer you hold real estate, the better it performs.[9]

Some people look for "creative" ways to purchase real estate: They borrow money from friends or family, they buy properties directly from sellers with no money down, they even use credit cards or short-term, high-rate loans to get started. While it is possible to start investing in real estate this way, it's certainly not advisable. For one, it's obviously risky. More importantly, those who have built sustainable wealth through real estate have done so using the value principles they developed in the workplace and in life. Making and

---

8   The Oracles, "Real Estate Is Still the Best Investment You Can Make Today, Millionaires Say—Here's Why," *CNBC*, October 2, 2019, https://www.cnbc.com/2019/10/01/real-estate-is-still-the-best-investment-you-can-make-today-millionaires-say.html.

9   "Barbara Corcoran's Wild Real Estate Tactics You'll Want to Repeat," interview by David Greene and Rob Abasolo, *BiggerPockets Real Estate Podcast*, BiggerPockets, May 9, 2023, www.biggerpockets.com/blog/real-estate-763

saving money to build your first down payment and eventually using that real estate purchase as the financial reserve (the equity), you can use to buy more real estate is the only smart way to grow your real estate portfolio safely, consistently, and over time. Those who use the discipline of earning and saving their own capital have an advantage over those who use other people's money: It means more to them.

The Danger in Skipping the Pillars

The three pillars—defense, offense, and investing—will give you the foundation for building your real estate wealth the right way. Wealth easily gained doesn't last long, as *Reader's Digest* will tell you: "Whether they win $500 million or $1 million, about 70 percent of lotto winners lose or spend all that money in five years or less."[10] Five years is an amazingly short period of time to lose that kind of money. How does it happen? Because most of those who inherit wealth quickly simply aren't prepared to manage it. Those who make their money through fame don't always fare so much better. For example:

- Singer Michael Jackson was over $400 million in debt,[11] and close to foreclosure on his Neverland Ranch at the time of his death.[12]
- Boxer Mike Tyson, who once amassed more than $300 million, later filed for bankruptcy.[13]
- Rapper MC Hammer went from having $30 million to being $13 million in debt.[14]
- Actor Burt Reynolds, by his own estimation, was worth over $60 million, and he lost it all. Reynolds admitted, "I've lost more

10 Michelle Crouch, "13 Things Lotto Winners Won't Tell You: Life After Winning the Lottery," *Reader's Digest*, April 27, 2023, https://www.rd.com/list/13-things-lottery-winners/.

11 Jeff Gottlieb, "Michael Jackson Trial: Pop Star Was 'Tapped Out,' Millions in Debt," *Los Angeles Times*, August 12, 2013, https://www.latimes.com/local/lanow/la-xpm-2013-aug-12-la-me-ln-michael-jackson-debt-20130812-story.html.

12 "Michael Jackson Died Deeply in Debt," *Billboard*, June 26, 2009, https://www.billboard.com/music/music-news/michael-jackson-died-deeply-in-debt-268276/.

13 Matt Egan, "Mike Tyson: I Didn't Think I'd Survive My 30s." *CNN Business*, May 24, 2017, https://money.cnn.com/2017/05/24/investing/mike-tyson-bankruptcy/index.html.

14 Kelly Phillips Erb, "IRS to Rapper: It's Hammertime!" *Forbes*, December 8, 2013, https://www.forbes.com/sites/kellyphillipserb/2013/12/08/irs-to-rapper-its-hammertime/.

money than is possible because I just haven't watched it."[15]

Were these people not intelligent enough to manage money? That's a hard argument to make when they all reached the pinnacle of their respective careers. The common thread woven into each story is that they made massive sums of money, but they also led outsized lives and did not properly manage their fortunes. Being a lottery winner, sports star, or performer can mean big bucks and no preparation on how to handle big wealth. When compared to the small business owner who learns strong financial fundamentals to keep their business in business, or the corporate employee who climbs the ladder by taking on more and higher responsibility over time, it's easy to see how quickly money leaves those who have no preparation, let alone preparation for that kind of wealth.

Building your three pillars will not only give you the best chance for success in real estate, but it also will make it difficult for you *not* to succeed.

KEY TAKEAWAYS

- True wealth—the kind that can be sustained over time—from real estate is built on the foundation of three pillars: defense, offense, and investing.
- Sustainable wealth takes time to create.
- Net worth is determined by adding the value of all your assets and subtracting the amount of liabilities.
- Cash flow is defined as the difference between the income a property produces and the expenses associated with it.
- Not all assets are created equal; beware the ones that require too much of your time, attention, and energy.
- Passive income is measured by tracking the numbers of hours you spend each week managing your portfolio.
- Be disciplined to earn and protect your wealth and know how to manage it.

---

15 Ned Zeman, "Burt Reynolds Isn't Broke, but He's Got a Few Regrets." *Vanity Fair*, November 5, 2015, https://www.vanityfair.com/hollywood/2015/11/burt-reynolds-on-career-bankruptcy-regrets.

PILLAR I

DEFENSE

Chapter 2
DEFENSE FIRST

Wealth, like a tree, grows from a tiny seed. The first copper you save is the seed from which your tree of wealth shall grow. The sooner you plant that seed the sooner shall the tree grow. And the more faithfully you nourish that seed, the sooner shall the tree grow. And the more faithfully you nourish and water that tree with consistent savings, the sooner may you bask in the contentment beneath its shade.
—GEORGE SAMUEL CLASON, *THE RICHEST MAN IN BABYLON*

Time is Money

The world we live in requires us to spend money. Anyone who goes out for a meal, pays for gas, makes a car payment, buys an app for their smartphone, watches cable TV, and even takes a hot shower incurs expenses.

The reality is that we trade our time (work hours) for money, and time is a precious commodity we never get back. Time is the ultimate form of currency, and it's flying out of our pockets faster than we realize. Take a pair of $140 Nike sneakers for example. For someone who makes $20 an hour and is taxed at 12.5 percent, those Nikes actually cost a day of work.

Defense is about limiting how much money leaves your pocket that you never get back—and how much time you spend that you never get back. When you spend money carelessly, you lose more than just today's time. How? Money saved and reinvested earns more money. Money invested today begins making more money tomorrow, and that money starts making more money the day after that. Over time, we develop an entire workforce of money that labors as we sleep, continually increasing our returns. Compound interest happens independent of us trading our time for it.

We are not free to do as we please when we're trapped in the cycle of trading time for money to pay for our needs. Most of us start our lives stuck in this pattern:

Time ➤ Money ➤ Things

Saving, investing, and reinvesting returns is the only way to break the cycle of trading time for money. This creates freedom and puts you in control of your life. The freedom pattern to wealth looks like this:

Time ➤ Money ➤ Investments ➤ Money ➤ Things

When *your* time is in *your* control, you can choose to spend it on making more money, or making it in smarter ways, or simply doing the things that you want to do.

Mantra: A Portion of What You Make is Yours to Keep

Gaining freedom over our time only occurs when we stop trading time for money. How do we do that? By buying cash-flowing assets. When you invest your money and it starts passively earning more money for you, you've begun the process of freeing yourself from trading time for money.

Having money to invest starts with saving the money you've already earned. Conventional wisdom says to save 10 percent of your income, but I have no idea where that number comes from. Maybe it's that it feels like an achievable yet impactful amount for the average American who has limited practice saving money and lives paycheck to paycheck. Regardless, it's a great place to start.

Saving 10 percent of your income requires discipline, focus, and drive. Saving more than that requires even more discipline, focus, and drive. This means you must focus on your future and your goals, not on your present and your comfort. Saving more of your income is a step toward becoming a wealthier version of yourself. You'll start to think, "How can I save more? How can I make more? How can I work harder? How can I improve my return?" The better you get at saving money and asking yourself questions like these, the faster you'll break the cycle of trading time for money.

Your Mission, Should You Choose to Accept it

None of us can avoid spending money. We need certain things to live, like food and shelter. We also need to *live* in our world. In addition to spending on your own needs, others spend your money as well—and not just in the ways you might think. Your friends want you to spend money by going out for drinks. Your nephew expects a birthday present every year. Your neighbor wants you to pay for half of the fence. These are expenditures that others expect you to make.

Your biggest threat won't be from those you love or are close to—it will be from strangers whose job it is to identify fools and separate them from their money. I'm talking about marketers, advertisers, and influencers. Take a walk through a shopping mall like a sociologist: The layout and store windows are carefully designed to simultaneously make you feel like you need something you didn't know you needed and make buying whatever it is they're selling easy for you. They must create the need before they can sell you their product.

Have you ever walked by a Cinnabon in the mall or airport, smelled the pastries, and then bought one, when you hadn't thought about Cinnabon until that very moment ?

Turns out Cinnabon's infamous scent is a deliberate and methodical tactic used to convince you to buy cinnamon rolls. According to *The Wall Street Journal*, the bakery chain really wants to lure customers in with the smell and employs many methods to do so: The stores are located in malls and airports so that the "smells can linger" in the buildings; cinnamon rolls are baked at least every thirty minutes; and to keep the scent in the air, some stores even warm up sheets of cinnamon and brown sugar. Ovens are also placed near the front of the store "so the enticing smell of warm cinnamon rolls escapes when oven doors open." Kat Cole, the former president of Cinnabon, told

WSJ that sales dropped "significantly" when ovens were put in the back at a test location.[16]

Clever, right? Create the hunger, provide the food. It's not just Cinnabon deploying these tactics. An article in *U.S. News & World Report* reveals seven methods that advertisers use to make us spend money.[17] I add my definition to these deeds in square brackets.

1. Appealing to our greed and other vices [finds our weakest points]
2. Exciting our emotions [removes us from logic and reason]
3. Suggesting everyone else is doing it [appeals to our FOMO, or fear of missing out]
4. Using attractive people in advertising [appeals to our sexuality]
5. Employing repetition [wears us down]
6. Glossing over cost [separates our decision-making from understanding that we are trading time for the product]
7. Making you laugh [lowers our defenses]

Have you ever felt confused and tired by the end of a trip to the shopping mall? Now you know why. You were led into a labyrinth of deceit intentionally created to separate you from your money by beating down your defenses and forcing you to struggle with your weakest parts. And this is just the mall! The same thing happens every day on TV, on social media and internet advertising, and in magazines. The aim is to take our money from us.

Before getting upset, let me caution you that it does no good to see yourself as a victim. Everyone is in this same struggle, battle, or game (however you see it), but it's lack of knowledge that makes you lose. When you are aware, you can turn the tide in your favor; you can fight back. Your mission, should you choose to accept it, is to engage in this battle for your money and stop the strangers who are trying to take it from you.

---

16 Sarah Nassauer, "Using Scent as a Marketing Tool, Stores Hope It—and Shoppers—Will Linger," *The Wall Street Journal*, May 20, 2014, https://www.wsj.com/articles/SB10001424052702303468704579573953132979382.

17 Geoff Williams, "7 Tricks Advertisers Use to Make You Spend Money," *U.S. News & World Report*, September 10, 2015, https://money.usnews.com/money/personal-finance/articles/2015/09/10/7-tricks-advertisers-use-to-make-you-spend-money.

Money as a Store of Energy

To the uninitiated, money is a means to an end. We've moved from trading our apples for someone else's chicken eggs to exchanging time for dollars, which can then be exchanged for anything else. The practical purpose of money is clear, but something powerful is being missed: Money is not just a practical tool, it's also a store of energy.

Michael Saylor, a co-founder of MicroStrategy and a bitcoin enthusiast, makes an interesting argument for why he believes cryptocurrency will continue to gain value over time. On *The David McWilliams Podcast*, Saylor stated "the inability to store your economic energy in the form of property or money over time is an economic death sentence." Saylor invested in bitcoin when he realized the U.S. government had introduced so many physical dollars into the U.S. supply that they had bled the value of the money already in existence. Bitcoin, Saylor believes, will hold its value because it cannot be deflated.

Saylor's comment that money is a store of economic energy is spot on. While I have no idea if bitcoin will end up as a store of economic value in the future, I do know that economic value must be stored *somewhere*. Unlike Saylor, I believe real estate is a safer bet than bitcoin. Later in the book, I share information and strategies related to using real estate as a store of energy. Before you can invest in real estate, however, you first need money.

When you go to work, you expend energy and are compensated for that energy. When you get paid, you are receiving energy from your job in the form of a paycheck; think of what you do with that money as how you store the energy you receive for working. You can store your eight-hour workday in the form of dollars in the bank or in the form of Nike sneakers in your closet. Which of those two are likely to hold their value? How much are those shoes worth to someone else after you've worn them? If the shoes do hold some value, how easy will it be to find someone to exchange their dollars for the energy the sneakers have been storing for you?

Clearly, storing your energy in the form of dollars is better than in the form of shoes. Unfortunately, we all have closets full of energy that is no longer useful for anything else. Standard currency is the easiest way to extract the energy you've stored from the work you've done. Spending money on stuff gives away that energy. When you bought those shoes, you received the benefit of wearing them, but you lost the energy of the eight hours of work you did. The shoe store gained that money energy and used it toward the expenses associated with running that business. With every purchase, you're taking energy from yourself and giving it to someone or something else. If you want to store the energy that money brings, you need to save that money, not trade it away.

The money you earned through hours at work, like those calories you burned doing CrossFit, are how you honor yourself. The hours build up your savings, so you can invest in real storages of value, like real estate or stocks or other investment opportunities. These investments are "energy generators" that grow your wealth, even without your involvement. They are better storage options because they increase in value the longer you hold them. The more energy (money) you can pour into these generators (real estate), the faster your energy (money) will multiply. But the more you spend on things, the less energy (money) you'll have to build your real wealth.

Schemes to Avoid

Before going further into the steps of building wealth, I want to discuss approaches offered by other authors, personalities, and so-called authorities. Most approaches focus on one element, such as saving money, but that doesn't lead to *complete* financial freedom. This is because their approach leads to wealth being created in one way. Let's do a quick review of alternative approaches and their inherent problems.

Jump Out of the Plane and Build the Parachute on the Way Down

This doesn't sound like good planning, does it? While I think there is a contingent of people who might work well under this stress, it's clearly too risky and an unwise way to build wealth. Quitting your job before you have another, or starting an endeavor before you've crafted a game plan for success, puts unnecessary stress and strain on you. This approach also decreases your chances of success by removing a vital part of wealth-building: creating a working plan.

Abraham Lincoln is credited with this saying: "Give me six hours

to chop down a tree and I will spend the first four sharpening the ax."
This book outlines a strategy that is relatively simple, but it requires
an "upfront investment" that you take the time to understand it fully.
Impulsive folks want to jump into a new endeavor and figure it out on
the way. Wiser investors takes the time to understand the principles
of investing so they can engage in the endeavor with passion and
intensity and smarts.

Save-a-Latte

What should you cut back on to save for buying real estate? The
strategy of not buying a morning coffee and instead investing the
money in the stock market was first popularized in David Bach's
Smart Women Finish Rich, published in 1999. The book made the
argument that saving the $5 you would spend on a daily coffee and
investing it at an 11 percent annualized return could explode into $2
million by the time you reached 65 years of age. With numbers like
that, who wouldn't put down the espresso and go on a savings spree?

The problem was that the math didn't work. An article published
by *Slate* discusses how the theory was disproved:

> Bach knew his archetypal latte guzzler could not be spending
> $5 on a single latte, not in 1999. So he added a biscotti to the
> bill and factored in the incidental Diet Cokes and candy bars
> he assumed his subject also bought. Even then his numbers
> didn't quite add up. Five dollars a day, 365 days a year is $1,825.
> So Bach "rounded" the number up to $2,000 annually. Other
> numbers were equally as suspect. A 10 or 11 percent average
> annual return on stock market investments? The Dow Jones
> Industrial Average showed a 9 percent average annual rate of
> return between 1929 and 2009. When *Bad Money Advice*, a
> popular personal finance blog, ran the numbers, remembering
> those two pesky financial details, he came up with $173,000.[18]

If anything, these rounding errors do more to highlight the power
of compound interest over time than the power of saving on small

---

18 Helaine Olen, "Buying Coffee Every Day Isn't Why You're in Debt," *Slate*, May 26, 2016,
https://slate.com/business/2016/05/the-latte-is-a-lie-and-buying-coffee-has-nothing-
to-do-with-debt-an-excerpt-from-helaine-olens-pound-foolish.html.

treats like coffee. Rather than eliminating the smallest expenses in your budget, you're much better off tackling the largest. For most people, this is their housing expense. While giving up coffee may not seem as much of a sacrifice as giving up the comfort of your own space, consider the impact of this at scale.

When comparing a daily $5 coffee (about $150 per month) to a $2,500 per month rent payment, you're talking about nearly seventeen times the difference in costs. In other words, eliminating your monthly rent is nearly seventeen times more significant than saving on cups of coffee. Compounded over thirty years, the results are simply beyond compare. To make things even crazier, this accounts for rent of only $2,500 a month. In reality, that gets larger every year with rent increases.

The amount you will collect from your tenants also increases, and it does not include how the property will appreciate over thirty years. This book will teach you the power of "house hacking," the simplest way to get others to pay your housing expenses and eliminate them from your budget.

Follow the Newest Trend

New ways to save and make money are always appealing, in large part because not enough time has passed to prove if the new method has pitfalls. I've seen the trends of buying timeshares, Beanie Babies, Pokémon cards, and NFTs, and the rise and fall of more cryptocurrencies than I can recall. Each asset class followed the same pattern: a new, cool thing was sold as "the future," excitement in the market was created as speculators bought in, and prices rose before bursting after people realized that these flash-in-the-pan schemes held no inherent value (or worse, companies went bankrupt and people lost their investments).

Real wealth isn't built in get-rich-quick ways. Wealth builds slowly, but it picks up speed because exponential growth takes place along the journey. It requires five ingredients: capital, knowledge, results, time, and leverage. None of these are quickly accumulated. And removing even one ingredient will significantly increase the time it takes to grow wealth and decrease any investment's performance.

Simply avoid the newest "hot" trends, especially if it's in an asset or space you don't understand.

Set It and Forget It

The most common investment strategy is the set-it-and-forget-it method. This is most often seen when employees contribute a consistent portion of their paycheck into a 401(k) or other type of tax-protected retirement plan. While this is better than not saving at all, it's certainly not a strategy in which you have much control over the outcome. In most cases, the employee does not understand what they own, cannot use leverage to scale or protect their investment, is not growing in knowledge about the asset class, and is not earning a return in more than one way.

In fact, most of these holdings are typically in stocks and make money only in one way: if the stocks become worth more later than they are worth now. There is no value add, no way to buy these assets below their market value, and (in most cases) the employee has no idea what is in their portfolio. The only real known factor is the value given in dollars at the bottom of the report.

Expressed within the CrossFit framework, this approach to wealth-building is like taking 5,000 to 10,000 steps a day, which is better than what most people do, but it is definitely not the same as pushing yourself to tears. The same is true for those looking to build real wealth. On its own, this method is just not enough.

Sir Save-a-Lot

The Sir Save-a-Lot person believes they can save their way to wealth. This was me at the beginning of my own journey. This method has a few problems, though.

- Inflation makes our savings worth less every year, in exponentially increasing amounts
- Only focusing on saving means ignoring earning and investing
- Taxes on earnings may mean there is not enough left over to make traction in saving
- Savings cannot grow exponentially without investing
- If humans lived to be 1,000 years old, this system would likely be the safest and most surefire way to grow your wealth. However, the average life expectancy in the U.S. is just over 76 years old,[19]

---

19 Elizabeth Arias et al., "Provisional Life Expectancy Estimates for 2021," *CDC's National Center for Health Statistics* (August 31, 2022): https://www.cdc.gov/nchs/data/vsrr/vsrr023.pdf.

which prevents this method from working effectively to create the life of influence and freedom most of us want.

Simply stated, saving will get you started, but it won't work by itself.

Pyramid Schemes

Pyramid schemes have been around forever. In wealth-building, this involves members joining an existing group of investors. As new members join, established members enjoy the benefits of high returns, which is based on money the new people invest into the scheme. Everything seems to work great until either new members stop joining or the economy tanks (consider the Bernie Madoff Ponzi scheme). When the base of the pyramid can no longer support those above it, the scheme topples and everyone loses their capital because there never was an investment asset—just unsuspecting people giving away their money to other people who didn't know where their returns were coming from.

These models can only fail, every time. Solid and sustainable wealth comes from a grounded framework, which I'll detail in full later in the book.

KEY TAKEAWAYS

- We must spend money to live, but discipline teaches us to save most of our earnings and then invest that money.
- We all start our journey working traditional jobs where we trade time for money. The objective is to break that cycle and to move from an entrapment pattern to a freedom pattern.
- Money reinvested earns more money. This is called passive income.
- Protect your earnings from those who want to take it from you, such as spending on stuff you don't need.
- Money is not only exchanged for things, it is also a store of energy. Spending money today is robbing yourself of what that energy could grow into in the future.

- It's crucial to employ a savings method that you can stick with and track your progress to see how saving money builds your wealth.
- Avoid strategies that teach only one approach to wealth-building, even if that approach is one you're most comfortable with.
- Keep focused on the big picture. Building wealth is about creating healthy habits, not making one-off moves.

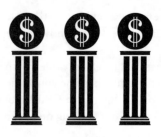

Chapter 3
DEFENSIVE PRINCIPLES

In real life, strategy is actually very straightforward. You pick a general direction and implement like hell.
—JACK WELCH, FORMER CEO OF GENERAL ELECTRIC

Strategies, Standards, and Games

When I first began my own wealth-building journey, I didn't know anything about wealth other than that I controlled how I spent my money. I had to create strategies, standards, and games for myself that would make it easier to save my money. While crudely simple, these ideas allowed me to save more than $100,000 before graduating college. If I could make it work without any of the information I've learned since then, I'm confident your financial life can change when you implement the same system.

My approach was simple: Make as much as I could and save as much as I could. At the time, I was waiting tables. Learning to be a better server allowed me to earn better tips. Keeping my expenses low by living at home with my parents instead of paying rent for "freedom," eating at home, driving a modest car, and only buying clothes on sale were all simple but effective methods.

To maximize the effectiveness of my earnings throughout my career, I have used these strategies, standards, and games.

My Strategies

I worked at the nicest restaurants I could, and worked every day that I could; plus, I showed up early and stayed late. I became good at my job so I could service more tables and maximize the tips I received. I studied the top performers in the restaurant, asked for constructive feedback from my supervisors, and consistently asked for more responsibility and more opportunity. This led to me being assigned the large parties as well as the better sections of the restaurant.

When I moved into law enforcement, my strategy became working overtime. I endeared myself to the sergeant who controlled the overtime schedule. I made myself available to work—even when I didn't want to—so I would be the first call when an opportunity arose. I asked my supervisors about anyone calling in sick or if additional shifts were needed, and I showed I was happy for the work. I presented myself as a stark contrast to my coworkers, who complained about being asked to work overtime or extra shifts.

When I became a real estate agent, I held more open houses than other agents. I made more phone calls, held more appointments, and gave more presentations to potential buyers and sellers. I tracked how many people I could add to my database in a week, and how many times I could legally contact them. This led to more closings and a deeper understanding of how to find clients, and to writing three books on these strategies for other real estate agents: *Sold*, *Skill*, and then *Scale*. Creating and working my strategy paid stronger dividends than I ever could have imaged.

My Standards

When I worked in restaurants, I promised myself that I'd deposit no less than $500 a week into my savings account. If I did not meet my goal, I required myself to work extra days or double shifts to make up the difference, even if that went into the following week. My standard did not change if there were slow days at the restaurant, if I was out sick, or if an unexpected bill occurred that I was responsible for. The amount of $500 was the *minimum* I would deposit.

When I found a better restaurant to work in, I increased my standard to $1,000 a week. Again, if I came up short, I'd work extra days or shifts. If I was tempted to not take late tables, I knew that I was risking the need to work double shifts the following week to make up the difference. Self-imposed standards made it easy for me to add shifts when others were going home.

When I started working in law enforcement, I increased the amount I saved to $10,000 a month. When I moved to a department that paid better, I strung longer shifts together. I changed my standard from how much I would save to how many hours I would work.

When I started my career in real estate, I had less control over outcomes than in my work with restaurant service or law enforcement. Some months I would sell one house; other months it'd be six to seven. Rather than focus on the money I made, I instead focused on the metrics I could control. Moving from lag measures (money I made) to lead measures (actions I took, as I mentioned under My Strategies) guaranteed I was outperforming others in my workplace. And in my first year of full-time real estate sales, I was the top agent in my office of one hundred agents.

My Games

When I was doing restaurant work, my aim wasn't to deposit just $500; it was to deposit *as much as I could* every week. I kept things interesting for myself by moving the goalpost whenever I accomplished my goal early. Three great nights in a row could give me $500 for savings, plus expenses for the week. When that happened, I'd see if I could deposit $1,000 that week. I loved the look on the cashier's face at the bank—I would have to bring in my tips in cash —when the person realized how fast my account was growing or the size of a deposit via a huge wad of money. My gratification wasn't in spending money; it was in exceeding my own savings goals.

These goals disciplined me to save my money, but they also forced me to step up my offense game. Setting a difficult standard for myself created stress, and the only way I could relieve it was by improving my performance. If a standard waitperson could serve four tables at a time, I pushed myself to serve eight. I taught myself efficiency, like how to move faster and with fewer steps. I memorized the menu so

I didn't have to look at the prices when writing them down on the ticket (this was before the days of computers), and I practiced manual dexterity so I could toss a salad or dress an entree faster than my colleagues.

This may sound over the top to some of you, and many of my coworkers did tell me I was "trying too hard," but this was my game. In retrospect, it's clear the skills I built during this time allowed me to learn future tasks faster as well. This game approach is something I've used in every job I've had. In law enforcement, I'd race myself to see if I could write a traffic citation before dispatch came back with the warrant results. In real estate, I'd race to see if I could find a house on the Multiple Listing Network before my client could find the Zillow link. The game was about challenging myself to improve my performance; it became an internal reward system that motivated me in pursuit of my goal of saving.

Oddly enough, I was motivated to approach my jobs this way because I knew I *didn't* want to work forever. When I see others who don't love their current job, and I see them putting in less effort, I scratch my head. The only way out of the rat race is to earn money, save money, and invest money. Giving less effort is the absolute worst thing you can do if your goal is to improve your situation. The game helped me stay focused, even if the job itself was redundant, predictable, or unexciting.

Make Defense Fun

When you start on this journey, saving money can feel a lot like eating vegetables. We all know we're supposed to eat them, and no one would argue that vegetables aren't good for you. Yet, when no one is looking, most of us don't eat them. That's why you have to make eating your vegetables fun. If you don't learn to enjoy pushing yourself when things are hard, or you don't want to do something "just because," you doom yourself to failure. To start your wealth-building journey, you will create strategies, standards, and games that make saving money fun and rewarding.

You will also track what you make and what you spend. This will reveal patterns in your spending habits—areas where you spend more than you realize and areas where you don't even realize you are spending at all. Tracking your income will also reveal areas of opportunity, like for overtime, promotions, or side hustles. You'll find ways to make more money you've likely never noticed before, so start tracking.

Is the process of saving money exciting enough to motivate you? While accumulating wealth may sound like the secret to happiness, according to experts, it's not. For example, Tony Robbins, the business and life strategist, says there is no fixed level of achievement or success that will allow you to live the rest of your life comfortably and happily on cruise control:

> I always tell people if you want to know the secret to happiness, I can give it to you in one word: progress. Progress equals happiness. … There are levels of making it in life and whatever you think 'making it' is, when you get there, you'll see there's another level. That never ends, because if you stop growing, you're going to be unhappy. … When you achieve a goal, it feels good for—how long? You know, a week? A month? Six months? A year? And then it doesn't feel so good. … I don't care what it is you've achieved, and the reason is because life is not about achieving the goals, life is about who you become in pursuit of those goals.[20]

When you don't have food, your hunger is all you can think about. Money works in the same way. While it can seem like all your problems will be solved with one good influx of cash, new problems will come up once you have some money. We continually chase goals. Once a goal is obtained, you get that temporary feeling of satisfaction, but a new goal shows up and a new journey will begin.

Progress
When it comes to something as disciplined and difficult as saving money, you want to hack into the power of progress to stay motivated and make the journey fun and enjoyable. Why take a journey if you can't have fun and enjoy yourself along the way? Tracking your

---

20 Catherine Clifford, "Tony Robbins: This Is the Secret to Happiness in One Word," CNBC, Oct 6, 2017, https://www.cnbc.com/2017/10/06/tony-robbins-this-is-the-secret-to-happiness-in-one-word.html.

progress is the first way to tap into the power of it. Seeing changes every month will reveal if you are going forward, backward, or staying in place. We do this by creating a budget to track where our money goes. If you're familiar with budgeting, you already understand its importance and power. If you've never budgeted your money, good news: You will find it easier to save money than ever before! Even if you don't make a lot of money right now and aren't able to save large amounts, you can still build powerful budgeting skills by focusing on income and spending. (Budgeting is discussed in detail in Chapter 4.)

Another way to hack into the power of progress comes down to how you approach a workday. The first approach is that of silent resignation, stoically accepting your lot in life, putting your work boots on every day, and making your way to your modern-day coal mine. This approach will get you through the day, but it won't make the next day or day after that any better. The second approach is to show up excited and with a great attitude, eager to serve and eager to learn. Those who use this approach give themselves a ladder for today, tomorrow, and all future days. When you improve your skills today, new opportunities appear tomorrow. Each step, however small, leads to the next step. And each step takes you further on your path. This powers your progress by keeping you motivated through the mundane parts of the journey toward building wealth.

Not only is this hack important for how far it will allow you to go but it also makes your steps along the way more fun. It is the promise of new opportunities and seeing your progress that removes the hopeless despair of a workday and turns it into an adventure. Showing up and doing the bare minimum reduces the power of your future. Showing up every day with vigor to do the best job possible improves the opportunities on your horizon. This puts the power of your future into your hands. You choose the skills you want to build and pick which opportunities you want to follow.

Building Momentum

Everything is easier with momentum. In fact, any forward motion can only be accomplished through momentum. Start-up businesses understand this. The first several years of their existence are spent with a single purpose: build momentum. A train isn't powerful when it first starts moving, but given a full head of steam, it roars forward.

Your momentum is based on your habits, as discussed in the last chapter. Saving money can be difficult before you're used to doing it. Just like working out or working longer hours, it's harder at first and becomes easier the longer we stick with it.

Identity

It's important to know how critical your identity is when it comes to saving money. When you're working, if you see yourself as a spender or only living paycheck to paycheck, you're wearing the wrong identity. You must tell yourself—and believe—that you are someone who enjoys saving money and watching it grow. A portion of what you make is yours to keep, and the more of it you keep and invest, the more of it you have to grow. When you see yourself as a saver, and you see your savings grow week after week, your brain starts to look at work differently. A 2021 study published by the *Public Library of Science (PLOS)* revealed just how large a role your identity plays in your decisions.

> According to identity theory, the decision an individual makes at a given point in time is affected by the identity that is salient during the decision process. The salient identity might relate to characteristics such as one's religious affiliation, workplace, place of residence, or political views. The identity that is salient depends on the situation and can be manipulated.[21]

Identity salience refers to how you perceive yourself in certain situations, and how you respond to those situations based on that identity. For example, you may be a daughter, a sister, a mother, a registered nurse, a manager, a homeowner, a PTA president, a devout churchgoer—the list goes on. While all those identities are within you, you don't bring every single one to every single situation. The identity that is present when you are making a decision—the identity that informs your decision-making based on your experiences and beliefs—is your salient identity.

The research published in *PLOS* showed that decisions made by

---

21 Dikla Perez et al., "Consistency in Identity-Related Sequential Decisions," *PLOS ONE* 16, no. 12 (December 8, 2021): e0260048. https://doi.org/10.1371/journal.pone.0260048.

those studied changed depending on their salient identity present at the time of the decision. It revealed an important fact: A change in your identity will lead to a change in your decision-making. In areas of deep struggle, where it seems you just can't change, the secret lies in identity.

When you see yourself as a saver, you have an easier time finding the discipline to save your money. If you see money as a tool to buy things (like the $140 Nike sneakers), you'll have a much more difficult time not spending it. To get good at saving money, and later making more of it, learn to see yourself differently. When you form the identity of someone who is good with money and sticks to a plan, it will affect your decision-making.

James Clear, author of *Atomic Habits*, gives the following advice regarding behavioral change:

> Changing your beliefs isn't nearly as hard as you might think. There are two steps.
>
> 1. Decide the type of person you want to be.
> 2. Prove it to yourself with small wins.
>
> First, decide who you want to be. This holds at any level—as an individual, as a team, as a community, as a nation. What do you want to stand for? What are your principles and values? Who do you wish to become?
>
> These are big questions, and many people aren't sure where to begin—but they do know what kind of results they want: to get six-pack abs or to feel less anxious or to double their salary. That's fine; start there and work backward from the results you want to the type of person who could get those results. Ask yourself, "Who is the type of person that could get the outcome I want?"[22]

Seeing yourself as a wealthy individual, as a disciplined individual, is a critical first step to achieving wealth. To bring this vision to fruition, start tracking your progress and notice each small win. As

---

22 James Clear, *Atomic Habits: An Easy & Proven Way to Build Good Habits & Break Bad Ones* (New York: Penguin Publishing Group, 2018).

the small wins accumulate, progress will motivate you to keep saving and get more wins. As your identity shifts, so will your spending decisions. As a result, the amount of money you save and the optimism you develop about working to make money will increase. Enjoy this part of the wealth-building journey!

Money Personalities

The process of changing spending habits includes changing personal habits, and those are tied to your personality. In her book *Know Yourself, Know Your Money*, Rachel Cruze outlines several money personality types. As you read through the types below, ask yourself which category you fall into, and what may hinder or help you in building your wealth.

Savers vs. Spenders

Savers: *Prioritize saving, wait patiently, ready for a rainy day*
Savers see money as a form of security, preferring to keep it tucked away for that proverbial rainy day. Putting money aside for a future purpose isn't a big sacrifice. Savers are more likely to experience buyer's remorse and need to see a clear and present value in the items they purchase.

Money is a poor form of security. Finding your security in money instead of people is a dangerous game that has disappointed many people. Money is a tool that can open doors and provide you a better life, but it is only a tool, and it is useful only when applied wisely. Look for ways to add security to your life that are not related to your savings.

Spenders: *Love shopping, give generously, budget creatively*
Spenders see money as a way to exercise creative possibilities. Money is made to be spent. Spenders struggle when there is money burning a hole in their pocket. Money is often a form of showing generosity, appreciation, and love. Putting money aside for the future feels like a great sacrifice and may not make sense. After all, can't you always make more later?

If you're a spender, look for ways to show your feelings without spending money. You can show your appreciation with kind words. And many folks would prefer your time or attention than a night out on the town or an expensive gift (and if they don't, they're not really your friends). You may be using money as a substitute for true connection or to avoid emotional vulnerability. Getting real with yourself about this tendency can unlock your ability to save your money and finally put yourself in a strong position financially.

Nerds vs. Free Spirits

Nerds: *Love spreadsheets, love budgeting, pay taxes early*
Nerds have their taxes complete and submitted well before April 15. They have a strong affinity for spreadsheets, amortization charts, and budgeting software. Nerds feel a strong sense of control over their money by budgeting. They have a laser focus on how to track money.

This focus doesn't necessarily translate well into the realm of family, friends, and relationships. The dopamine that comes from tracking progress can create an addiction to focusing on the money at the expense of relationships. Because relationships and even creativity are significant in building a winning offense, nerds can lose money by getting too bogged down in details.

Free Spirits: *Live life to the fullest, don't like budgeting, aren't worried about the details*
Free spirits forget about April 15. They don't have an interest in money or finances, and their "let's enjoy life" mentality drives their decision-making. The word "budget" is not in their vocabulary.

Free spirits aren't intentional about their money, so they may well reach the latter years of their life and wonder why they don't have any. It's particularly crucial for free spirits to practice financial discipline, no matter how boring it may seem. It helps for free spirits to see money as a tool that will support their preferred lifestyle for decades to come.

Things People vs. Experience People

Things People: *Enjoy tangible things, love getting gifts, enjoy collecting and tracking assets*

If you enjoy spending on physical things like clothes, shoes, or the latest tech gadget, then you're a things person. This works against you when you're trying to save money, as it may appear you're depriving yourself of the newest iPhone or car. Continually remind yourself that saving money will allow you to invest in real estate, and that passive income will provide enough cash flow to buy whatever you like later. The goal of wealth is to lead a better life, not just collect more things.

Experience People: *Love going out to eat, enjoy making memories, look forward to the next opportunity to connect*

Experience people value other people and making memories more than buying things. If you prefer to spend your money on concerts, eating out, or a day at the spa, you're an experience person. Experience people are initially drawn to the idea of building wealth when they think about stays to exotic locations, day trips, and family vacations. This initial motivation can quickly dwindle when the hard work of saving money, staying disciplined, and delaying gratification means delaying experiences. To stay focused, this personality type needs to create quality experiences that don't cost much money: A day at the local beach, a hike in a nearby forest, or a home-cooked dinner with friends are all low-cost but high-value substitutions.

Quality People vs. Quantity People

Quality People: *Pay more for quality, research their purchases, don't impulse buy*

This type of person wants things that are going to last and will do their research before making a purchase. They look for detailed reviews and don't do well when forced to make big money decisions on short notice. In relation to buying real estate, quality people will spend weeks on Zillow analyzing homes without ever seeing one in person.

If you're a quality person, ask yourself why it is so important to have the "best" of whatever you want. Are these things a reflection of you? Quality people may objectively believe higher quality is better; or it may be something deeper, like hiding a lifelong embarrassment over being poor in their childhood.

Quantity People: *Like variety, love a good deal, want one in every color*
Quantity people enjoy variety. They prefer having ten options to using the same item over and over. Quantity people have closets full of clothes (one in every color) and love being able to mix and match to create multiple outfits. This personality type may be great bargain shoppers and willing to shop for the best price, if not the best quality. They pride themselves in the art of the deal.

In real estate, this trait can lead you into troubled waters. I've seen many people with this personality type focus on the wrong metrics when building their portfolio. Quantity people can easily focus on volume metrics—bigger is better—and select the wrong locations, completely missing the mark of buying real estate.

Safety People versus Status People
Safety People: *Value the security money can bring, prioritize an emergency fund, invest in low-risk/low-reward assets*
Safety people try to mitigate the unknown, including job loss, emergencies, or changes in the economy. This money personality type is more interested in building a fortress than frolicking on a private island.

This type must fight to keep their desire for safety at bay or they'll lead a life filled with fear. Continually remind yourself that inflation is eating away at your money, robbing it of the energy it's meant to store for you, and that doing nothing is the surest way to fail. On that same note, this personality type needs to get comfortable with failing because it often leads to improvement, and improving your decision-making is the safest thing to do.

Status People: *Like name brands, enjoy the finer things in life*
Status people buy things for the image it gives them, not for their practical use. They pay attention to what other people are driving, wearing, or using, and are always comparing themselves. Status

people see themselves as a reflection of their values and will put only their best foot forward. This money personality type is an expert at justifying large expenditures.

This type must learn the uncomfortable lesson that what they own does not define them; their character and values are a much more accurate reflection. Status people must remind themselves that they can't buy the image they want; at least not an image that they want to last.

Abundance People vs. Scarcity People
Abundance People: *Have a glass-half-full view, natural givers, take risks*

Those with an abundance mindset believe there is more than enough for everyone. They tend to take more risks as they believe everything will work out just fine. These people give their money away freely because they believe there will always be more coming.

While it may appear that an abundance mindset is "good" and a scarcity mindset is "bad," this isn't necessarily true. Those with an abundance mindset can easily give away their hard-earned savings assuming there will always be more, only to find that's not the case. A friend of mine gave away or loaned out nearly all of the $100,000 awarded to her in a class-action lawsuit to various family members. When I asked why, she told me it was simply because they asked. Not one person has repaid their loan or shown her the same generosity she showed them.

Those with an abundance mindset must start seeing their money as a store of energy that they value for themselves. This shift in perspective can save abundance personality types from making foolish money choices.

Scarcity People: *Hold on to possessions tightly, fear losing things, naturally distrusting*

Those with a scarcity mindset operate under the assumption that resources are finite, and they constantly prepare for a worst-case scenario. An ounce of faith can go far for those with a scarcity mindset.

Jesus said: "Look at the birds of the air; they do not sow or reap or store away in barns, and yet your heavenly Father feeds them. Are you not much more valuable than they? Can any of you by worrying add a single hour to your life?"[23]

For those who believe in a higher power, it is a strong source of comfort that their basic needs will be provided for. For those who don't, consider the Law of Reciprocity. When you think of someone who has given generously to you, doesn't it create a desire in you to give back, or to pay it forward? Scarcity is often only a mindset.

Seven Lessons from *The Richest Man in Babylon*

One of the most influential and widely respected books in the wealth-building genre is George Clason's *The Richest Man in Babylon* (I'll refer to it as *RMIB* through the rest of this book). Written in 1926, *RMIB* dispenses advice in the form of short parables highlighting financial principles. Widely regarded as a classic in financial literature, I highly recommend it because it is a strong companion to the information contained in this book.

The following lessons from *RMIB* are echoed with practical application in this book:

1. *RMIB:* Start thy purse to fattening.
   This book: Put your emphasis on growing your savings account rather than spending your money.
2. *RMIB:* Control thy expenditures.
   This book: A crucial step in wealth-building is learning to budget. If you don't know what and where you spend, you don't control your finances; you will find it exceedingly difficult to make the right decisions to earn more income and invest your money wisely and safely.
3. *RMIB:* Make thy gold multiply.
   This book: Learn, understand, practice, and pursue the power of compound interest.
4. *RMIB:* Guard thy treasures from loss.
   This book: Avoid risky investments or get-rich-quick schemes, and never invest in anything you don't understand.

---

23 Matthew 6:26–27 (NIV).

5. **RMIB:** Make of thy dwelling a profitable investment.

   This book: Own your home, especially when you can use your residence to generate additional income (such as having a rental unit or roommates).

6. **RMIB:** Ensure a future income.

   This book: Build up your passive income to ensure you are never without money; then use your money to make more money.

7. **RMIB:** Increase thy ability to earn.

   This book: Build your skills, experience, and value so you can earn more money in the future. Put an emphasis on self-improvement (see the Strategies, Standards, and Games section at the beginning of this chapter) to increase your value in the workplace. Do what you need to so you can save more money and then eventually give up your day job.

I will expand on these seven lessons in the following chapters and share how they can be applied. I encourage you to read *RMIB* in conjunction with this book. Follow these principles and stay focused on the goal!

KEY TAKEAWAYS

- Creating strategies, standards, and games for yourself is the best way to start your journey of building wealth.
- Saving money is hard, so make it fun.
- Tracking your spending reveals patterns in your spending habits.
- Showing up and doing the bare minimum gives away the power of your future.
- Moving forward is easier with momentum. Change is difficult at first, but it becomes easier the longer we stick to our goals.
- A portion of what you make is yours to keep; the more of it you keep, the more you have to invest. Money makes money.
- Knowing your identity type can help you learn to make smarter decisions; developing an identity of someone who is good with money is crucial to becoming good with money.

Chapter 4

BUDGETING

*A budget is telling your money where to go
instead of wondering where it went.*
—JOHN MAXWELL

What Is a Budget

The first step to building wealth is saving more of what you earn, and a budget is a tool that helps you do that. Budgets are made up of two parts:

1. Money coming in (income, alimony, etc.)
2. Money going out (expenses, bills, etc.)

A budget forces you to look at where you get your money and where you spend it. When you spend money without tracking it, you never know where it's going, and suddenly your wallet or bank account is low. Having a budget will help you build your savings account, which—as you know—is how you start building wealth.

One of the better-known strategies for creating a budget first appeared in a book called *All Your Worth* by Elizabeth Warren and Amelia Warren Tyagi. The book introduced the 50/20/30 rule, which is more often called the 50/30/20 rule. This approach divides your expenses into three categories: needs (50 percent), wants (30 percent), and savings (20 percent). This allocation works for those whose objectives are to maintain the status quo, avoid going into debt, and live a relatively comfortable life.

If your goals, however, are to build wealth, stop trading time for money, and live like no one else, you need to shift your thinking on how you budget. Let's pause for a moment to analyze this.

Self-made millionaire Steve Siebold spent twenty-six years interviewing wealthy people for his book, *How Rich People Think*. There are several ways Siebold says the rich view the world differently from the masses. [24]

- Rich people believe being wealthy is a right, while the average person believes being wealthy is a privilege.
- Rich people believe the wealthy are more savvy, while the average person believes the wealthy are smarter.
- Rich people believe money is earned through thinking, while the average person believes money is earned through time and labor.
- Rich people believe money is liberating, while the average person believes money is controlling.
- Rich people believe in working for fulfillment, while the average person believes in working for money.

Earlier in the book, I shared how I made saving my restaurant tips a game in an attempt to train myself to save as much as possible. To win at this game, I was willing to make sacrifices, like living with my parents, eating at home, not going out, etc. My goal dictated my decisions.

Saving money became fun when I saw the progress I was making in an ever-growing savings account. The more fun it became, the more I wanted to save. It may seem insignificant, but the subtle shift from thinking about how much I *must* save to thinking about how much I'm *able* to save supercharged my results and made the process enjoyable. This gamification was so important to the results I achieved that I'm not sure I would have succeeded without it.

As you implement your own budget, ask yourself this question: How much *must* you save versus how much *can* you save? The more

---

24 Kathleen Elkins, "8 Ways Rich People View the World Differently than the Average Person," *CNBC*, October 11, 2016, https://www.cnbc.com/2016/10/11/8-ways-rich-people-view-the-world-differently-than-the-average-person.html.

willing you are to set aside immediate wants and save your money, the faster you'll see your account grow.

Actionable steps you can take now to begin saving more:

- Watch movies at home on streaming services rather than go to the movie theater
- Work out at home, not in a gym
- Eat at home, not in restaurants
- Pay with cash whenever possible
- Avoid spending money when you're bored
- Track every dollar you spend
- If you need a car, buy it used
- Look for ways to reduce your largest expenses

How to Make a Budget

There are many ways to make a budget. Some prefer the old-school method of writing on paper. Others prefer going digital with software like Microsoft Excel or Google Sheets, or apps that use bank statements to track expenses and automatically assign your spending to categories.

Here are my suggested steps for you to create your budget:

Step 1: Determine How You Want to Track Your Money

I prefer to use an app, and my favorite is Mint. The app connects with your credit card or bank statements and classifies your expenses. It allows you to set a budget for each category, and it reports how much room you have left in that budget category before the month ends. It's available on your smartphone or computer, and it's extremely easy to use.

Know that any app will show you exactly where you're spending your money. The point is to find a system that *you'll use*. If you prefer another app, use it. If you prefer Excel, use it. If you prefer a paper notebook, use it.

Step 2: Audit Your Accounts and Review Your Financial Situation

To determine where your money is going, you'll need to know all your expenses, most likely found on your bank and credit card statements. Reviewing your statements will show you what monthly bills are currently being debited from your bank accounts or charged to your credit cards. The only exception to this method would be if you make yearly payments that don't show up as monthly expenses. This can occur with gyms, club memberships, etc. Look at one year of statements, just to see if you've missed any recurring yearly items.

Once you know how much money is being spent (your expenses), it's important to compare that with how much money you make (your income). It goes without saying, but you should never spend more than you make. Putting yourself in debt will only delay your wealth-building journey that much more.

If you already have consumer debt, make sure you put those into your budget software or spreadsheet (Mint can do this after you've connected it with your accounts). My advice is to put your largest debts at the top and move progressively lower to the smallest amount.

Step 3: Determine Needs vs. Wants

Look at your expenses and categorize them as a need or a want. Be honest with yourself in these classifications because it's important to get these right for your percentages. Is your spending on a need (food shopping) versus a want (eating out)? Note that both relate to feeding yourself. Ask yourself tough questions: How many of your wants are you willing to sacrifice to achieve your financial goals? How much of your need costs can be reduced (say, shopping at a grocery store rather than using a meal site that ships ingredients to you)?

Step 4: Review

Review your spending to make sure every category has a column on your spreadsheet. Once your spreadsheet is complete, you'll have a good understanding of how you spend your money.

Now ask yourself a few more questions.

- Was I unaware of what I was spending money on?
- Am I happy or disappointed in how I spend my money?
- Who is separating my money from me? How are they doing it?
- If I continue on this path, can I build my wealth and achieve financial freedom?

Step 5: Set Goals

Here's another tough question to ask yourself: How much of my income am I willing to save? Knowing where you spend your money and pondering how that made you feel are helpful exercises in deciding how much of your money you will commit to saving. The 50/30/20 ratio, for example, breaks your income into 50 percent needs, 30 percent wants, and 20 percent savings. My questions to you:

- Are you willing to save a significant percentage of your income to get where you want to go?
- What is your time horizon; that is, how fast do you want to save enough money to invest in appreciating assets?
- How much are you willing to sacrifice to achieve your goals sooner?

Your wants category is your low-hanging fruit. This is a category where, technically, all your expenses could be cut. "What must I part with?" is one question, though it's negative in tone. A better, more positive, one is, "Which of these expenses am I willing to keep, knowing it will slow me in reaching my savings goal?" Your old way of thinking likely rewarded yourself with wants. The new way of thinking is to reward yourself with the progress of watching your savings grow.

At the same time, you need to stay motivated to stick with the goal. Allow yourself the comforts in life you *really* enjoy and cut out the rest. Remember, this is only for the short term. You add wants back in as you progress on the journey and the money starts to accumulate from real estate.

You cannot eliminate the needs category, but you can make changes to reduce your expenses in this category. Start with the biggest expenses. Can you reduce your rent, perhaps by moving somewhere less expensive or renting with a friend? Can you waste less food? Can you buy less expensive items? This is where you get to set up and play your game. If you want to win, where can you start making cuts?

At this point, you should have the categories of needs, wants, debts, and savings; this is a good defense pillar. This audit and ongoing budgeting will expand as you progress into building your offense and investment pillars.

Step 6: Create Your Budget

Once you've determined the percentages of your income allocation, you will need to reconcile your current expenses. Avoid the temptation to create a budget that's convenient and based on your current spending. The idea is to create your ideal budget, then change your spending habits to fit that.

If it feels tight and uncomfortable, you've done well! You want a scenario in which you are forced to find creative ways to save. This can be fun if you let it. Spending less on gas, food, entertainment, and other areas will force you to find ways to enjoy life that don't cost money. I'm not saying you can't enjoy life; I'm saying you can find less expensive ways to do so. For example, riding your bikes to the beach or a park and bringing sandwiches for a picnic is cheaper than driving several hours to a paid campground and needing to load up on food and alcohol. This strategy can be applied across all categories. Enjoy the game you create.

Lifestyle Creep

Lifestyle creep is when you increase your spending after you get an increase in income. That usually happens when you get a raise at work, but it can also happen when you've paid off a debt or received an inheritance. Instead of saving the extra money, the extra money goes to a more expensive lifestyle—think nicer clothes, a new car, fancier vacations, etc. Those expenses that you were previously living without now seem like a "need." Instead of using the increased income to speed up your wealth-building journey, you can cause serious damage to the hard work you've already put in.

Working hard to get a raise only to spend all that money and not save it is a problem for many Americans. And it's a huge deterrent to wealth-building. When I was younger I would go through spurts of consistent and focused weightlifting, working out every day and growing stronger. I was burning calories, so I needed to eat more than I had burned to gain mass. This created a situation in which I was eating early, often, and a lot. When I would stop lifting due to injury, sickness, or travel, I'd keep eating nearly the same way. I wasn't tracking my calories, and that created a situation where I experienced "calorie creep."

Creating a budget early in your journey before you focus on making more money will put systems in place that help prevent lifestyle creep from eroding your hard work. The following are common ways lifestyle creep can happen, and advice on how to monitor it.

Retail Therapy

Retail therapy, the practice of shopping to lift your mood when you're sad, stressed, or depressed, can be a major threat to your savings plan. A WebMD article on retail therapy refers to a study that found 62 percent of shoppers bought something to cheer themselves up. A further 28 percent made a purchase to celebrate something.[25] As you proceed on this new journey, you can expect trials and tribulations of many kinds. New challenges will make themselves known. Higher levels of income are often associated with higher levels of responsibility and stress. This can create feelings of discouragement and anxiety. During these times, the temptation to shop can be very real. Having a budget in place that dictates how much you will spend on clothing and miscellaneous items can stop retail therapy from destroying your hard work. You can feel good splurging on a mocha and forgoing that new coat you don't even need.

More Travel

Travel is a powerful motivator for establishing financial independence. It becomes a problem though when it's funded by money you must earn as opposed to money your investments have earned on your behalf. Whether you pay off your house and decide to put all the money you used to spend on your mortgage toward fun trips or you increase your vacation spending as your salary increases, travel can easily become part of lifestyle creep. As you're building your investing pillar, stay mindful of how much money you spend on travel.

Eating Out

A fun way to spend money is eating at nice restaurants. Not only is the food usually better than what you make at home, the environment and the experience are too. Throw in the fact that there are no dishes to do, and you've got a clear winner! The problem is it's far

---

25 Sharlene Tan, "Is Retail Therapy for Real?" WebMD, September 10, 2021, https://www. webmd.com/balance/features/is-retail-therapy-real.

more expensive than eating at home. Here's what financial services company SoFi has to say about it:[26]

> There's almost no way around it—eating out will almost always cost more than cooking a meal at home. While the average cost of eating out varies dramatically depending on the restaurant you go to, most restaurants charge a large markup on the items they serve. When you eat out, you're paying less for the food and more for the service, convenience, and ambiance.

When you start making more money, avoid the temptation to eat out more often by allotting a little extra money in your budget toward dining out and then sticking to that new amount. And make the most of each dining experience!

Habits of Luxuries

Remember when people made coffee at home, and Folgers® was the norm? Drive Research found that 32 percent of Americans purchase coffee from a coffee shop one to three days a week.[27] And the spending doesn't stop there.

- A survey of 1,000 people in the U.S. found more than half of the respondents who eat out—which included eating in restaurants, and ordering takeout and delivery—did so at least two to three times per week.[28]
- The average American spends between $244 and $313 on cosmetics every month.[29]

26 Kayla McCormack, "Examining the Price of Eating at Home vs Eating Out," SoFi Learn, April 27, 2023, https://www.sofi.com/learn/content/price-of-eating-at-home-vs-eating-out/.

27 Lark Allen, "2022 Coffee Statistics: Consumption, Purchases, and Preferences," Drive Research, July 27, 2022, https://www.driveresearch.com/market-research-company-blog/coffee-survey.

28 "Fourth's Truth about Dining Out Survey Report," *Fourth* (May 15, 2019): https://www.fourth.com/wp-content/uploads/2023/01/US_White_Paper_Truth_About_Dining_Out_Survey_Report_110119.pdf

29 Chris Kolmar, "24 Powerful Cosmetics Industry Statistics [2023]: What's Trending in the Beauty Business?" Zippia, May 12, 2023, https://www.zippia.com/advice/cosmetics-industry-statistics/.

And this is all despite the fact that more than 60 percent of Americans live paycheck to paycheck.[30] Lifestyle creep takes items that were once considered luxuries and makes them necessities. Don't let lifestyle creep affect your future.

New/Better Car

Many people who get a raise immediately look for ways to spend the money. And a new car is one of the first things people buy. If you think about it, it makes sense. Most people want a new or better car more than anything else. When you combine that with the fact that cars are easy to finance and don't require a huge down payment, it becomes easy to take on the new debt, especially after a raise—but that financing can be for five years (or longer, now). Having a set amount of money for your transportation budget, regardless of your income, will eliminate the temptation to upgrade your ride as you make more money.

The Importance of Accountability

The point of a budget is to have a money plan—not just for today's money but also for your future money. As you learn offense, expect to earn more money every year. How you handle raises is important, as is your desire to earn more income. As you walk this journey and commit yourself to the pillars that grow wealth, you should expect to rely more and more on your budget. Having a plan for future wealth is every bit as important as having a plan for today's money.

As Clason wrote in *The Richest Man in Babylon*:

As a man perfecteth himself in his calling even so doth his ability to earn increase. In those days when I was a humble scribe carving upon the clay for a few coppers each day, I observed that other workers did more than I and were paid more. Therefore, did I determine that I would be exceeded by none. Nor did it take long for me to discover the reason for their

---

30 "69% of Americans in Urban Areas Are Living Paycheck to Paycheck; 14 Percentage Points Higher than Suburban Consumers," LendingClub, May 24, 2023, https://ir.lendingclub.com/news/news-details/2023/69-of-Americans-in-Urban-Areas-are-Living-Paycheck-to-Paycheck-14-Percentage-Points-Higher-than-Suburban-Consumers/default.aspx.

greater success. More interest in my work, more concentration upon my task, more persistence in my effort, and, behold, few men could carve more tablets in a day than I. With reasonable promptness my increased skill was rewarded.[31]

Plan to save more, not spend more, when your income increases. What would it look like to save 100 percent of your raise every month? Budgeting will make this easier by keeping your savings goal front and center. Finding a community of like-minded people will help as well. Odds are, most of the people in your life right now aren't great at money management. When you're surrounded by others on the same mission, it can be both encouraging and inspiring. Different people bring different skills and strengths to a group, and there will certainly be times when your motivation lags. In these moments, having other people to encourage you, keep you focused, and share their wins can be incredibly helpful. Plus, you'll be learning from people while teaching others less experienced than you. If you don't know of any groups, recommend this book to someone and create a book club together. Your wealth-building curve will be significantly shortened when you share this journey with others.

Kyle and Katie's Story

Kyle and Katie were college sweethearts who married right after graduation. He continued his education, earning several graduate degrees. A former college basketball player, Kyle's first job was as an assistant coach for a college basketball team, so he and Katie moved to Southern California. When he began his new career, he and Katie owed more than $100,000 in student loans. Much to their surprise, the coach of the team was soon fired, and so was Kyle. They then moved to Northern California, where Kyle took an IT job at a university, which paid significantly less than the coaching job, and Katie stayed home with their son. It wasn't long before Kyle and Katie realized they were now carrying even more debt, having added credit card payments to school loan payments.

Kyle and Katie were forced to play better defense to avoid falling

---

31 George S. Clason, *The Richest Man in Babylon* (Denver, CO: BiggerPockets Publishing, 2022), 63.

deeper into debt. They committed to finding ways to spend less money and came up with a plan to do so. Using a budget, they made significant and immediate cuts in their spending. Embracing the "envelope method," they took their predetermined amounts for food, rent, gas, student loans, credit card debt, entertainment, and so on, and put the money in envelopes labeled with that category. They would pull from the appropriate envelope when money was needed to pay bills or make purchases.

Their debt created pressure, and the budget forced the couple to be creative. They moved into a smaller apartment to cut their rent in half. They eliminated eating out and travel. They wrote heartfelt letters rather than buy expensive gifts, and the couple attended inexpensive movie matinees to save money on entertainment. Kyle developed a love of reading as an inexpensive way to grow personally. In one year alone, he read one hundred books, most of which were borrowed from the library.

If the money in an envelope ran out before the next paycheck, they did without. This caused some quarreling and discomfort in the relationship, but it wasn't long before they adapted to this new standard of living and started to see their savings grow. The progress became fun, and they shared their excitement with other couples. They found that others were struggling with these same issues, and not talking about it. Kyle and Katie found personal reward in their own progress and in serving others, so their sacrifices over luxuries became less painful. They felt gratitude for the things they had, rather than missing what they didn't have.

Eventually, Kyle got a better-paying job as a speech-language pathologist and Katie began her career as a nurse. While their income increased significantly, their spending did not. Sticking with the envelope method, Kyle and Katie deposited nearly 100 percent of their increased income directly into their savings account. This became the down payment on their first house (with a thirty-year mortgage at a great interest rate), where they celebrated bringing home their first child. They now had financial freedom and they kept their spending habits in check. Kyle and Katie became an example of hope and a source of encouragement to their friends who struggled with controlling their own spending.

KEY TAKEAWAYS

- A budget is a tool to help you control how you spend your money. It is made up of two parts: money coming in and expenses going out.
- A budget forces you to look at where your money is going now and to plan for where it will go in the future.
- Rich people do not see money the same way as other people.
- Choose how to track your money: Apps like Mint make creating a budget easy, but you must choose what you will use.
- Allocate as much as you can into your savings account.
- Make your budget based on your goals, not your comfort. The more difficult a budget you create for yourself, the more creativity you will unlock, and the faster you will achieve your goals.
- Lifestyle creep shows up in several ways; it needs to be planned for and kept in check.
- Find others to join you on this journey. It's difficult to go alone and more encouraging with others.

Chapter 5
SAVINGS, EXPENSES, AND DEBT

Do not save what is left after spending,
but spend what is left after saving.
—WARREN BUFFETT

Pay Yourself First

Here's a quick recap of what you've learned so far.
- Escaping the entrapment pattern is your ultimate goal.
- If you don't save your money, you'll never be able to stop trading your time for it.
- Your defense pillar is to save as much money as possible so it can be invested. A budget is your tool to accomplish this goal.

An oft-used concept to show prioritization is the "big rocks," popularized by Stephen Covey in *The 7 Habits of Highly Effective People*. The big rocks symbolize the most important things, while the pebbles items of medium importance. And the sand represents the smallest items with the least consequence. If you start by filling the jar with sand and then adding pebbles, there isn't enough room for the big rocks; but if you do the reverse, everything fits in the jar. The lesson? If you don't put the "big rocks" in the jar first, they won't fit in later.

Money works in a similar fashion. The big rocks are your budget priorities. If your first inclination on payday is to treat your friends to a round of beers, that's your big rock. Now, we're going to get scientific here. Everyone has a reticular activating system (RAS) in their brain stem. Essentially, the RAS connects the subconscious part of your brain with the conscious part of your brain. What does that have to do with budgeting? Your RAS takes what you value or focus on most and steers your brain (your decisions, your attention) toward it. For example, when someone says your name in a crowded room, your brain filters out the noise and hears your name because it's.important to you. Similarly, when you have money, you'll first buy what you value: a round of beers, a better car, a shopping spree; whatever you fancy, you'll buy it.

To break this habit, you need to retrain your brain. The simplest way to accomplish this is to make paying yourself first your biggest rock, your highest priority. Designate the amount you are committed to saving every day, week, or month, and move it to a separate banking account *immediately* upon receiving it. This small but significant event will change the entire dynamic of your financial life. Rather than using savings as your sand so that you save only what is left over from your paycheck, you are now saving first and only spending what is left over. Doing this repeatedly trains your brain into thinking that your savings goal is your big rock. Your RAS is sure to notice.

To accomplish this savings goal and rethinking process, you'll need three accounts.

1. A savings account to build momentum
2. A checking account for your budgeted expenses
3. An emergency account for, well, emergencies

When your paycheck hits your checking account, set up an automatic transfer of the amount you want to save into your savings account (remember, that's your big rock account). A caveat to this: If you don't have three-to-six months of living expenses set aside for emergencies, then first send the money to your emergency account. Once the emergency fund is full (three-to-six months of expenses), redirect that amount into the savings account. The trick is to move your money automatically, and after the money is there, it must stay there. You can only spend what is left in your checking account.

This becomes simple when you've already allocated in your budget how much you can spend on "wants" each month. You'll simultaneously be doing the difficult task of forming new habits and adjusting to this new spending pattern. Making saving your money less reliant on your willpower and more an automated process will have a big impact on your success in saving money and changing your habits.

Nevertheless, expect some early resistance, as you'll likely feel deprived. This is part of the adjustment period. Don't fall into the trap of believing you make more money than you really do and can afford to spend more than you really can. Also, be aware of the following ways your old spending patterns may fight back.

Spending from Gross, Not Net

It's easy to justify spending when your RAS tricks you into believing you have more money than you really do. Let's consider the urge to buy a new BMW after a big raise. Spending from gross leads you to think, "I make $90,000 a year. I can afford to spend $700 a month on this new BMW."

Spending from gross takes your entire annual income ($90,000/year) and compares it to the smaller amount ($700/month, or $8,400/year). The large discrepancy between dollar amounts makes it easy to assume the new payment is a small portion of your income. Spending from net is different; that's what is left after taxes, health insurance premiums, and money set aside in a company 401(k). Spending from net sounds like, "I have to account for taxes each paycheck. Then I need to consider rent, food, utilities, and other needs. That leaves me with $20,000 per year to save. At $8,400 a year, this new car payment represents 42 percent of my savings for the year."

The difference between comparing the $8,400/year car payments to your before-tax income rather than what is left after expenses is remarkable, and it shows you the choice you're really making to buy the car. Forty-two percent of your total savings *for the year* is an incredibly large sacrifice, while 9.2 percent (the percentage of your gross) feels easy to justify. This is how your mind plays these tricks on you. Your RAS knows you want the car and will use the trick of subtracting from gross to help you justify it.

Feeling Self-Pity

Self-pity can be an extremely enticing and effective way to justify self-indulgence. Seeing yourself as a victim leads to deceptive self-talk that can be used to keep you in debt. It works like this:

First you tell yourself, "I haven't taken a day off in over twelve months. This pace is impossible to keep up. Rewarding myself with a new BMW will keep me motivated."

Then you tell yourself, "What's the point of working so hard if I can't enjoy myself?"

Then you tell yourself, "The ad said BMWs hold their value better than comparable brands. It's really a form of an investment."

And so on! This type of talk can run in the background of your decision-making for years without ever being exposed, even though the thinking can easily be proven both false and foolish when examined closely. It's not until we start using a budget and tracking our savings that we realize the presence and impact such thoughts have. Think like a victor in control of your outcome as opposed to a victim. Victors think like this:

First you tell yourself, "That BMW is more than just monthly payments. The oil changes, maintenance, tires, and more all cost significantly more than other models. I'm smarter than to overpay like that."

Then you tell yourself, "A BMW is just a status symbol."

Then you tell yourself, "When I have enough assets, I'll let my investments buy me anything I want. If I still want a BMW, I'll buy it for its value to me."

Comparison to Others

Looking to others for comparison when they are not on the same journey as you will cause confusion. Your mind will point out how your friends are driving nice cars and they seem "just fine" with their money, and you don't know anyone else getting this serious about budgeting every dollar with this much detail. Sure, it won't be hard to find people saving less, but those people are not pursuing financial freedom; you are. Compare yourself to the ideal version of yourself, not to others who haven't taken your journey.

The RAS is seductive. It plays tricks. It will tell you what you want to hear to stay in your old pattern of entrapment. You can actively combat this by tracking your savings and sticking to a budget that will lead to your goals. Part of the process of following a budget is changing your thinking. It exposes faulty beliefs and allows a rewiring of unhealthy habits. As your thoughts and value system changes so will your capacity to say no to things you once said yes to.

Take Control of Your Expenses

Some advice from *The Richest Man in Babylon* is to "study thoughtfully thy accustomed habits of living. Herein may be most often found certain accepted expenses that may wisely be reduced or eliminated."

As you automatically transfer money into your emergency or savings accounts, you are building momentum. Still, sticking to your budgeted needs and wants is difficult until it becomes a habit. It's also difficult to decide what to continue spending money on and what needs to be changed or cut. As you've likely noticed after reviewing your budget, a significant portion of your income may go toward consumer debt payments, which is money you have borrowed and agreed to repay. Much of this borrowing was likely to fund the lifestyle you wanted but couldn't afford.

To reduce spending and increase savings, you must eliminate these debt payments. I recommend evaluating the things you have bought with debt (particularly your wants) and assigning them a value between 1 and 10 (10 being highest) to determine how much enjoyment you actually received from that particular expense. (You can find your categories on your budget.) These values will guide you to a better understanding of how to spend your money most efficiently and enjoyably.

Expense	Enjoyment Level
Internet	7
Cable	3
Clothing	4
Gym membership	5
Travel	9
Dining out	2

Let's say this is your table. Dining out has a relatively low value for you, while travel brings much more enjoyment. When looking at ways to make additional cuts to your budget, this offers clarity on the areas you prioritize (such as travel) and the areas that are easy to make cuts (such as dining out). This exercise will highlight the importance—or not—of what you have spent your money on and thus traded your energy for. Are these things bringing you happiness or quality of life, or are they stealing from your future and providing little enjoyment in return?

As noted earlier in the book, wealthy people see money as a tool to provide them with freedom more than as a means of short-term gratification. That means part of your journey to becoming wealthy is developing a new relationship with your money. If spending less on things you didn't enjoy meant spending less time working somewhere you disliked or spending more on things that energize you, wouldn't that be a win? Could you quit a job you hated and take a new one that you enjoyed more but paid less? Would your quality of life immediately improve? Evaluating the satisfaction you receive from your wants will bring clarity on if they are worth the energy you are trading for them.

It's also worth noting that a penny saved is worth more than a penny earned. Money you earn is taxed. It typically requires going to work, which has several additional costs associated, like money on gas, clothing, and lunches out (particularly pre-COVID). Time spent driving to and from work is typically not compensated and rarely enjoyable.

Because of taxes, it's much less efficient to earn money than to save it. Money you earn is taxed. Money you save isn't. In other words, if you earn $100, you may keep $75 of it. If you save $100, you keep all of it. Early in the stages of your journey, your capacity to earn is somewhat limited in comparison to your capacity to save.

Top-Down Cuts

To figure out how to maximize your savings, I recommend evaluating your monthly budget, beginning with your largest expenses:

Rent	$3,500
Groceries	$2,200
Car payment	$750
Personal care	$550
Vehicle maintenance	$350
Coffee	$150

You'll notice a few expenses that jump out. Let's begin with rent. Many people assume rent is a fixed expense, but it isn't. Some people rent places that are nicer or bigger or in a location they don't need, such as a single-family home with a big backyard and great school district when they don't even have kids. Housing is likely your biggest expense, so start by finding ways to reduce it first.

The key to controlling housing expenses is to recognize that housing decisions are often based more on comfort than on necessity. We all need a place to live, and our sneaky subconscious tells us we *need* that $3,500 apartment. Housing is a need, of course, but we don't *need* a large single-family home or an apartment in the best part of town; we just prefer it. This thinking leads us to skip over the housing allowance in our budget and make our way down the list. As we come up with a new excuse for each line item, we eventually end on that pointless $5/day coffee expense as what we will sacrifice. While every dollar you can save is a good thing, you can do better than only addressing the smallest expense.

The problem can be solved by asking yourself a differently worded question. Change "I have to live somewhere, right?" to "What safe options do I have for living arrangements that would be cheaper than my current situation?" In many cases, there are ways to reduce housing expenses. We just don't like considering the options.

- Move to a smaller place.
- Move farther away.
- Move in with a friend.

- Buy a home and rent out the other bedrooms.
- Rent a bedroom in someone's home.
- Live in an RV and pay for parking on someone's property.
- Be willing to move around as a house sitter.
- Agree to do cleaning or cooking in exchange for free room and board.
- Move in with your parents.

I'll be the first to admit that none of these options are comfortable. People spend so much money on housing because they assume comfort is more important than their future. Considering options like these forces you to look at your subconscious decision in a new light. There's nothing wrong with deciding to continue paying a high percentage of your income toward housing; you just need to be fully aware of your decision and make it consciously.

We also often assume that food is an expense we can't reduce. Maybe you can trade your food costs by offering to cook the food that your roommates buy. If you're a good cook, maybe you can pick up work as a private cook in someone else's home and then arrange to also eat what you make. One question you might be asking yourself: Could either of these be an uncomfortable change? Probably. The right question is: Is your future worth it?

For more realistic options, you can reduce your food budget by shopping at different stores. Get to know the stores in your area as a fast way to shave money off your food budget. Different foods are often on sale at certain stores at certain times. Grocery outlets or bargain markets sell overstocked food at discounted prices. Coupons can be found online.

Your car payment—or transportation budget—is the easiest way to make a change. Those with a modest car or no car payment won't have the same option because you're already doing great in this category. For those who have splurged on a car before achieving financial freedom, the price is often steeper than you'd think.

If you had to pay cash for a car, what you could afford would be significantly different than what you think you can afford. Rewarding yourself with a fancy car, or anything else that you really want but can't afford too early in your journey, will remove your incentive to work, grind, and sacrifice to truly escape your entrapment pattern.

Debt often robs people of the drive and ambition needed to stay on this hero's journey to wealth.

If you already have an expensive car, I strongly suggest you consider selling. If you took on debt to buy it, this act will immediately reduce your expenses and give a boost to your savings rate. If you own a fancy car outright, selling it and buying a cheaper one can still make sense. Fancier cars tend to require higher-cost maintenance, repairs, and parts. More expensive tires, oil changes, gasoline, and even windshield wipers add up over the lifetime of the car. Selling your expensive car and buying one with lower yearly costs might leave you with additional capital to invest or pay off other debt.

Compound Interest

As Benjamin Franklin said, "Money makes money. And the money that money makes, makes money." Compound interest occurs when you allow the interest of your initial investment (the principal) to stay in the account rather than take the interest as a withdrawal. This larger principal-plus-interest amount then earns more interest, and when you invest that new interest, your balance keeps growing and you get the snowball effect.

Over time, this compound effect can create massive momentum. Does a snowball stay the same size as it rolls down a hill? Absolutely not. Once it's rolling, it grows effortlessly. Good luck stopping it once it has momentum! The effort is in the initial stages. Scooping up the snow, packing it into a ball, rolling it down the snowiest hill; wealth-building is the same concept. It's more effort in the beginning to create a budget, followed by accumulation of cash through the power of savings momentum. Forming the right money habits will keep your money snowball rolling your entire life.

Albert Einstein once said, "Compound interest is the eighth wonder of the world. He who understands it, earns it; he who doesn't, pays it." Everybody knows that paying interest is bad, but only a few people decide to do something about it. And, if I can be quite frank, it explains why broke people are broke and rich people are rich. When you get into high-interest loan debt, you are now fighting against the inevitable force of compounding interest instead of using it in your favor. Why trudge up a hill when you can instead run down it?

Building momentum based on compound interest is the goal, but there's more to it than you'd think. When you go into debt and you must *pay* the interest instead of earning it on your investment, compound interest is working against you, not for you. Consider the typical credit card debt situation. The following example is from Bankrate:

Here's a quick overview of how long it can take to pay off a balance if you only make the minimum payment on your credit cards every month—and how much interest can accrue over time. In this example, you're paying off a credit card with a $1,000 balance and a 17 percent interest rate, in which the minimum payment is calculated at 1 percent of the balance plus new interest.

Month	Minimum Payment	Interest Paid	Principal Paid	Remaining Balance
1	$24.17	$14.17	$10.00	$990.00
2	$23.92	$14.02	$9.90	$980.10
3	$23.69	$13.88	$9.81	$970.30
4	$23.45	$13.75	$9.70	$960.59
5	$23.21	$13.61	$9.60	$950.99
6	$22.98	$13.47	$9.51	$941.48
7	$22.75	$13.34	$9.41	$932.07
8	$22.53	$13.20	$9.33	$922.75
9	$22.30	$13.07	$9.23	$913.52
10	$22.08	$12.94	$9.14	$904.38
11	$21.86	$12.81	$9.05	$895.33
12	$21.64	$12.68	$8.96	$886.37

At the end of your first year, you'll have made $274.58 in payments while only reducing your $1,000 balance by $113.63. If you continued to only make the minimum payment, it would take you over nine years to pay off your debt—during which time you'd pay $857.52 in interest charges.[32]

In this example, you borrowed $1,000 but paid back $1,857.52. Most people would never agree to receiving zero percent interest on an investment, yet when you borrow money you receive a *negative* return. Paying a minimum payment at 17 percent interest means spending nearly double what you borrowed and taking nine years to pay it back. Why do people do this?

If your spending habits—meaning car loans, credit card loans, consumer loan debt of any kind—cause you to climb a monthly hill against interest, you're going to be climbing that hill for the rest of your life. You'll have no hope of getting rich. However, if your saving habits are focused, then you can relax. You will be rich in time, because you have compounding interest doing some of the work for you, and you won't be spending your money on someone else's compounding interest. Your habits define your wealth. Bad habits and good money don't stay together.

Opportunity Cost

The problem is worse when you consider the money that you lost by not investing the same $1,000 into something that paid *you* compound interest. According to the Oxford Languages dictionary, opportunity cost is defined as "the loss of potential gain from other alternatives when one alternative is chosen." Opportunity cost is an economic term used to weigh the full impact of decisions, particularly when it comes to the deployment of capital.

The U.S. Securities and Exchange Commission runs a site called Investor.gov. By using their calculator, you can plug in what would have happened had you invested that $1,000 at 17 percent for nine years: You would be $3,108.40 richer.

---

32 Nicole Dieker, "Guide to Credit Card Minimum Payments," Bankrate, May 25, 2022, https://www.bankrate.com/finance/credit-cards/guide-to-credit-card-minimum-payments/.

Total Savings

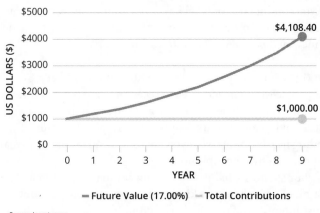

Source: Investor.gov

In summary, you can see what happens when you spend $1,000 on a credit card with 17 percent interest and only make minimum payments for nine years: You *lose* an additional $857.52 to the card company. If you invest that $1,000 for the same nine years at 17 percent interest, you *gain* an additional $3,108.40 in your account. Opportunity cost describes the full impact of this decision: You did not just lose $1,000 in credit card spending plus $857.52 in credit card interest; you also lost the $1,000 you could have saved plus the $3,108.40 in interest you could have earned on that investment. This is a difference of nearly $6,000, all based on what you decided to do with $1,000.

What if I told you that in twenty years, with only compound interest of 17 percent and no additional principal, that same $1,000 would become $23,105.60? And if the initial investment was $10,000, growing at 17 percent over 20 years, you'd have $231,000 in your account. The longer we let the compound interest snowball, the bigger, faster, and more powerful it becomes. And that doesn't include adding more savings into the investment. This is not a trivial matter.

In case you are wondering if a 17 percent return is possible, it is. I earn well over that on nearly every real estate asset I own, but even if you can't find that high of a return, you can absolutely prevent yourself from paying that 17 percent to someone else. The goal of paying off your debt is to move the power of compound interest from working *against* you to working *for* you.

Pay Down Debt

The Richest Man in Babylon tells us:

> Thy debts are thy enemies. They ran thee out of Babylon. You left them alone and they grew too strong for thee. Hadst thou fought them as a man, thou couldst have conquered them and been one honored among the townspeople. But thou had not the soul to fight them and behold they pride hast gone down until thou art a slave.[33]

Paying down debt is an important step in wealth-building because it makes it possible to save money. But before you can pay down your debt, you need clarity on how much of it you have. In the previous chapter, we discussed auditing your bank and credit card statements and entering that information into the "debt" section of your budget software, Excel sheet, etc. Now we'll focus on your approach to paying off that category.

You receive no benefit from holding credit card debt. It is the echo of previous purchases likely made when you could not afford them and did not understand their true cost. It is easy to see a $700/month car payment as $700/month. It is more difficult to see it as $42,000 over the life of a five-year loan (and add interest to that) when it could have been $42,000 saved over five years to become a down payment on a property that might someday be valued at more than $1 million.

Those who understand wealth use the power of compound interest to create a future where they buy assets and let those assets make their car payment for them. Better yet, they don't have car payments, now or in the future. When your assets are producing enough wealth for you, you can pay for a car in cash for the rest of your life. Those who don't understand how wealth works buy the car via a car loan and end up with no assets and need to buy another car with debt when the first one has to be replaced.

---

33 Clason, *The Richest Man in Babylon*, 108.

According to Bankrate, 35 percent of U.S. adults carry credit card debt,[34] and Debt.org says 340 million Americans are carrying debt in some form (mortgages, car loans, student loans, and credit cards).[35] When everyone around you is taking on debt, it can seem sensible and reasonable to do the same, but you are smarter than that.

If you've been following the path so far, your expenses are clearly laid out.

1. You know where you have been spending your money
2. You know where your money is going with your budget
3. You use tracking tools to help you stick to that budget
4. You set automatic transfers to put a predetermined amount into an emergency fund, followed by a savings account
5. You know your debts and are ready to pay them off

The only thing left to do is determine which method you will use to pay off your debt and get started! There are two basic methods, and each has strengths that will appeal to people differently. My advice is to consider each method, choose the one that best fits your personality, and make progress from there. There is no "right" method. What's important is that you choose a method you're more likely to stick with.

1. The Snowball Method

This method approaches your debt by paying off your smallest debt first (and thereby paying it off the fastest). While continuing to make the minimum payments on all your debts, put every extra cent toward the smallest debt. After you pay off the smallest debt, combine that extra money with the minimum payment of that loan, and put it toward the next-smallest debt. You'll pay that one off even faster and continue gaining momentum as you attack your larger debts. For example, let's say your smallest debt is $200. If you put $100 toward it each month, your smallest debt is paid off in two months. Your next-smallest debt has a minimum payment of $50 per month;

---

34 Erica Sandberg, "Survey: More Americans Are Carrying Debt, and Many of Them Don't Know Their APRs," Bankrate, January 10, 2023, https://www.bankrate.com/finance/credit-cards/more-americans-carrying-debt-and-many-dont-know-apr/.

35 Bill Fay, "Debt in America: Statistics and Demographics," Debt.org, April 3, 2023, https://www.debt.org/faqs/americans-in-debt/demographics/.

now you have the $100 you were putting toward the smallest debt, plus the $50 minimum payment you were making on this debt. That means you're putting $150 toward the second-smallest debt. After that's paid off, you'll put the extra $150 toward the third-smallest debt, plus the minimum payment you were already making. This method is psychologically rewarding and a good option for those who need encouragement and to see progress.

2. The Avalanche Method
This method involves paying down your debt with the highest interest rate first, then moving to the next-highest rate and paying that off. Again, you must keep making the minimum payments on all your debts during this time. I find this to be the more practical method, because paying off your highest-interest debt first should technically get you out of debt faster than the snowball method. The downside is it's less psychologically rewarding if your debts with higher rates are the larger ones. It will simply take longer to pay them off, which can slow the feeling of progress. This is the method for those who won't lose motivation and can stick to the plan without seeing fast progress.

The most important thing is to stick to whichever plan you select. Every month, you must take your extra pay-down money and apply it toward the next debt in your method. As you pay off each debt, take time to celebrate these wins. Each debt you pay off will lead to paying off the next debt even faster—the power of momentum is on your side.

Patterns for Tracking

To ensure you're consistently tracking your income, sticking to your budget, and paying down your debts, you'll need to schedule regular reviews with yourself to go over your numbers and keep them top of mind. Frequent reviews will train your RAS to pay attention to where your money is going and rewire your brain to reward you for making progress on your goals.

I recommend weekly reviews of your budget tracking, asking yourself these questions.

1. How well are you staying on budget with your needs?
2. How well are you staying on budget with your wants?
3. How are your emergency fund or savings accounts growing?

4. How much debt have you paid off?

5. When you're ready to tackle your next debt, which one will it be?

An accountability partner or group can keep you encouraged and focused. You can all share tips, tricks, or strategies to improve your budgets, accelerate the pace at which you grow savings, and celebrate together as debts are paid off. Time is of the essence, especially when you consider the opportunity cost of not having savings with interest that compounds over time in your favor.

This is a simple concept, but it's also hard because it requires discipline, focus, and commitment to your budget, your tracking, and paying down your debt. As long as you stick to your plan, you'll win. The pillar of strong defense is priceless.

In the next section, we will discuss how to make more money and track your income. The offense pillar requires a different skillset, mindset, and approach. While saving your money is simple, making more money is fun.

KEY TAKEAWAYS

- Pay yourself first by setting your checking account to automatically transfer money to your savings account or emergency account.
- Budget from your net paycheck, not your gross income.
- Give a numerical order to your expenses to see which are giving you pleasure and which are not.
- Review your most expensive budget items to see if they can be eliminated or reduced.
- Compound interest is the eighth wonder of the world. Those who understand it, make it; those who don't, pay it.
- Opportunity cost is the true cost of spending money, such as the interest you could have earned by saving money instead of having to pay off debt.
- Outline your debt obligations and determine if you will use the snowball method or avalanche method.
- Track your budget weekly.
- Look for a group or accountability partner to receive and offer help from like-minded people on the same journey.

PILLAR II

OFFENSE

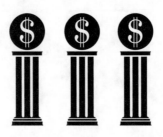

Chapter 6
OFFENSIVE PRINCIPLES

*Your level of success will rarely exceed your level
of personal development, because success is something
you attract by the person you become.*
—JIM ROHN

Earning a higher income comes down to developing your skills, abilities, and performances—and having the mindset of a winner. This section will share how to build up each of these areas, from receiving promotions to taking on new jobs or roles in a job that will earn you more income.

My Professional Progression

I told you a bit about my work history in Chapter 3, but I want to give more details here to show the push it takes to put your future first.

As a teenager, after months of applying for any job anywhere and getting nowhere, I told a friend about my troubles. He got me an interview the next day where he worked: a Baskin-Robbins ice cream shop. I was paid 80 percent of minimum wage because where I lived, there was a law that high school students could be paid less than minimum wage while still in school.

Next door to the Baskin-Robbins was a sandwich shop called Togo's. My friend and I got to know the employees there because we frequently picked up sandwiches for lunch. One particular shift manager at Togo's liked my work ethic and got me an interview with the hiring manager. I was offered a job with not only more hours but that also paid the full minimum wage. Togo's had a better training system and more involved management than Baskin-Robbins. After six months, I was promoted to shift manager, received a raise, and learned how to order food for the shop, take inventory, reconcile the cash register, make schedules, and more.

My younger brother landed a job at the Mexican restaurant next door to Togo's. As a busser, he was tipped by the servers, not the patrons. Even with this second-hand tipping system, he would frequently leave with an additional $20 or $30 at the end of the night. A quick analysis revealed that, as a new employee with no skills, he was making an additional three-to-four hours of wages just from tips. With most shifts, he increased his income by 50 percent for no extra time or work.

This motivated me to find a restaurant job of my own, and I went after the nicest place in town. I started as a busboy and a host, eventually winning over my coworkers and the owners. Helping the waiters, working with urgency, and taking care of all the guests led to me being promoted to waiter before any of the other support staff who had worked there longer than me. This quintupled my income, led to more responsibility, and incentivized me to work my hardest every day. My skills, mindset, and commitment to excellence improved, and the fires of my ambition grew hotter.

Unfortunately, a high school basketball injury led to ankle reconstruction surgery that left me on crutches for six months. During that time I asked myself some tough questions regarding my education and employment options.

After I healed, a friend told me about a restaurant an hour away that had a much more expensive menu. He introduced me to his neighbor who worked there, and the neighbor got me an interview. I was hired and now working in an upper-echelon restaurant that doubled my income, which required that I up my game again. I also changed the friends I was spending time with to people who were more mature and committed to success than living in the moment.

I worked at that restaurant through college and graduated with my car paid for, my schooling paid for, and more than $100,000 in the bank. Eighteen months of applying to enforcement agencies finally resulted in landing a job as a sheriff's deputy. This was a pay cut from what I made at the restaurant, and when I started at the police academy, I prayed that I would graduate and be able to stay on this new career path. For six months, I lived with continual fear that I'd fail a test, get injured, or make a mistake that would disqualify me.

I did graduate though, and I took my first assignment as a deputy sheriff at a maximum security detention center. I learned to be very aware of my surroundings; I was in a perpetual state of alert, trying to seem comfortable and relaxed in a dangerous environment where no one could afford to be comfortable or relaxed. I learned an important lesson there: The mind will adapt to the environment you put it in.

For the first few weeks on the job, my adrenaline was pumping the entire shift. I would get home and be unable to sleep because my sub-conscious still believed someone could jump out at me at any time. It took time to compartmentalize my hormonal responses. After a while, I could stay vigilant mentally while still calm hormonally. This allowed me to survive in the work environment and sleep in my home environment.

To make more money, I had no choice but to work more hours. I got on the sergeant's good side so that he'd call me first when over-time was available. As a single man with no family, I worked every shift I could. I made friends with the right people, studied the right things, and performed well; eventually I was being asked to work in the coveted positions other deputies wanted.

Everything was going well until the Great Recession in the late 2000s. Property taxes crashed, the sheriff's office budget was cut, and all the younger deputies were laid off—including me. I took a law enforcement job with a different agency that I believed was less likely to suffer budget cuts. This new job, as it turned out, offered better benefits and more overtime opportunities. I maximized my hours. By working up to one hundred hours a week for several years, I saved as much money as I could and invested it in real estate. I was receiving promotions and special assignments and making friends with the right people. Many of my financial pieces were coming together at this stage. Everything was going great, except for my health. The lack of sleep, always eating out, and not taking care of myself were catching up with me.

Friends from a group I belonged to called Gobundance challenged me: Knowing I was good at real estate investing, they told me to get my real estate license and stop working any unforced overtime for the rest of the year. If it went well, leave law enforcement and start a healthier life.

For the next twelve months, I learned how to sell homes as a real estate agent instead of working overtime as a law enforcement agent. I found my first clients by talking about real estate to officers, friends, and family. I eventually developed a presentation to give to potential clients and began giving it as often as I could. My initial steps into being an agent were painful, messy, and hilarious. I manually input my entire phone's contact list, one person at a time, into a customer relationship management system, not knowing how easily I could have downloaded it and imported it as a CSV file. My attempts at building rapport with potential clients were ridiculous until I figured out how to do it. I left police work after a year, started selling homes, and became the top agent in my office my first year working full-time in real estate.

I eventually put systems together, hired agents and admin staff, and started The David Greene Team. I used this same systemic approach to start a mortgage company, The One Brokerage. I began writing books for BiggerPockets and hosting a BiggerPockets podcast with Brandon Turner. I bought more real estate, started my mastermind Spartan League, and hosted retreats to teach business, budgeting, and real estate investing to others.

I was able to get through those times because I knew they weren't the whole journey, just a season of it—and we can all get through a season. Seasons are meant to teach us something. The lessons we learn during the difficult seasons of our lives are emotionally expensive. We go through so much pain to learn them, but that's also what makes them valuable.

I wanted to share an overview of some of the lessons I've learned on my own journey to show how those lessons made my future success easier. Lessons accumulate and build, eventually making each new lesson better, easier, and more lucrative than the last. Your first day working out is miserable, full of pain, sore muscles, and negative thoughts. None of us would continue to work out if it stayed that way. It doesn't. Working out becomes easier, more fun, and more productive the more you do it. So, too, does building your pillar of offense.

Lessons from My Journey

While no two journeys will be exactly the same, there are certain principles that will either help you or hinder you. Look for the lesson, learn from it, then master it as quickly as possible to speed up your progress. This can be done by adopting a winner's mindset, acting like a leader, and learning lessons with as much humility as possible. The following are success principles I learned in my journey.

Success Principle: Action Is Always Better Than Inaction

When I wanted a job in high school, I applied everywhere. After not finding anything, it was only talking with my friend that led me to my first job at Baskin-Robbins. I didn't realize it at the time, but that action of talking to someone about my job search was vital.

Success Principle: Help Others Whenever Possible

In the restaurant, I was known as the person to help others, and completing my tasks efficiently gave me more time to help others. This led to me having a good reputation and earning a promotion at work. Being helpful gets noticed.

Success Principle: How You Show Up Matters

The people who have put in a good word for me did so because they have worked with me and have seen my work ethic, integrity, and passion for excellence. Those are traits you can't just manufacture. How you show up every day matters for your future.

Success Principle: Make Friends Everywhere You Go

Earning the respect of my coworkers led to my boss hearing positive things about me, which eventually led to promotion opportunities. These coworkers then became clients and referrals when I earned my real estate license. Make friends everywhere you go. It forces you to put others first, be unselfish, and bring value to your environment.

Success Principle: Work Hard

When others see you doing your best, it's hard not to like and respect you (even if you're not that good at what you do yet). Skills take time to build, but hard work is possible from Day 1. Even if you're still on a learning curve, be the hardest worker in the room.

Success Principle: People Pay Attention

While it's true that everyone cares about their own interests, you can still make yourself useful to the people around you. At certain points in your journey, you will need help. You may need a day off for a health matter, be overwhelmed with work, or be going through a difficult personal time. Be there for others when they need it too, and make sure you deposit more into the accounts of your coworkers than you withdraw from them. They'll notice.

Success Principle: Earn Your Boss's Approval

It's common to hear people complain about their boss; in fact, it's unusual *not* to hear this. The irony is that the complainer is usually making themselves look worse than their boss. It's rarely personal when a boss seems like they don't like you. Just make sure the team wins, and your boss will appreciate you.

Success Principle: Make Your Desires for Promotion Known

Like a baby bird in a nest, a closed mouth doesn't get fed. I've blown opportunities by being too scared to speak up about what I want. When I made my intentions clear, I did better. In most cases, my boss explained to me what I needed to change or improve to be ready for a promotion. For those chasing excellence, this kind of feedback is precious. Don't let your ego get in the way of receiving information about how you can improve.

Success Principle: Save Your Money

This should go without saying by this point. It's more than discouraging to improve your pillar of offense only to spend all your money and have nothing to show for it.

Success Principle: Be Positive

I nearly quit the academy because of negative thoughts. It was only when I realized I would be envious of someone else graduating if I failed that I snapped out of my dark thinking.

Success Principle: Look for the 20 Percent

Twenty percent of your actions will bring you 80 percent of your results (the Pareto principle). Staying late to serve the last tables increased my income by 30 to 50 percent. Overtime paid 50 percent more than regular hours, and double time paid even better. Saving my money and watching it grow motivated me to keep working, even when I wanted to stay home or leave early. Look for the small decisions that lead to greater results. Do you know what your 20 percent is? Every opportunity has one. Make it a priority to find it, then stay in it as much as humanly possible to increase your income.

Success Principle: Double Down When You Find Something That Works

Saying yes to overtime when others said no allowed me to be the first one called when it was available. I certainly worked double-time OT whenever I could: I picked up more shifts at the restaurant, I showed houses before my police shift. I doubled down and prioritized overtime.

Success Principle: Avoid the Things That Don't Matter

I worked, studied, and exercised. I read books. I didn't smoke, party, drink, or stay in situations that did not have a clear upward path. I didn't take vacations or rack up debt for an "experience." I made only purposeful and calculated moves. Though none of them were impressive on their own—I didn't attend an Ivy League school, for example—their combined total led to impressive results in investing.

Success Principle: Do Hard Things

Working in a maximum security detention facility was hard. Training at the police academy was hard. Learning to be a real estate agent and holding open houses and figuring out my database were hard. When I didn't know what I was doing, taking the position of shift manager at Togo's was hard. Hiring and firing ten real estate assistants in a row was hard (and expensive). Taking over the biggest real estate podcast in the world was hard. And writing books is still hard. Consistently doing the hard things, and striving to do them well, built my skills and revealed patterns that made future struggles feel easier. This also will happen for you if you push yourself to keep learning.

Success Principle: Build Momentum

The hardest part of your journey to wealth is at the beginning, like with everything else in life. Whether it's working out, starting a new job, or changing your eating habits, the first steps are front-loaded with difficulty. With time and consistency, it gets much, much easier. As you build your wealth momentum, you'll enjoy the step you're on a bit more than the last, and it gets a bit easier and faster. Focus on building momentum, not achieving immediate results.

Success Principle: Look for Synergy

You've probably heard the Mark Twain quote, "Synergy is the bonus that is achieved when things work together harmoniously." Synergy with other ventures will help you build momentum faster, and conversely transfer some of the momentum you've built in one venture into new ventures. I built the majority of my wealth buying real estate. It got easier the more times I analyzed, offered, rehabbed, and managed a new rental. The multiple businesses I have started are in the same sphere. Synergy, paired with momentum, made building the pillar of offense easier with each business.

Offensive Principles

Saving money is a result of simple actions you can take, but making money is much more about who you are than what you do. Seeing yourself as a magnet that draws or repels opportunity will help you to understand this. Find the problems that need to be solved, and be the person to solve them. Rather than asking how you can make your day as easy as possible, ask yourself what struggles your boss or coworkers are having and look to relieve their burdens.

Increasing your value in the marketplace will have a direct correlation to increasing your income, and increasing your level of responsibility will build your skills and your value in the workplace. Changing your spending, your value system, your habits, and your mental approach is more challenging than most people are willing to accept. Not everyone really wants financial success.

This is the straightforward reason why the minority of people earn the majority of the money. Rich people believe there are unlimited opportunities and ways to earn money. They see the opportunities and are willing to make the changes necessary to take advantage of them. According to Zippia, the top 10 percent of Americans earn 30.2 percent of total U.S. income, whereas the bottom 90 percent split the remaining 69.8 percent of total income.[36] There are many arguments to be made about the disparity of income, but one thing is certain in a capitalist society like ours: You absolutely have the ability to adopt the habits, traits, and values of the wealthy for yourself.

Offensive Principle: Don't Look for Fulfillment in Life through Your Job

College students and others have been set up for failure when they're encouraged to pursue a career in a field that brings them fulfillment. While fulfillment, of course, is not a bad thing, many things can bring fulfillment in life *outside of work*. This can include raising a family, supporting a charity, coaching a team, volunteering at a house of worship, or starting a cultural movement. People should not expect emotional fulfillment *and* a high wage in the same place; it's often not realistic. The market doesn't care what anyone wants. The market cares about the highest level of goods or services possible. That's where the money is located, and those who do the best in the marketplace often have the means and experience to undertake benevolent endeavors across the globe on their own time.

Offensive Principle: Welcome Challenges

Every job, industry, or enterprise has areas of responsibility that are more difficult to succeed in than others. Look for them. Train your RAS to look for the opportunities that improve your chances to make

---

36 Jack Flynn, "Average American Income | 25 U.S. Salary Statistics," Zippia, Oct. 26, 2022, https://www.zippia.com/advice/average-american-income/.

yourself known at work and to make more money. This makes you more valuable to your company.

Offensive Principle: Approach Improvement Like an Athlete

Former high school and college athletes tend to have higher-status careers and earn 5 to 15 percent more than nonathletes,[37] an advantage that doesn't exist for any other extracurricular school activity.[38] This appears related to the approach that dedicated athletes use to improve their performance, along with learning other valuable qualities like leadership, proactivity, and confidence. The good news? You don't have to be a former athlete to behave like one. All of us have something we want to get better at, whether that's a hobby, a video game, or a craft. To do so, we focus on that goal. This approach works for improving your vocational skills as well.

Offensive Principle: Create Raving Fans

While doing your job "well enough" can keep you from getting fired, it's not enough if you want to ascend in the workplace hierarchy. People don't support mediocrity. That's why you must do more for others, so people will go out of their way to support you in return. Make it your job to create raving fans, and you'll see your career explode. This requires significantly more effort and will force you to outwork and outperform your marketplace competition. As noted earlier in the book, setting a standard for yourself that is significantly higher than others in your field is a simple and effective way to ensure you offer (and receive in return) superior performance and service.

Offensive Principle: Embrace Responsibility

It can be seductive to avoid responsibility at work. If you don't own the business, there will always be opportunities to avoid the hardest parts of the job or the most difficult tasks and leave them up to someone else. Employees who avoid responsibility create bad habits for themselves. For these people, they won't have the stamina to start their own

---

37 Kevin M.Kniffin, Brian Wansink, and Mitsuru Shimizu, "Sports at Work," *Journal of Leadership & Organizational Studies* 22, no. 2 (June 16, 2014): 217–230, https://doi.org/10.1177/1548051814538099.

38 Betsey Stevenson, "Beyond the Classroom: Using Title IX to Measure the Return to High School Sports," *National Bureau of Economic Research* (February 1, 2010): https://doi.org/10.3386/w15728.

enterprise, and the shock can be so substantial that it's overwhelming. This leads to entrepreneurial failure and a return to the employee trap.

Change your thinking on how you see responsibility from "pain point" to "possibilities for improvement." Making this subtle shift will radically improve your mood and optimism. Responsibility is like exercise: It gets easier with practice. Look for ways to take on small areas of responsibility wherever you can, ask for feedback on ways you can do better, and seek additional responsibility when the opportunity arises. Look at it as if you're getting paid to get better every day. You may not see a big bump in your salary, but your improved knowledge is of great value to the market *and* when you want to move on to being your own boss.

Offensive Principle: Act Like a Leader Now

Avoid the trap of "I'll work harder when they pay me more" and learn to look at work from the perspective of those in higher positions. Can you imagine a basketball player telling a coach, "I'll try harder later?" Continuing this analogy, if you want your coach (boss) to put you in the game (give you promotions), you need to give them a reason to want to.

Go to work every day with the mindset of proving to your boss why they should pay you more, promote you more, give you more opportunities. The best way to do this is to act like a leader before being promoted to one. When a leadership position becomes available, you will be the first name to come to mind. With promotions comes a higher salary, and with a higher salary comes more savings.

Offensive Principle: Don't Make Excuses

Feeling sorry for ourselves is a seductive trait, as is believing we are better than we really are. It's easy to see ourselves in the best possible light and make excuses for poor performance: I didn't sleep well last night, my kid is sick, etc. Those we work with and who depend on us don't know our story, and usually don't care. Excuses only prevent us from doing our best. Recognizing this is a big step toward maturity.

Practice extreme ownership. How you show up is completely within your control, and nobody but you stops you from being the best version of you. If you make a mistake or an outcome isn't right, resist the urge to make excuses for yourself.

Sales vs. Operations

Offense is about more than just principles. It also comes down to acquiring the skills that generate revenue, create value, and make the bacon. For most, acquiring sales skills will lead to a more lucrative career. Salespeople tend to make more money than operational people but have to accept less stability. Operational success is developed through acquiring different skills than sales. Understanding the difference between the two will help you decide which career path to choose and how to progress on it.

Almost all businesses can be classified into two divisions: sales and operations. Sales is like fishing: You look for customers, entice them with your goods or product, then try to reel in the revenue. Operations is everything else.

Consider restaurants: The cooks, managers, and dishwashers are the operations, and no restaurant could function without delicious food being prepared in the kitchen and served on clean plates. These positions are compensated by the hour, with the hourly rate based on seniority. People in sales—those who work to get the customers into the restaurant—are more likely to be compensated by salary.

The servers are in a hybrid role. They are part of operations—getting food to the table—*and* sales—upselling diners with a glass of wine or dessert at the end of the meal. These sales are obviously valuable to the restaurant's bottom line. As a result, successful servers are in line for advancement, such as being assigned the large parties and best tables and getting their preferred shifts. This keeps the best staff happy and in turn they provide the guests with the best experience possible. This then improves the restaurant's likelihood of staying in business and maximizing profits. It creates a symbiotic relationship between the best staff and restaurant managers and owners.

Why are those on the sales side compensated better than the operations side? Because they generate revenue that pays the operation staff and are therefore more valuable to a company's bottom line. This should not be confused with the value provided by those in operations. The moral here is that it's better to pursue excellence in the areas that pay better. That means focusing on sales.

Another reason it pays better is that learning how to make sales is usually more difficult than learning how to master operations. Additionally, operations depend on sales.

Fish, like customers, are notoriously difficult to catch. You have to choose the right bait and present it in the right way. You have to do sales at the right time of day and in a place where customers can be found. You can get everything right and the customer seems interested, and then just as quickly they're gone.

Learning how to make sales takes nuance and time. To sum it up, if you want to earn more money, you need to learn how to make sales.

KEY TAKEAWAYS

- To earn more, pursue excellence, develop your skills, and learn leadership.
- Look at obstacles not as problems but as possibilities for improvement. How you look at challenges determines how you feel and your success level.
- Twenty percent of your actions will bring you 80 percent of your results. Find your 20 percent.
- Create raving fans and see your career explode.
- Don't wait for a leadership position to act like a leader.
- Increasing your level of responsibility builds your skills and your value in the workplace. Increasing your value in the marketplace directly correlates to increasing your income.

Chapter 7

THE PURSUIT OF EXCELLENCE

We are what we repeatedly do. Excellence,
therefore, is not an act, but a habit.
—ARISTOTLE

The Seduction of Excellence

People seek out excellence. When in need of a contractor, don't you ask around for recommendations of someone who's good? When was the last time you wanted to eat at a mediocre restaurant or visit a doctor who was simply okay? When we search on Yelp or Amazon, we look at the number of stars a business has, because more stars equals excellence. Life is too short to settle for mediocrity. We even refer to doing our best as "bringing our A game" to indicate excellence.

Those we highly respect are known for their excellence. Chuck Yeager is unquestionably the most famous test pilot of all time, winning a place in aviation history as the first pilot to fly faster than the speed of sound. Albert Einstein achieved greatness in science with his theory of relativity. Mozart is unquestionably a genius in music. I even chose the epigraph to start this chapter because of Aristotle's known excellence in teaching.

Excellence captivates us so much that we will trade our hard-earned money (and energy) to watch professional sports teams, rock stars, and race car drivers do their work.

The Nature of Excellence

The lesson here is that excellence transcends competition. For example, Tony Robbins, one of the best-known self-help gurus in the world, is reputed to charge seven figures to coach his students. How does he get away with that? The people who pay Tony Robbins don't look at money the same way you do. One, they have more of it than most people; and two, being coached by Robbins has more value to them than a million dollars. Understanding the financial implications of excellence is easy: When you become excellent at something (like Tony Robbins is at life coaching), you have something to offer people who are willing to pay you exorbitant amounts of money, because that money means less to them than what they get in return: you.

Let's examine the opposite approach. Can a mediocre product demand a high price? Going further, how difficult would it be to get a buyer interested enough to part with their money (energy)? And do you want to spend your time with someone looking to buy a mediocre product—or worse, to live a mediocre life?

We all want to be associated with excellence. If I gave you the choice between the gift of a Rolex or a Casio watch, which would you prefer? My next question to you: What if you had the choice to become like the Rolex or the Casio? Knowing how much easier money, opportunity, and wealth flow toward excellence, what would you be willing to do to become the Rolex?

You're reading this book because you want a Rolex life. You don't want to worry about money. You don't want to feel poor, stretched thin, or anxious about your next bill. When you order an expensive meal at a restaurant, you don't want to feel guilty for it. This doesn't mean you want money to burn, but by the same token, you don't want money to consume your thoughts. A person buying a $15,000 used car is agonizing over every possible scenario that could go wrong, trying to prevent a loss, mistake, or problem. A person buying a Bugatti probably doesn't even know what it costs. These two shoppers have very different relationships with money. And quality. And excellence.

To become the Rolex, you must pursue excellence. The Rolex is known for its superior design, materials, and branding. How did the company achieve this? It's not complicated. The manufacturer asked a specific question: "How do we make the best watch in the world?" By asking yourself the same question and pursuing the same path, you'll get a similar result for yourself.

When it comes to the offense pillar, your goal is to increase the value you bring to the marketplace (your job, your boss, your customers, and so on).

Benefits of Greatness

A popular episode of the TV show *Seinfeld* involved a trip to buy the best soup in the city. The owner, known as the "Soup Nazi," makes soup that is so incredible a line extends around the block with people hungrily waiting for it. The soup comes with one caveat: You must follow the precise rules of the rude owner. Only a certain number of soups are available for purchase, and they may or may not come with bread. On George's first order, he notices he's not given bread. When he asks for some, he's told he must pay extra. When he complains, his order is canceled, and he gets no soup at all.

The episode humorously shows that the characters cannot figure out how to play by the rules. They say the wrong thing, ask for too much, or offend the owner. While the owner violates every rule of customer service, the line for his product never shortens. Why? His soup is so good, people are willing to do anything to buy some. Some customers win by learning the rules of the game. The biggest winner, though, is the owner who created the soup everyone wants. He could name his own (ludicrous) terms, and people still lined up for his soup. This didn't just happen; he had to first make excellent soup.

Excellence Manifested

The clearer and bigger your target, the easier it is to hit. Understand for yourself what you are pursuing. Aim for excellence in your workplace, but don't stop there. Recognize what excellence looks like in all its forms in your life.

As you read through the following, ask yourself: What improvements in these areas would increase the value you bring to the table?

Beauty and Confidence

While beauty comes in many forms, it is most easily recognized in someone's looks. I use this as my first example because how we feel about our physical appearance has a profound impact on our emotional state. The more attractive we feel, the more powerful we feel. It affects our emotions.

Not surprisingly, we find good-looking people to be more trustworthy. Studies have shown that attractive people are hired sooner, get promotions more quickly, and are higher-ranking in their companies. In *Beauty Pays: Why Attractive People Are More Successful*, economist Daniel Hamermesh explains that attractive people tend to have desirable personality traits, like higher self-confidence, that appeal to employers.[39] With confidence comes more job offers, higher salaries, and promotions. While we are born with our looks, everyone can build their confidence through doing more for themselves, like working out and dressing for the job you want. And that leads to knowing that confidence is belief in yourself. Confidence that you know what to say and when to say it, and what to do and when to do it.

IQ

The Oxford Languages dictionary defines intelligence as "the ability to acquire and apply knowledge and skills." Knowing how to apply what we learn increases our value at work and in life, and as a by-product, increases our income. Part of intelligence is being willing to take on new challenges, so look for ways to build your knowledge and skillsets.

Likeability

It is hard to objectively define what makes someone likable, but we know it when we see it. It's not a leap to assume that being likable can improve your opportunities in life and at work. Robert Cialdini, a social psychologist, has spent years researching what makes people

---

39 Daniel S. Hamermesh, *Beauty Pays: Why Attractive People Are More Successful* (Princeton, NJ: Princeton University Press, 2011).

more influential and persuasive. He says, "We like people who are similar to us, we like people who pay us compliments, and we like people who cooperate with us towards mutual goals."[40] Being likable means highlighting the areas we have in common with someone while downplaying the areas that we don't.

EQ

In *Emotional Intelligence*, Daniel Goleman suggests that our emotional intelligence quotient (EQ) might be more important than our IQ, because the latter doesn't account for the full range of intelligence.[41] Psychologist Howard Gardner suggests in *Frames of Mind: The Theory of Multiple Intelligences* that people are intelligent in multiple ways, including interpersonal intelligence.[42] We all know or have heard of people who study black holes but are shy around others at a picnic, or someone who is a brilliant artist but can't change a tire on their car. Intelligence comes in multiple forms. No matter which forms of intelligence you are gifted with, develop them, improve them, and use them to bring value to the marketplace.

Enemies of Excellence

Committing yourself to the pursuit of excellence means recognizing the forces working against you. Be aware of the following things that will hold you back.

Asking the Wrong Question

The default state for many of us is, "What's in it for me?" This is a dangerous question because the market—also known as your boss or customers—asks a very different question, and any time you separate yourself from the market, you will find yourself at odds with it. The market is asking, "Who has what I want? Who has what I need? Who sells the value I want?" That means you need to ask yourself

---

40 Robert Cialdini, "The Science of Persuasion: Seven Principles of Persuasion," Influence at Work, https://www.influenceatwork.com/7-principles-of-persuasion.

41 Daniel Goleman, *Emotional Intelligence: Why It Can Matter More than IQ* (New York: Random House, 2012).

42 Howard Gardner, *Frames of Mind: The Theory of Multiple Intelligences* (New York: Basic Books, 1983).

instead, "How can I provide what the market wants?" This will reveal opportunities and open your creative energies.

Looking for a Shortcut

We often look for the easiest path or shortest distance from A to B, or view obstacles as things to be avoided. However, the pursuit of excellence involves the opposite. In *The Obstacle Is the Way*, Ryan Holiday highlights the importance of seeing life's difficulties or struggles as incredibly important parts of our journey: "The obstacle in the path becomes the path. Never forget, within every obstacle is an opportunity to improve our condition."[43]

He also wrote:

> Andrew Carnegie famously put it. There's nothing shameful about sweeping. It's just another opportunity to excel—and to learn. But you, you're so busy thinking about the future, you don't take any pride in the tasks you're given right now. You just phone it all in, cash your paycheck, and dream of some higher station in life. Or you think, this is just a job, it isn't who I am, it doesn't matter. Foolishness. Everything we do matters—whether it's making smoothies while you save up money or studying for the bar—even after you already achieved the success you sought.

As Aristotle taught, excellence is not an act but a habit. If we are not pursuing excellence in the small things, how can we expect to pursue it in the big things?

Spending Time with the Wrong People

Tanya L. Chartrand and John A. Bargh are two psychologists who explored the chameleon effect, which refers to nonconscious mimicry of the postures, mannerisms, facial expressions, and other behaviors of one's interaction partners such that one's behavior passively and unintentionally changes to match that of others in one's current

---

43 Ryan Holiday, *The Obstacle Is the Way: The Timeless Art of Turning Trials into Triumph*, (New York: Portfolio/Penguin, 2014).

social environment.[44] In other words, when you live or interact with other people for long enough, you pick up some of their habits and behaviors—good or bad.

Who you spend time with matters. There's the saying that we are the average of the five people we spend the most time with. That's why I suggest joining a group of people who are on this same journey. Spending time with the right people—people who want to succeed as much as you do—will lead you to pick up on their behaviors, value systems, and perspectives. Of course, the same holds true for spending time with the wrong people.

Seeking Comfort

The desire for comfort is natural, but it's dangerous when comfort becomes *too* comfortable. Examine your relationship with comfort, and make sure it's not stifling your growth. Approach work with the intention of facing what might be hard, knowing that you can only improve yourself by stepping outside of your comfort zone. This will not only improve you, it also will improve your earnings capacity.

Allies of Excellence

The following actions will cultivate your passion and drive for excellence and assist you on the wealth-building journey.

Falling in Love with the Process of Becoming Great

If you remember only one thing from the Offense section of this book, make it this: Falling in love with the process of becoming great will propel you much further and faster on this journey. Don't start this work begrudgingly; eagerly approach every day looking for the opportunities life can bring you, and see any resistance as a blessing to make you stronger. The positivity you bring toward your obstacles is vital for moving forward.

Tracking What Matters

Research published by the American Psychological Association

---

44 Tanya L. Chartrand and John A. Bargh, "The Chameleon Effect: The Perception–Behavior Link and Social Interaction," *Journal of Personality and Social Psychology* 76, no. 6 (January 1, 1999): 893–910, https://doi.org/10.1037/0022-3514.76.6.893.

shows the more often that you monitor your progress toward a goal, the more likely you are to achieve the goal.[45] The study's lead author, Benjamin Harkin, PhD, said:

> Monitoring goal progress is a crucial process that comes into play between setting and attaining a goal, ensuring that the goals are translated into action. … prompting progress monitoring improves behavioral performance and the likelihood of attaining one's goals.

Put simply, successful people track their progress. Whether it's for business or fitness, monitoring your progress is essential. This will prevent you from backsliding too far during bad times and keep you focused on achieving your best during good times. Tracking improves your motivation and keeps you in the game.

Loving Accountability

The American Society of Training and Development found there is a 65 percent higher chance of completing a goal if you tell someone about it. That goes up to a whopping 95 percent if you keep accountability appointments with that someone. The study also found decreasing probability of success the further you remove yourself from accountability.[46] For example, deciding you'll take an action but not telling anyone gives you only a 25 percent chance of success. Even planning how to do it but not telling anyone only gives you a 50 percent shot. Successful people learn to love accountability as a process because it delivers results.

Harnessing Your Subconscious

Dr. Bruce Lipton, a stem cell biologist, is quoted in "The Power of the Subconscious Mind" by Judith Pierson: "Most people don't even acknowledge that their subconscious mind is at play when the fact is it is a million times more powerful than the conscious mind."

---

45 Benjamin Harkin et al., "Frequently Monitoring Progress toward Goals Increases Chance of Success," *American Psychological Association* (October 28, 2015): https://www.apa.org/news/press/releases/2015/10/progress-goals.

46 Thomas Oppong, "Psychological Secrets to Hack Your Way to Better Life Habits," Observer, March 22, 2017, https://observer.com/2017/03/psychological-secrets-hack-better-life-habits-psychology-productivity/.

Pierson adds, "Your subconscious can sabotage your best efforts or be recruited to enhance your life."[47]

Our subconscious can be a wonderful ally or a cruel master. It's up to us to decide which role it will play. If it believes you want to achieve excellence, it will point out opportunities to do so. If it believes you want to avoid hard work, it will provide the excuses you need. Harnessing your subconscious will give you the power to change your habits and the path you are on.

Seeing Yourself in Others

Mahatma Gandhi famously said that we should be the change we wish to see in the world. Be the friend you wish you to have. Be the person who gladly shares others' accomplishments. Be the best you can be to bring out the best in others. Focus not on yourself, but on others. This is a powerful exercise in increasing value wherever you go.

Meritocracy vs. Seniority

We've all been in a situation where we've patiently waited for "our time" to come, only to see others receive the promotion or contract or bonus we thought we'd get. It's tempting to feel taken advantage of in those moments, but these experiences are a normal part of life.

The problem is how the value system is set up to work. One system is meritocracy: Those who deserve something the most—because of their skills or hard work—will receive it. Capitalism is supposedly based on meritocracy. The employee who generates the most revenue for their company makes the most per hour. In sports, the athlete who performs the best gets the gold. Meritocracies feel natural.

The other value system is seniority. Here, the employee with the most years is the most valuable. They are compensated with better shifts, assignments, or pay. This system is commonly found in industries where merit is difficult to measure. A car dealership that measures sales is more like a meritocracy, while a factory that requires workers to assemble car parts is more likely to operate by seniority.

---

47 Judith Pierson, "The Power of the Subconscious Mind," *ResearchGate* (November 9, 2022): https://www.researchgate.net/publication/365211107_The_Power_of_the_ Subconscious_Mind.

However, most enterprises function in a hybrid system. Salespeople get a base pay but also performance incentives. Office work is harder to quantify value, so the salaries and benefits for the same position tend to be the same. When a salesperson receives base pay and performance incentives, or an office worker receives an hourly wage and a bonus when the company hits its goals, they are working in a hybrid system.

There is danger in thinking you operate in a seniority-based society when, in fact, you are in a merit-based one, especially in a shifting economy. Many employees who think they're secure in their positions find themselves unemployed. Those higher in seniority often find themselves the first out the door. Working in a meritocracy, and knowing exactly where you stand in that system, is usually safer.

This is why it's important to take advantage of valuable opportunities to take on more responsibility. There are only so many management or senior or specialized positions, and it's rare when one of them has an opening. Being unaware of how to get those positions puts you at a workplace disadvantage. The bussers where I first worked didn't realize we could be promoted to server until they saw me do it. They thought they were operating under a seniority system and had to learn the hard way that our boss was operating from a meritocracy. I understood it, and I took advantage to better myself.

If you've never owned a company, you may find it difficult to understand an owner's unique perspective. Owners have only their bottom line in mind when making any hiring, firing, or promoting decisions. Understanding that businesses are built on, fed by, and designed around revenue streams will help you figure out how to increase your value—and your take-home pay. This is especially important to learn when you become your own boss in real estate.

Hiding from Greatness

Revenue-generating skills—that is, sales—clearly pay more than operational skills. With this being the case, why do so many people choose operations over sales?

Operations Are More Secure

Because sales positions have a higher ceiling (the ability to make more from bonuses or commissions), they usually also come with a lower floor (base salary). This is an uncomfortable idea to a lot of people who enter the workforce, especially if they have debt. Operational positions feel more secure because the salary is known.

Operations Are More Comfortable

Your jobs have likely been in operations; most are. If you received a more challenging position, you were given the impression that you were making progress. But in operations, you only learn your job in a hierarchy. With sales, you are more of your own boss—that can be uncomfortable, but it also comes with the ability to grow your skills and your income far higher.

There Are More Jobs in Operations

There are far more McDonald's employees working in the operations end of the business than in the sales and marketing departments. That's because it takes highly paid, highly skilled, and highly experienced corporate executives to make the business decisions. They work with the PR and marketing agencies, and they decide which ads to run, in which markets to run them, and what prices should be. McDonald's doesn't leave the most important business decisions to those who make the food, clean the restaurants, and collect the money from patrons. Those workers keep the operation running; they don't work with improving the business model.

Operation Jobs and Consumer Debt

Consumer debt is the cause of so much pain and lost opportunities. Some people who want to make the jump to sales often can't because of their debt and financial constraints. They have taken on so much debt that they cannot afford to make less money in the short term while they build the skills that will make them more money in the long term. With growing debt obligations, the window gets smaller for moving from the operations track to the sales track. Consumer debt is your enemy for making professional progress.

Operations and Performance

Most operational structures are formed as divisions in companies. Poor performance is easier to hide in an operational setting because it's more difficult for management to measure productivity at the individual level than at the divisional level. This increases the likelihood that a handful of individuals are carrying the load of the entire team, making it easier for poor performers to remain unexposed while the division looks great to the CEO.

Remember my restaurant example? When I was bussing, I would frequently complete my job, then help the servers with their jobs, then help the other bussers with theirs. The result from my hard work was that tables were readied for new guests at a faster rate. The problem is that my boss saw it generally as "the bussers" doing their job. It was only after the servers specifically named me to the manager that I was recognized for my excellence.

Sales works differently than operations because you're at the individual level. A quick computerized report shows results from those in sales—and quickly reveals the top and bottom performers.

Operations Are Less Stressful

Few people naturally enjoy stress, but it is valuable when we have a scary goal—and all goals should be scary. For those on a journey to financial freedom and who need to build their pillar of offense, stress is a blessing. Look for ways to improve your income and money-saving skills, and look to any stress as your fuel.

Work in operations requires less business and personal growth than work in sales. This is not to say operations do not require growth. It's just that work in sales provides immediate and unavoidable feedback. Mistakes in sales are more obvious. It is impossible to improve your ability in sales without also improving yourself.

Show Your Merit through Problem-Solving

So now that you understand that working in sales is a better system to advance your goal of building wealth, how do you make that happen? The short answer is to focus on building your skills, which is covered in the next chapter. Before we get there, I want to share how one's merit is determined. It can be summed up as *your ability to solve problems*. This one skill will make you more valuable to your employer and the marketplace.

Elon Musk, who is one of the richest people in the world, has said, "You are paid in direct proportion to the difficulty of problems you solve." The market values those who do the hard things. The harder the problem, the fewer people who can do it. And if you're one of the problem-solvers, you can usually make more income. Problem-solving usually shows in three ways: difficulty, quantity, and quality.

Difficulty

Those who can solve more difficult problems are compensated at a higher amount than those who solve simple problems. For example, Elon Musk has taken on the problems of the world's changing environment by creating fully electric vehicles, and has lowered the cost of spaceflight by creating SpaceX.

While Musk has a reputation for being notoriously difficult to work for, it's likely because he demands excellence from those associated with his businesses. He frequently seeks the brightest engineers to help solve truly difficult problems. These people are highly compensated, and their problem-solving abilities have made Musk's companies some of the most successful in the world.

Quantity

You can also make more money if you solve more problems, even if they're not difficult. I made more money as a waiter than my colleagues because I could handle more tables. The same was true in my real estate sales career working for other people. Selling higher-priced homes was harder than selling townhouses, but it led to more revenue and was more important to my (and the company's) bottom line. Improving your knowledge and skill level will teach you to solve difficult problems, but working more efficiently than others will help you to solve more problems. Improving your productivity each day leads to improvement over the month. Doing this for years will lead to a lifetime of more revenue and more investing opportunities.

Quality

Working in a more expensive restaurant meant solving more problems with higher-paying customers. My skills had to be sharpened, but the result was the opportunity to work on larger parties and banquets. Doing my job *better*, not just faster, improved my income.

You know quality in the difference someone makes you feel. Interacting with someone who takes your order *and* brightens your day improves your mood and shows that they like their job. We all can control the quality of our problem-solving by having a positive attitude.

These are straightforward examples of ways to pursue excellence. Solving problems can be broken down by quality, difficulty, and quantity.

KEY TAKEAWAYS

- The people we most respect are known for excellence in their achievements.
- The financial implications of excellence are simple: You can charge more for your abilities.
- When it comes to building your pillar of offense, look to increase the value you bring to the marketplace.
- Confidence shows in the belief you have in yourself; with confidence comes more job offers, higher salaries, and promotions.
- IQ is important, but so is emotional intelligence (your EQ).
- Spend time with successful people so that you subconsciously pick up on their behaviors, value systems, and perspectives.
- Too much comfort is dangerous for growth.
- Fall in love with the process of becoming great.
- Successful people track their progress and share their goals for accountability.
- Consumer debt can keep you stuck in lower-paying operations jobs rather than a sales job that has lower base pay but no ceiling on what you can make.
- You are paid in direct proportion to your problem-solving abilities.

Chapter 8
SKILL DEVELOPMENT

Life is like a tango; fortunate are the few who can master it.
—A.J. GARCES

Why We've Lost Touch with Developing Our Skills

For centuries, getting an apprenticeship was a requirement to enter a trade. Benjamin Franklin was an apprentice printer, George Washington an apprentice surveyor.[48] Centuries later, we have replaced skill-building with education in many ways; college is now the de facto step after high school. While blue-collar trades have kept apprenticeships, many people see higher education as the path to their future—and the effect on society has been large.

The apprenticeship model focuses on building skills for the purpose of creating a specialized labor pool. Centuries ago, learning how to shoe a horse, set a newspaper, or build a barn were necessary skills one needed to become a tradesperson. It was a linear progression from apprentice to skilled tradesperson.

---

48 "Old Idea, New Economy: Rediscovering Apprenticeships," interview by Sasha Aslanian, *The Educate Podcast*, APM Reports, September 3, 2018, https://www.apmreports.org/episode/2018/09/03/old-idea-new-economy-rediscovering-apprenticeships.

Today, the labor pool is muddied. Education has removed skill-building as the path to success. As a result, Americans now value education over skills in the trades.

Is this good? Yes, a student seeking to practice law needs an extensive education in law. The same could be said about education for doctors, engineers, and scientists. These career paths have a direct correlation between higher levels of education and higher levels of pay. Other career paths are far different. For most of us, our skills are typically learned on the job or through experience. That leads us to ask, is education or learning skills better? The better question you should ask is, "Is my education building my skills?"

An article published on Study Finds discusses research from Professor Jeroma Adda from Bocconi University in Milan and Christian Dustmann from University College London, who examined the short- and long-term benefits of certain decisions workers make when entering the labor market.

Workers who pick up more job skills and undergo more job training before entering the market generally make more money than their peers. The study found acquiring more skills, both physical and mental, increases a worker's chances of getting high-paying jobs, receiving better offers from competing companies, and avoiding unemployment.[49]

Why Skill-Building Is Important

Once you've acquired a skill, that knowledge cannot be taken away from you. Say you work at an auto repair shop. Most of your clients drive similar model cars, but occasionally someone brings in a European brand vehicle. Your coworkers don't like working on these cars because they are unfamiliar with them, but you take a different approach and volunteer for the rare and valuable skill-building opportunity in front of you.

You watch online videos, talk to knowledgeable mechanics, and read the instruction manual for each new model. Through a slow process, your skill set with these cars grows. You build a reputation

---

49 Chris Melore, "Want a Higher Salary? Acquiring New Skills Is More Important than Having Connections," Study Finds, August 24, 2022, https://studyfinds.org/higher-salary-acquiring-new-skills/.

for yourself. Your boss gets referrals from other mechanics who can't fix European models, and he gives them all to you. You now have an invaluable skill, and you can command a higher wage. You can go to almost any mechanic shop and quickly get hired. That's not true for your colleagues, who decided to take the easy route and pass up the opportunity to educate themselves.

In this example, the only thing separating you from your colleagues is your desire to build your skill set. And with that, you improved your marketplace value.

Your schedule, position, or job may be taken from you, but your skills cannot. Supervisors come and go, and economies are constantly shifting. There are so many things you cannot control, but your skill sets and your ability to build skills are within your control. Those who know how to adapt the quickest have the easiest time in the marketplace.

From Darkness to Light

The streets in London are notoriously complicated and difficult to memorize. They were laid out with little rhyme or reason, so taxi drivers are required to pass a difficult test that often requires three or four years of studying. Because of the vast knowledge required to memorize all the streets in London, neuroscientist Eleanor Maguire was curious if the cab drivers who passed the exam had a hippocampus that was larger than normal, similar to those found in animals who were known for burying their food and finding it later.

Maguire and her colleagues Katherine Woollett and Hugo Spiers studied a group of seventy-nine aspiring taxi drivers over a four-year period, measuring the growth of their hippocampi with magnetic resonance imaging (MRI). Additionally, they measured brain growth in another thirty-one people who did not drive taxis to compare them to. Both groups had similar-sized hippocampi to start the study.

After four years, thirty-nine of the seventy-nine trainees had earned their licenses, while twenty trainees who failed their exams agreed to continue participating in the study. Maguire gave the successful and disappointed trainees the same tests she had given them before their training, with the intention of determining if they would do better. Maguire found the drivers who earned their licenses performed far better than those who failed, even though they had performed equally before the training. The MRIs showed the successful drivers hippocampi had grown during this time. It appeared the longer someone had been driving a taxi, the larger their hippocampus grew, as though it had expanded to accommodate the cognitive demand of memorizing London streets.[50]

The results from Maguire's study showed that the more people focus on learning new information, the more their brains will adapt to prioritize it.

Similarly, we track our income and expenses because we are training our brain to value this new information. Looking at the budget frequently and learning ways to improve it can have a similar effect to the London taxi driver study. Budgeting, like learning the streets of London, is a discipline that can be learned, studied, and improved upon.

As David Allen notes in his book *Getting Things Done*:

> Just like a computer, your brain has a search function—but it's even more phenomenal than a computer's. It seems to be programmed by what we focus on and, more primarily, what we identify with. ... We notice only what matches our internal belief systems and identified contexts. If you're an optometrist, for example, you'll tend to notice people wearing eyeglasses across a crowded room; if you're a building contractor, you may notice the room's physical details.[51]

This explains the phenomenon of why we notice other cars on the road of the same make and model we want to purchase when previously our brains didn't detect a difference in any cars on the road. Imagine the power you could unlock if you could literally train your RAS (your reticular activating system, part of the brain stem connecting the subconscious part of your brain with the conscious part of your brain; this was introduced in Chapter 5) to call attention to the things

50 Eleanor A Maguire, Katherine Woollett, and Hugo J Spiers. "London taxi drivers and bus drivers: a structural MRI and neuropsychological analysis," *Hippocampus*, 16, no. 12 (2006): 1091-101, https://doi.org/10.1002/hipo.20233.

51 David Allen, *Getting Things Done: The Art of Stress-Free Productivity* (New York: Penguin, 2015).

you believed were most important. Focusing on your budget every week begins the process of teaching your RAS that you want it to notice how you are spending and making money; the opportunities to make more money and save more money are everywhere.

Your brain will adapt and reconfigure to support your savings goals. It's wired and designed to focus on what you tell it is most important, but before it can readjust, you must clearly direct it to what you want. The habits you have now came from training your subconscious to direct you toward certain actions. Whether you realize it or not, you created the habits and the life you have now. This means you can recreate them. Your subconscious is a powerful ally when recruited to work toward your new goals. It's also a powerful enemy if left unchecked, continuing to steer you toward old patterns, habits, and values.

I improved my ability to build my skills—and to earn more money—by reading *The Richest Man in Babylon*. Those lessons still apply as much as ever, and the following is my advice based on that literary classic.

Fall in Love with the Process Itself
After a night in the restaurant, my routine was to walk to my car after clocking out and ask myself if I had as much money in my pocket as possible. Had I taken advantage of every available opportunity to grow? Had I set myself up for tomorrow's success? I would reflect on the day's work and consider if I had cut corners, had a poor attitude, or had missed an opportunity for growth. If yes, then I'd think about how I could handle those situations better the next day.

This is my process for falling in love with greatness. It requires stoking the fires of my ambition to be as hot as possible. I am driven to learn new things, perform better, and welcome obstacles that get in the way of my ambition. Without this drive, you wouldn't be reading this book.

You may be nervous to stoke this fire because you're afraid you will change into a more ambitious and greedier version of yourself. Only one of those things is negative.

Differentiate between Ambition and Greed
The Oxford Languages dictionary defines greed as an "intense and selfish desire for something, especially wealth, power, or food." The

key word is "selfish"—that is what prompts us to do something that benefits us at the expense of someone else. It ranges from eating the last piece of cake just because you don't want someone else to have it to taking a final shot to score at the last second when someone else is in a better position.

Ambition is defined as "desire and determination to achieve success." It's the impulse or emotional drive to achieve or have more. It can have a negative connotation, but well-placed ambition is likely to create win-win scenarios. When an athlete wants to win the game, they'll give the best player, or the player in the best position, the final shot, because that's the best chance for the team to win.

Someone who is ambitious can create opportunities for themselves *and* others. They inspire their coworkers, family members, and friends to be better. My promotion from busboy to server led the other bussers to follow in my footsteps. They ended up making more money, and it made a better labor force for the restaurant. When I became the top-producing real estate agent in my office, I started a team. I didn't take business away from the other Realtors; I set an example for growth. There are now four teams in the same office that originally had none.

The right ambition will always create more than it takes. Greed does the opposite. Greed wants to take what others have without creating value or giving back. Greed is theft. It will lead you to give intentionally poor advice to others, to manipulate them, or even to sabotage their advancement. The negative stereotypes about wealth come from examples of greedy people; avoid being greedy and you will be free of guilt about building your wealth.

Create Focused Effort

A laser can cut through incredibly dense or hard objects. Symbolically, our own internal energy and ambition—our laser—allow us to cut through obstacles in our way. Light bulbs are different from lasers in that the energy they produce is neither contained nor amplified but spread out. Light bulbs allow you to see everything, but they do not have a specific focus.

Treat your ambition like a laser. Keep your energy contained, learning one skill set that will amplify and grow. Then learn another one. You'll eventually be able to laser through any of the obstacles in your job and in learning real estate. Bigger obstacles require more energy, but that's okay. Spend the time growing your skill sets to blast through them.

Immerse Yourself in Your Craft

When I first got my real estate license, I listened to three podcasts a day on how to be a better agent and how to improve my sales skills. I devoted nearly half a standard workday to listening to other professionals explain how they found success. This led to the inspiration and development of many of the tools The David Greene Team uses today, including our listing presentations, buyer presentations, branded moving boxes, client gifts, database management, in-person events, and more.

Agents on The DGT are required to give several presentations to their database a week, which builds both their confidence and delivery skills. It also spreads the word that they know their stuff. I review news and updates about the real estate market and share this information with the team, which improves both my knowledge and that of my team members. Even as the CEO—especially as the CEO—I want to learn even more about my craft. This rewards both me and my staff with more opportunities to make money.

Build a Fan Base

Building a fan base is all about the art of getting others to learn more about your skills or the quality of your work and who you are. Putting the best interests of others first is one way that will set you apart in a good way. Focus on building a great reputation, and fans will start to find you and tell others about you.

Supply and Demand in the Marketplace

Have you heard of Adam Smith? He's often referred to as the Father of Economics; in his 1776 book, *Wealth of Nations*, he described the concept of supply and demand as an "invisible hand" that naturally guides the economy. Smith said the invisible hand is the automatic pricing and distribution mechanisms in the economy. He described a society in which bakers and butchers provide products that individuals need and want (this was the eighteenth century, after all), creating a supply that meets demand and developing an economy that benefits everyone.[52]

Understanding this concept simplifies complex economic structures, like real estate prices. If there were an unlimited supply of homes, it'd be difficult, if not impossible, for housing prices to rise. Even if the demand for homes was strong and the market full of buyers, the supply would more than meet the demand. In real estate, price fluctuations occur only when supply and demand are out of balance. If the supply of homes shrinks but demand remains constant, there will be increased competition and sellers can increase their prices (seller's market). If supply remains constant but demand drops, it will be harder to sell homes and prices will have to drop (buyer's market).

The Advantage of a Supply-Side Market

Your income-earning potential follows the same principle. Choosing a career where there is limited competition gives you a demand-side advantage. Entering a heavily populated career puts you at a supply-side disadvantage. Consider this carefully when deciding where to start your real estate career. Following the herd may feel safer, but that's not always the case.

This applies to the earlier example about the mechanic who learned to work on European-made cars. He put himself in a demand-side market: Very few mechanics could do what he does. Meanwhile, his colleagues kept themselves in the supply-side market, along with many other mechanics who had the same skills. Staying aware of market trends in any job sector is important, because things can change rapidly and without warning.

For example, the late 1900s and early 2000s saw computer networking jobs in high demand; computer technology and workplace needs had evolved faster than the job market could provide laborers to meet them. The lack of supply in computer networkers, paired with the high demand for their services, led to very high salaries. I heard about this and wanted in, quickly signing up for classes that taught this skill. Apparently, I wasn't the only one with that idea. Thousands

---

52 "The Origins of the Law of Supply and Demand," Investopedia, September 21, 2021, https://www.investopedia.com/ask/answers/030415/who-discovered-law-supply-and-demand.asp.

upon thousands rushed into the field at the same time.

Within a few years, the field was flooded with qualified professionals. The rapid increase in supply, paired with a steady demand, led to wages plummeting for computer networking laborers. I went looking for a new career path. Had I stayed committed to that career path, not only would I have made much less money, but I would have soon been out of a job completely when technology quickly replaced humans to make computers communicate.

The Advantage of a Demand-Side Market
One advantage on the demand side is related to your skill-building abilities. The smartest way to improve your position is to improve your skills. The key is not to just get better, but to focus on being the best. Anyone can get better; it takes real work to become the best.

Improving your skills, getting certifications, and working more hours will certainly make it easier to be hired and hold a job. More experience leads to higher levels of competence, which in turn improves your value. You win by becoming noticeably better than everyone else and providing a better experience to your customer, your boss, or your coworkers.

The Process of Building Skills
To a large degree, your skills will determine your quality of life. Those with better skills will find it easier to make friends, attract partners, and make money. Learning how to acquire skills is an incredibly valuable skill in and of itself. For those who are younger, I recommend making this your top priority. Learning sales skills, communication skills, problem-solving skills, and more will pay huge dividends later. For those with more life experience, you likely have a better understanding of yourself and your strengths and can therefore identity the best skills for you to create the career you want.

Seeking Feedback Early
In my professional career I have always asked for feedback and instruction from my supervisors. It's a strategy I picked up when I played sports in my youth. I craved advice from my coaches in

the hopes that their feedback would make me better. Bringing this approach to my professional life led to the growth of my skills, and the money followed.

You might be surprised to hear that the reason this approach works is because it involves allowing yourself to not just make mistakes, but seek out and celebrate them. In a society focused on success, this might be hard to believe, so let me explain with a story from Researcher Jude King, PhD:

> In their book *Art & Fear,* authors David Bayles and Ted Orland tell the story of a teacher in a pottery class. ... On the first day of class, the ceramics teacher divided the class into two groups. All those on the left side of the class, he announced, would be graded solely on the *quantity of work* they produced, all those on the right solely on *its quality.*
>
> His procedure was simple: On the final day of class he would bring in his bathroom scale and weigh the work of the "quantity" group. Fifty pounds of pots rated an "A," forty a "B," and so on. Those being graded on "quality," however, needed to produce only one pot—albeit a perfect one—to get an A.

> When grading time came, the results were surprising but emphatic.

> The works of highest quality, the most beautiful and creative designs, were all produced by the group graded for quantity.

> As Bayles and Orland put it, "It seems that while the quantity group was busily churning out piles of work—and learning from their mistakes—the 'quality' group had sat theorizing about perfection, and in the end had little more to show for their efforts than grandiose theories and a pile of dead clay."[53]

This supports my theory on why I found success in sports. Rather than *talking* about how to improve, I was playing, seeking feedback,

---

53 Jude King, PhD, "The Science-Backed Secret to Rapidly Improving Any Skill," *Medium,* June 11, 2019, https://medium.com/swlh/the-science-backed-secret-to-rapidly-improving-any-skill-530e573aa546.

and immediately incorporating what I learned into the next day's practice. Both the pottery students (who were graded on quality) and I (who was judged on sports and athleticism) learned from our ongoing mistakes—an important type of feedback and a powerful teacher!

The Learning Feedback Cycle

Through the practical examples of athletics and art, it is easy to see that improvement is driven by learning. What's less obvious is that learning does not automatically lead to improvement. The key to turning learning into improvement is *using feedback*, which means using early results to modify your subsequent action(s). Scott Young describes the learning feedback cycle as having three stages: input, process, and result.

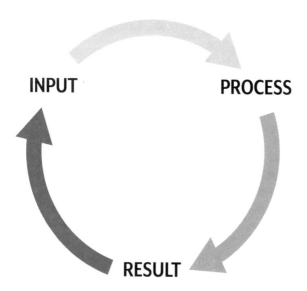

According to Young, real learning doesn't occur until all three parts of the learning feedback cycle have been completed.[54] In the pottery example, the quantity group completed learning feedback

54 King, "The Science-Backed Secret."

cycles for each pot, so their design and craftsmanship improved with each new piece. The quality group gained hypothetical knowledge, but received no feedback on the success or workability of that information because it only existed as a concept in their mind. Until they put those ideas to use, that knowledge was unproductive.

Seeing it spelled out like that, it seems simple. The application of knowledge is greater than the hoarding of knowledge. But let's take it a step further. You can tip the scales in your favor by finding ways to shorten your feedback loop. Dr. Anders Ericsson, a cognitive psychologist, specialized in the science of peak performance. He shed light on the importance of *timely* feedback to learning and improvement. In one study of medical professionals, he observed that surgeons (who see the results of their efforts almost immediately) tend to gain skills much faster than general practitioners (who may not see the impact of an incorrect diagnosis for years). He concluded that because work in the operating room offers feedback and success (or failure) quickly, surgeons are able to learn, adapt, and grow their skills faster.[55]

Ask yourself how you can shorten your feedback loop. In what situations could you put your knowledge and skills to the test quickly? And how will you identify the mistakes you've made and learn from them?

Most people are not proactive about learning cycles; they not only delay seeking feedback, they actively avoid it. Take the example of a car salesperson who does not proactively seek feedback. At the monthly review, their supervisor reviews their sales, which are strong but not the best at the dealership. A deeper dive into their sales technique reveals the salesperson does not ask customers enough questions to understand what they really want. The customers leave the dealership without buying a car and with questions they didn't ask. The supervisor teaches the salesperson how to ask better questions to build rapport. At the next review, the salesperson's numbers have improved. The supervisor provides more feedback to further improve the salesperson's skills.

This is the learning feedback cycle. The salesperson receives *input* about asking better questions, which they then *process* and

---

55 King, "The Science-Backed Secret."

implement, then they see the *result*: improved sales numbers. The level of growth is directly affected by the amount of time of the cycle. The more frequent the cycle, the faster the growth. The more infrequent, the slower the growth.

A salesperson who seeks continual feedback has a faster cycle than someone afraid of feedback. They receive constructive criticism, implement better processes, and see results by seeking *continual* feedback. When compared to the salespeople who receive feedback only every month or quarter, they have a clear advantage in doing better in the job. If the salesperson in the example had proactively sought out feedback, they could have shortened the time of their learning feedback cycle, and likely would have made faster improvements (and more money).

I witnessed this for myself in police department training. Those who were most coachable with the best attitudes were rewarded with additional attention from the instructors. Receiving more feedback from a firearms instructor, an emergency vehicle operations instructor, or a legal expert meant more learning and more skills being sharpened. My proactive requests for feedback led to me earning a reputation of being highly competent and receiving promotions and leadership opportunities. I climbed the ladder faster than other officers for two reasons: I knew I was competing with them while they were unaware of that, and I received more frequent feedback from department experts and supervisors.

I have implemented the same proactive learning feedback cycle at many stages in my life.

1. In the restaurant, I sought knowledge on restaurant etiquette from the manager while my competition didn't.
2. When I was playing high school basketball, I stayed after practice and asked for more coaching on strategies.
3. In college, I asked more questions during class and stayed after to learn more about topics that interested me.
4. At the police academy, I stayed late to seek additional martial arts instruction.
5. At the jail, I asked senior deputies questions about department policy and best practices.

6. In real estate, I offered to help the top-producing agents with tasks they did not enjoy, attended as many training sessions as possible, shadowed successful agents in other offices, and paid for coaching to improve my real estate business.
7. When I began writing books, I sought feedback and criticism on my writing style from best-selling authors.

In each of these circumstances, I was using the learning feedback cycle before I even knew that's what it was called. Once you make the conscious decision to grow your skills, the logical next step is to look for ways to implement your learning cycle.

Choose Opportunities Wisely

In the fable of the tortoise and the hare, the fast hare jumps out to a quick lead against the slower-moving tortoise. The hare's ability to move quickly actually backfires when his huge lead causes him to lose focus, making frequent stops and engaging in multiple distractions. The tortoise, having to compete without the hare's natural abilities, wins because his slow but steady progress is more effective over the length of the race. The lesson we've all learned from this tale is that steady progress beats shortsighted thinking.

We all have a hare inside us: It's the voice that tells us to do what is easiest, rely on our natural abilities, and engage in distractions when we can get away with it. There's nothing sexy about the tortoise's approach. It's so unattractive, we need a fable to remind us there's more wisdom in steady progress than rapid speed. One obvious way we can hurt our career earnings is by choosing the short path to "fast money" over the slow path to real wealth. Shortsighted thinking is expensive. It becomes even more expensive over time and with the power of compound interest.

I took a pay cut to attend the police academy. For six months I made less than what I earned waiting tables. This was not easy, and it bothered me. Even though I knew I had made the right move, it felt wrong. As a college student working in restaurants, I was making more money than anyone else my age. Meanwhile, my coworkers were adults with families to support. I felt like a big shot making an adult's wages as a kid, but had I stayed in that job, it would have been a disaster for my future. Others face the same temptation to take the most money *now* without considering the future. To put my focus on the next step—attend college and then the police academy—I had to be willing to let go of the fast money and instead pursue the career opportunities that would expand over time.

I provided a brief example about my computer networking career plan. Had I stuck with that plan, I would have made fast money for a few years but then been out of a job and looking for a plan B. The money I would have lost out on while I was unemployed and looking for my next opportunity would have been more than the fast money I made in the short term. It was the right decision to choose to finish college and look for steady income and overtime opportunities with law enforcement. That consistent income allowed me to save money that I then invested aggressively in real estate. I have built far more wealth than I could have hoped for in working a full-time job.

You may have already faced similar dilemmas in the journey toward financial freedom.

Would you rather...	Or...
Take a job with a higher salary at a start-up with no established reputation?	Take a job with a lower starting salary at an established company with a great reputation?
Be promoted to management with a pay increase but no sales exposure or opportunity?	Continue in a sales department making less money but receiving valuable on-the-job training?
Be promoted to a management position with higher pay but no overtime opportunities?	Stay at a lower base pay position with more overtime opportunities?
Pay for a college education when you don't have a career path established?	Take a position in the trades that won't pay well now but will later in life?
Buy an expensive car to look like you've "made it" or feel better about yourself?	Drive an unassuming car that keeps more money in the bank for investing?
Buy a big home, seriously increasing your debt and housing expenses?	Buy a modest home with space you can rent out, decreasing your housing costs?

Follow the hot new career field or investing opportunity?	Build skills or buy investments that others aren't pursuing?
Stay in a stable, comfortable position?	Try and possibly fail several times, learning a more challenging position that can move you forward?
Buy stuff you like?	Save money for investing in real estate?

We all face choices, but we often miss their significance in our lives. I spoke openly to work colleagues about my career goals and even encouraged others to join me in the journey. Sadly, most did not.

The people who make the choice to go down the easy path are motivated by either the attraction to fast money or the fear of having to start over. Career progression often involves taking a step backward before taking two steps forward. As you learn new skills, you cannot expect to be as immediately successful as those who started learning before you. Comparing yourself to others already in the field can cause discouragement. It's better to strive toward becoming like those you admire in a few years if you commit to the process. Looking forward, not backward, will change your perspective.

Time on Task

Some actions improve your skills; others don't. Learning which are which is an important piece in the skill-building puzzle. We forget about this when we fail to see every day as an opportunity to improve. It's only when a company begins the process of layoffs or the market enters a recession that we are forced to deal with these uncomfortable realities.

If you are running your own business or you're in a sales-based environment, keeping your attention on revenue-generating activities is vital. I tell the agents on The David Greene Team their goal is to spend as much time as possible in PLAN mode: Prospect (generate leads), Lead (follow up), Appointments, and Negotiate. If they aren't doing one of these four things, they aren't making money.

PLAN is a key performance indicator (KPI) for agents. KPIs are metrics that measure the most important things to achieve. These are the 20 percent of activities that lead to the 80 percent of results. If your goal is to build skills, you must understand which KPIs to focus on, as well things to avoid. A few examples include:

Profession	KPIs	What to Avoid
Salesperson	· Communicate with as many people as possible · Have as many conversations about business as possible · Follow up with as many leads as possible	· Reviewing emails from non-clients · Waiting for your clients to approach you · Placing business cards in random locations · Taking too much time serving clients you've already sold to
House flipper	· Contact as many distressed homeowners as possible · Meet with as many private money lenders as possible · Meet as many contractors as possible	· Obsessing over details the contractors should be handling · Reviewing the types of materials used by the rehab team · Improving your company logo
Management	· Encourage your staff and give due credit · Look for ways to improve productivity · Create better, more efficient systems	· Waiting for problems to arise instead of being proactive · Leaving things as status quo · Taking credit for staff accomplishments

Make this a familiar pattern:
1. Determine the KPI of your skill-building goal
2. Put as much time as possible into it
3. Review the results of the learning feedback cycle
4. Repeat

Michael Jordan wrote the following about goal-setting in his book *I Can't Accept Not Trying: Michael Jordan on the Pursuit of Excellence*:

> I approach everything step by step. ... As I look back, each one of the steps or successes led to the next one. ... I guess I approached it with the end in mind. I knew exactly where I wanted to go, and I focused on getting there. As I reached those goals, they built on one another. All those steps are like pieces of a puzzle. They all come together to form a picture. ... Step by step, I can't see any other way of accomplishing anything.[56]

Jordan is a pure example of excellence. His work ethic, tenacity, and commitment to basketball are second to none. Even with his remarkable athletic ability and superior skills, he was relentless in his commitment to improving them. Jordan's athletic trainer Tim Grover says in his book *Winning*:

> Winners don't fear reality, they don't hide from the truth, and they're not afraid to confront their own flaws and weaknesses. ... Every minute, you have the potential to recognize an opportunity, push yourself harder, let go of the insecurity and fear, stop listening to what others tell you, and decide to own that moment. And not just that one single moment, but the next one, and the next.[57]

Remind yourself daily you are in a competition to be the best you possible. Keep your focus on building your skills, measuring your KPIs, and seeking feedback. This will tip the scales of success in your favor. Above all else, remember these actions will improve your marketplace demand and put you in a position to succeed. When you take control of your finances and the direction of your life, you take control of building your skills.

---

56 Michael Jordan and Mark Vancil, *I Can't Accept Not Trying: Michael Jordan on the Pursuit of Excellence* (San Francisco: HarperSanFrancisco, 1994).

57 Tim S. Grover and Shari Wenk, *Winning: The Unforgiving Race to Greatness* (New York: Simon and Schuster, 2021).

KEY TAKEAWAYS

- Workers who pick up more skills and undergo more training before entering the job market generally make more money than their peers.
- You created the habits and the life you have now; this means you can also recreate them.
- Your subconscious is a powerful ally when recruited to work toward your new goals. It's also a powerful enemy if left unchecked, continuing to steer you toward old patterns, habits, and values.
- Ambition differs from greed in that it does not come at the expense of another. The right ambition will always create more than it takes.
- Those who seek feedback gain the advantage over those who do not. Asking for feedback will significantly improve the rate at which you improve.
- Choosing the short path to "fast money" over the slow path to real wealth can hurt your career earnings.
- Career progression often involves taking a step backward before taking two steps forward.
- Keep your focus on building your skills, knowing your crucial KPIs, and seeking as much feedback as possible. These will tip the scales of success in your favor.
- Take control of your finances and the direction of your life to take control of building your skills.

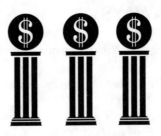

Chapter 9
LEADERSHIP

On any team, in any organization, all responsibility for success and failure rests with the leader. The leader must own everything in his or her world. There is no one else to blame.
—JOCKO WILLINK

House painting was my family's business when I was a child. My dad and his father-in-law owned a painting company, so I grew up smelling lacquer thinner and seeing my dad come home in white clothes covered in various colors. When I turned 11 years old, my grandfather took me painting with him. My jobs were to sand the door frames or cabinets before he painted them, mask off the areas that shouldn't get painted, and put drop cloths on the carpets and floors.

The problem was, at that age, I didn't want to be there and didn't know how to think on my own. That meant I stood around until my grandfather told me what to do. When given direction, I'd go do it and then wait for further instruction. Can you relate? One day, my grandfather told me about another young boy who worked for his friend. That boy would get out of the truck and immediately begin unloading the equipment. He was planting a seed in my mind that it was okay to be proactive, to think for myself, and to look for ways to contribute. Unfortunately for him, the seed didn't take root. I completely missed the lesson, instead thinking, "Well, you should hire him to come work with you."

I'm sure many of you can see that I received this well-intentioned direction from my kind grandfather as criticism because I had the wrong attitude. What happened between my job helping my grandfather and when I started working at Togo's? The only thing I can think to explain the shift in my attitude toward hard work and being a go-getter is that I better understood the value of money as I got older. It only took me a few years to realize that I *didn't* want to work a j-o-b forever, and the best way to accomplish that was by being proactive and showing my bosses the value I provided—leading to more money and more freedom in the long run.

Fast forward a few decades, and I now run a real estate team rather than sell houses myself. My main hurdle? Agents who want someone to tell them what to do. It's not a coincidence that my top agents have one thing in common: They proactively seek ways to improve their service, skills, and knowledge. They take responsibility for training newer team members, and then they seek more responsibility. Hands down, my best people are the ones who take a proactive approach to their work and want to be the best leaders possible.

Extreme Ownership

In his best-selling book *Extreme Ownership: How U.S. Navy SEALs Lead and Win*, retired U.S. Navy SEAL officer Jocko Willink presents a compelling argument that leadership plays a bigger role in success than anything else. According to him, everything is your fault. Everything. When something goes wrong, assume blame and look deeply at how you could be better. If someone else made the poor decision or the mistake, ask yourself how you could have helped prepare, train, or influence them to avoid it. If you don't like how something is going, make it better. Leaders never believe they are helpless, even if they aren't in charge.

Willink spent 20 years in the U.S. Navy SEAL Teams; during his military career, he was awarded the Silver Star, the Bronze Star, as well as other personal and unit awards. After retiring from the Navy in 2010, he started teaching the leadership principles he learned during his military career. He's a nationally recognized authority on leadership, as is his concept of extreme ownership. Like its name states, the concept is extreme—especially when so many of us have spent our lives blaming others for our poor outcomes. Our subconscious is programmed to do this, because blaming others is easy. Forcing yourself to look deeply at your own actions and listen to the whisper that points out where you could have done more takes discipline. Those who embrace this narrow path will learn what Willink teaches: It pays to win.

Leadership Patterns

The word leadership is often used to mean different things in different contexts. I see leadership manifest in several ways.

There is the leadership *position*. This refers to the person in charge; more specifically, to the person who is held responsible for the outcome. Leaders are often supervisors, bosses, or senior employees. Those in the position of leader are often held to higher standards and considered to be the example for others to follow.

Then there is the *spirit* of leadership, which is the drive or compulsion to improve a team's odds of winning through right action. It is the desire to make others around you better as a whole, not just your specific position within that group. When we speak of born leaders, we are often referring to the spirit of leadership. These folks are named team captain or squad leader, and are obvious choices for fast promotions due to their higher confidence levels and concern for the organization's outcome. Those in positions of leadership notice this spirit of leadership in others.

Those with a spirit of leadership have an advantage over those who avoid it. They proactively study information, arrive prepared for tests or meetings, and take initiative in asking questions and seeking to improve. They're viewed as team players because of their natural desire to work as a team and because they assist their coworkers without being asked to. Their desire to win drives them to improve their skills, which puts them on the path to better performance and leads to winning. This spirit of leadership is often contagious. It affects the attitudes and work ethic of others around them, improving the team as a whole and making their supervisors' jobs easier.

Finally, there is the *act* of leadership. One acts like a leader when they make decisions without explicit direction or take initiative in accomplishing an organization's goals. A busser who sees a patron walk into the restaurant when the host is not at the front has two choices: They can say it's not their job to greet the patron, or they can welcome the guest and let them know someone will be with them shortly and then find the host to inform them someone needs to be seated. The busser who does the latter is doing what is in the restaurant's best interest without being specifically directed; that's the act of leadership. I did not act like a leader when I worked with my grandfather.

Having the spirit of leadership increases the odds that someone acts as a leader. When you give someone positive reinforcement about their natural leadership skills, others notice. This eventually creates team momentum. As this momentum grows, people with the *spirit* of a leader are considered for a leadership *position*. This requires additional acts of leadership. With each increase in responsibility comes promotions, more pay, more benefits, and more perks.

Once promoted, a new cycle starts. You can relax and enjoy the perks of your new position, or you can continue building skills and taking on new responsibilities until the next promotion comes.

Lack of Leadership

Granted, it's much easier to ignore the things we aren't responsible for. We do it every time we see something that can be done but tell ourselves that someone else will do it, or every time we know we could do more but choose not to. This includes every skipped workout session, every time we could say something kind to someone but don't, and every time we miss a chance to feed our leadership spirit.

According to Apollo Technical, an IT and engineering recruitment agency, leadership is a critical yet missing piece for many companies:

> More than 77 percent of organizations report that leadership is lacking, and while that is a big number, it should not come as a surprise given that 10,000 Baby Boomers retire every single day. At the same time, 83 percent of businesses say it's important to develop leaders at all levels; yet, less than 5 percent of companies have implemented leadership development across all levels.[58]

---

58 "25 Surprising Leadership Statistics to Take Note Of," Apollo Technical LLC, May 25, 2022, https://www.apollotechnical.com/leadership-statistics/.

And the Association for Talent Development reported that most companies have skills gaps that may hamper their ability to prepare for the future:

> Survey results show reason to be concerned about a succession planning crisis. It appears that organizations aren't effective at preparing people for senior leadership positions. Half of the respondents said their companies had insufficient leadership bench talent, and 47 percent said they expect a gap of leadership or executive-level skills in the future.[59]

And these data were published before "quiet quitting" hit the zeitgeist. The issue is not one of lack of opportunity—not in America at least. The demand for leadership currently far outweighs the supply. Those who meet the need can expect the price they can command to rise.

It's not just within organizations that we see this occur. The pattern exists in the entrepreneurial/self-employed world as well. Failing to do what's best for your clients will lead to the same result as failing to do what's best for the team. The contractor who cuts corners, does poor work, and doesn't take advantage of opportunities to help their clients may not miss out on a promotion, but they'll definitely miss out on referrals. Over the course of a career, these missed opportunities are devastating to one's ability to grow a business.

Contrast that with the contractor who makes additional repairs while doing the original job, who proactively looks for ways to save the client money. This approach leaves the client feeling cared for and protected. They are more likely to leave positive reviews and go out of their way to tell others about their great experience. As referrals lead to more customers and more referrals, a business is born where a job once stood.

Growing a Business through Leadership

As one becomes a leader, more doors begin to open. Joe starts his career

59 "83 Percent of Organizations Have Skills Gaps, according to ATD Research," Association for Talent Development, December 19, 2018, https://www.td.org/press-release/83-percent-of-organizations-have-skills-gaps-according-to-atd-research.

young and unskilled. He apprentices for an established tradesperson and gains experience. His positive attitude and "team first" mentality make him an asset for the business. Joe helps build his boss's business as he builds his own skills under this tutelage. Joe's skills increase until he falls in love with the process of becoming great, and he reaches a level of excellence he couldn't have imagined previously.

Eventually, Joe starts his own enterprise. Each happy client leads to more referrals, and what starts as a tough time without many jobs soon becomes a business filled with opportunities. Joe can afford to take only the highest-paying jobs; in time, he can't keep up with demand and brings on apprentices of his own. Joe shifts his focus from "doing" the work to "teaching" the work, and he concentrates on marketing his business to new clients.

The apprentices at Joe's company who show the most aptitude and passion are promoted. They get the better jobs, earning more income for the company and themselves in the process. They then train the new apprentices. Joe uses his additional free time to get a contractor's license, making his company eligible for even bigger jobs and even more business opportunities. With each level of advancement, Joe embraces his own challenges and difficulties as a leader, as do those on his team who have the spirit of a leader. Some of his staff fail in the job or leave the company, but Joe is undeterred. He continues to improve his skill sets and the value he brings to his business, which sparks more growth.

Note that Joe was never officially promoted at his own company, because promotions only exist in someone else's business. When you do not own the company, you are at the mercy of opportunities being created by those above you. If you work for a company with strong leadership, promotions happen. If you work for poor leadership, it probably doesn't.

Those who choose to work for themselves have a different promotion pattern. With every staff member or apprentice that Joe hired, he effectively gave himself a promotion—along with more responsibility. He was freed up to do other things for the business, but he was also responsible for training the new hires, because his success depended on how well they did their jobs. If Joe decided to not act like a leader or to not try and instill those leadership skills in his employees, he could have faced a much different situation: failure.

There Are No Bad Teams, Only Bad Leaders

Jocko Willink's book *Extreme Ownership* opens with a story about a Navy SEAL recruitment group competing against each other during training. Boat Crew II consistently outperformed the other teams and frequently won the competitions, with the prize being breaks for its team members. Boat Crew VI, however, was a different story. Infighting, blaming, and a lack of teamwork led to the crew's subpar performance and frequent tongue-lashings from SEAL training staff.

This pattern continued until the senior chief made an insightful move to switch the leaders of the crews. All other rules of the competition stayed the same. The two leaders were not told why the change was taking place. For the next race, those two boats were locked in competition for the lead, significantly ahead of the rest of the pack. To everyone's surprise, Boat Crew VI, previously the worst crew, won. Of the event, Willink says:

> Had I not witnessed this amazing transformation, I might have doubted it. But it was a glaring, undeniable example of one of the most fundamental and important truths at the heart of Extreme Ownership: There are no bad teams, only bad leaders. How is it possible that switching a single individual—only the leader—had completely turned around the performance of an entire group? The answer: Leadership is the single greatest factor in any team's performance. Whether a team succeeds or fails is all up to the leader. The leader's attitude sets the tone for the entire team. The leader drives performance—or doesn't.[60]

Great leaders brings out the best of those under them. The former leader of Boat Crew II said or did something to harness the natural abilities of Boat Crew VI and get them to perform better. The talent had been there all along; the former leader of Boat Crew VI just didn't know how to tap into it. This is an important point because it challenges the conventional understanding of leadership. If leadership is viewed as simply telling others what to do or being the best at something, the story of Boat Crew VI's turnaround makes no sense. However, if leadership is viewed through the prism of a flame that can

---

60 Jocko Willink and Leif Babin, *Extreme Ownership: How U.S. Navy SEALs Lead and Win* (New York: St. Martin's Press, 2015): 49.

be stoked and grown, causing others around you to perform better, the story makes sense. Strong acts of leadership add fuel to the fire in others, improving their performance. Leadership is contagious and it benefits everyone in its midst.

Dean Smith, the University of North Carolina at Chapel Hill's head basketball coach for thirty-six years, said, "Basketball is a beautiful game when the five players on the court play with one heartbeat." Smith retired in 1997 as the winningest coach in college basketball,[61] so he understood leadership. The leader of the team sets the heartbeat, and the other players match it.

Phil Jackson, one of the winningest coaches in NBA history, is credited with the quote, "Basketball is a sport that involves the subtle interweaving of players at full speed to the point where they are thinking and moving as one." This is Jackson's description of teamwork. Boat Crew VI, under their new leader, moved with teamwork not previously seen. The results of strong leadership speak for themselves.

Imagine what you could do in business or in your career path if each team you worked on could achieve such oneness. Imagine if every group you were associated with was known for winning. Imagine if, at each stage in your evolution to become great, the spirit of leadership inside you grew stronger and stronger. How much would this be worth to you? How many doors might this open for you? Many of us spend our lives looking for the right leader to follow, but imagine if you became that leader for others instead.

The Blessings of Responsibility

As a teenager, basketball was my life. I loved to play it, I loved to study it, I loved to think about it. I loved the architecture of how five players created one moving organism. How there was always something I could do, at any moment, to make that organism stronger or make up for the weakness of one link. My coaches often demanded more of me than the other players, but at the time I didn't understand why.

When I was team captain, one of my responsibilities was to make

---

61 "225 Years of Tar Heels: Dean Smith," The University of North Carolina at Chapel Hill, May 13, 2019, https://www.unc.edu/posts/2019/03/08/225-years-of-tar-heels-dean-smith/.

sure every team member knew every play we ran. If a teammate made a mistake in practice by not being in the right position, practice would stop, and the team would watch me—not the player who screwed up—run laps as punishment. This was a form of extreme ownership that I did not understand at the time. Our star player was notorious for being late or missing practice completely. If he was not at practice on time, *I* was not eligible to play in the next game. My coach made me responsible for him because he had proved he could not be responsible for himself.

Was this unfair? From one perspective, yes. My parents encouraged me to quit the team as a message to the coach. I knew the treatment wasn't fair, but I could also see it was valuable. At 17 years old, I was being exposed to the facts that life is not always fair and responsibility is hard. My coach was instilling an adult mindset in me, while the rest of my teammates still acted like children.

The early exposure to leadership and responsibility imposed by my coach paid dividends later. In each job I had, I subconsciously looked for more responsibility while others avoided it; this felt natural to me. This proactive responsibility led to higher pay, more opportunities to learn, and a constantly increasing standard I placed on myself. Many others have life experiences that helped them in similar ways, such as a child needing to cook and clean when mom and dad have to work late or taking jobs as a teenager to help the family pay bills. These circumstances aren't fair, but they are valuable if the weight of responsibility bestows blessings.

In a 2007 survey of nearly 1,600 CEOs, 43 percent reported being the firstborn in their families.[62] Another survey discovered that firstborns are 55 percent more likely than the rest of the population to be founders of companies or organizations.[63] The weight of the responsibility of being the eldest child is likely to contribute to the higher levels of financial success.

We can't change our birth order, but we don't have to. Understanding that responsibility, not the luck of birth order, is what strengthens

---

62 Chelsea Greenwood, "Firstborn Children Are More Likely to Be CEOs, and Other Things Your Birth Order Can Predict about Your Future," *Business Insider*, April 8, 2019, https://www.businessinsider.com/siblings-birth-order-2018-4.

63 Pokin Yeung, "Why You're a Startup Founder: Nature and Nurture," *TechCrunch*, April 7, 2012, https://techcrunch.com/2012/04/07/founder-nature-vs-nurture/.

our leadership qualities puts the power in our own hands to improve our position. Responsibility does more than just make us better at our jobs; it can also improve the overall quality of our lives.

Look around. Do you see areas where you can step up and take initiative? Are there places in need of leadership? Leaders win, and winning pays.

Reasons We Avoid Leadership

With all the benefits that leadership provides, you'd think people would be eager to assume leadership positions. They're not. Several factors work against us in taking on the mantle of leadership, pursuing its benefits, and stoking its spirit within us and others. Understanding these forces will help you to avoid them and instead make wise decisions on which leadership opportunities are best for you.

No Self-Awareness

The leader of Boat Crew II turned Boat Crew VI around quickly, but not everyone is a Navy SEAL. However, all of us *can* develop our leadership spirit and act as a leader; you just have to be aware that you can.

Ego

Those with large or frail egos can find themselves pursuing the *position* of leader without having the *spirit* of leadership. This can lead to disaster. Those with an oversized ego normally can't handle the blame that comes with being a leader, or the extreme ownership required to do it well. If you find yourself shrinking from leadership opportunities, check in with your ego.

No Commitment to Excellence

Those uninterested in self-improvement often find no reason to pursue leadership because they see the sacrifice it requires but not the value it provides. From that view, there is only the downside of constant work to be better without the payoff. Leaders, on the other hand, are committed to excellence, winning, and success.

Fear of Blame

You cannot lead without receiving blame. In fact, leaders receive the most blame. When the Chicago Bulls suffered a disappointing playoff defeat at the hands of the Detroit Pistons in 1990, it was Michael Jordan who was labeled the disappointment. He subsequently hit the weight room to improve his body and led his team to sweep the Pistons in the playoffs the following year. If you can't take the blame for failing as a leader, you'll never get better as a leader.

Unresolved Wounds

When we are forced to admit we are wrong or made a mistake, we must admit that the current version of ourselves needs improving. For those who live with trauma of any sort, the message of needing improvement or "not being enough" can open old wounds that are too painful. The subconscious desire to protect ourselves from that pain will manifest in avoiding responsibility or the opportunities for scrutiny that accompany leadership.

In your pursuit of excellence and on your journey to financial freedom, you may find old wounds you buried long ago rising back up. Are you good enough? Are you smart enough? Do you have what it takes? Parts of the journey may reveal areas that still need healing; only by stepping out of your comfort zone are they exposed. And only by their exposure can they be dealt with appropriately. Unresolved wounds can lead to avoiding or thinking you dislike leadership. These old wounds, left alone, can cost you greatly on your journey to wealth and happiness in life.

Desire for the Wrong Kind of Freedom

Financial freedom allows you to do what you want with your life and not work according to someone else's plan. This kind of freedom is worth pursuing, but many desire the freedom from responsibility. If your desire is to take life easy and dodge hard things, commitment, or challenges, you'll steer clear of leadership opportunities. Look at those who have avoided responsibility, and you can see they don't have fulfilled lives. Joy is found in using and developing your skills and achieving financial freedom, not freedom from responsibility.

No respect for Your Gifts

Those who see their talents as gifts and use them as such benefit themselves and others. Those who don't see their gifts can't rise to the best of their abilities. Those who don't respect their gifts can't become constructive leaders. If you don't respect your gifts or, worse, don't believe you have any, you'll either be a poor leader or avoid leadership.

Lack of Faith

If you believe there's no point in improving or don't believe you can improve, you won't even try. A lack of faith in yourself or the mission will cause you to avoid leadership. I've been in situations when I did not believe in the mission or cause that I was associated with and found myself avoiding commitment. When this happened, I knew it was time to move on. If I didn't, I'd have given less than my best, which would have cheated myself and the mission. Leaders must have a strong faith in the cause, the mission, and their team members.

Listen to the Right Voices

Our words flow from our hearts. What we feel and what we believe is reflected in our language. If, deep in your heart, you want to avoid leadership at work, you may find yourself responding in the following ways:

- Why are they asking me to do that? It's not my job.
- That's not my problem.
- Shoot, there's the boss. Look busy!
- Go ask Steve. He's not busy.
- I'm not paid enough to care.

Those who are leaders or want to be leaders respond with:

- I can help you with that.
- What do you need? Let's work on it together.
- What can I do to develop myself?
- I can do it. It isn't my task, but the team deadline is approaching.

Note how so many of the positive responses are communication we usually have externally with our supervisor or coworkers. When we are operating from integrity, we show the world. Conversely, much negative talk is internal and an indication of what's in your heart. We think these thoughts in our heads but rarely dare to say them out loud. We subconsciously know we don't want others hearing how we really feel because we know it will make us look bad. When you're aware of it, you have the ability to change it.

Benefits of Extreme Ownership

The easiest way to avoid taking responsibilty for an outcome is not being involved in the decisions leading to the negative result. When I first began selling homes, I would refer my clients to a lender to get them preapproved for their mortgage. These lenders would often make mistakes, fail to communicate, or need to be reminded about the next steps. Inevitably, I'd end up explaining to the client what they needed to follow up with the lender on and what the next steps were. Though helping my clients get financing approval wasn't part of my job, I wanted the deal to close. Working with the lender and my clients in whatever way was needed not only got my deals to close, it also taught me quite a bit about lending.

I eventually included checking in on the lender as part of my process and taught my agents to do the same. On our selling listings, we would call the *buyer's lender*, even though it wasn't our responsibility, to make sure the buyer was turning in the required information. If it looked like they weren't going to be approved for the loan, we didn't grant extensions and would let the buyer's agent know the property would be going back on the market.

For our clients who were buying homes, part of our checklist was to make sure the loan officer ordered the appraisal, verified income, and received "clear to close" from the lender. This was more than other agents would do, even though they should. I included it in my process because I operate my business with extreme ownership (EO), and getting deals to close is how you win for your clients.

This attitude spread to other areas of my business. I learned how appraisers made their conclusions, how pest inspections worked, and how contractors solved construction problems. I became known as the agent who "knew everything." This was great for business because I was getting more clients, and those clients would refer me to their friends. This exponential growth was all a result of EO and skill-building. I avoided the "that's not my job" attitude and expected my team to never say *or* think it. Our clients didn't care whose job something was; they just wanted it done.

In addition to closing more deals, practicing EO led to an unexpected benefit: I started my own mortgage company, The One Brokerage, based largely on the information I learned doing loan officers' jobs for them. This additional revenue stream not only makes me more money, it also makes it easier for my Realtors to communicate with their lenders and for our clients to have the same team working for them throughout the process. This synergy is wonderful, and it never would have happened without EO.

Just like eating vegetables, EO does not come naturally; it becomes easier when you remember you are in a competition for a raise, a new customer, or larger market share. Everyone has the same opportunities to practice EO and improve every day. You will lose to the competition if you don't practice it.

Think of EO and its impact on leadership skills as the price you pay for excellence. In the Defense section of this book, we discussed the price you pay to keep your money: delayed gratification, giving up luxuries now to have more later, and paying down debt. While discipline is the price you pay to win at defense, EO is the price you pay to win at offense. When you accept that you have complete control over your attitude, approach, and skill-building, you take control of your financial future.

The Three Dimensions of Success

You might recall that when Joe started his business he had to learn new skills. Then he had to perfect them. When he could no longer earn more by learning more, he started his own business and hired others. This allowed him to scale, but it also created new challenges. Before he could leverage his employees' skills, he had to train them; he also had to create a process for teaching training, so his employees could eventually take over the training of new hires. He then concentrated on his marketing efforts to get new business and transitioned the company into a licensed construction business.

Joe's story highlights the three dimensions of leadership: learn, leverage, and lead. Each required him to start at zero and move along a spectrum toward excellence. When one dimension was completed, he started over at zero again on the next dimension. Let's dive into each of these dimensions.

Learn

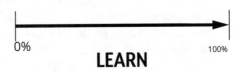

You start off knowing nothing, but as you learn, you gain knowledge and skills. The further along the learn spectrum you go, the more value you develop and the more money you make. Those who reach the end point achieve 100 percent competency and excellence in their field, and they are highly compensated. Before Michael Jordan won championships with the Chicago Bulls, he was focused on learning. He became the league's best scorer, and was well compensated for his achievements.

When one reaches the end of the learn spectrum, they are earning a great income but have no way to progress further. When you're at 100 percent here, you have two options: Stay put until you burn out, or start over at zero percent in the leverage dimension.

Leverage

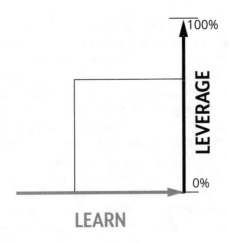

When Joe decided to transition from working a job to owning a business, he started over in the second dimension. Leverage functions like Iron Man's suit of armor: Joe's still doing the work, but he's able to do a hell of a lot more.

Building skills in the leverage dimension includes identifying talent and teaching them how to do the work. This is completely different than learning to do the work yourself. While excelling with learning is a difficult endeavor, excelling with leverage is even harder.

It can be difficult to achieve excellence and be the best at what you do, and then decide to start over. Excellence can become its own comfort zone. Jordan could have been satisfied being the highest scorer and best player in the league; many other NBA players who achieved the highest levels of the game stayed where they were. The difference with Jordan was his drive to win championships.

The Pistons developed the "Jordan Rules," a defense strategy that prioritized forcing Jordan into situations where he couldn't do his job. As great as he was, Jordan couldn't beat all five players by himself, and the Pistons knew it. This strategy is how Detroit knocked Chicago out of the playoffs in 1990, and why Jordan spent the postseason fuming.

Jordan took an interest in improving himself and his teammates. This was extreme ownership, and an indication that Jordan's leadership skills were improving. He held his teammates to a higher standard and pushed them to improve, which earned him a rough reputation in the league. It also made his team perform much better. With Jordan's competitive fire—his leadership spirit—spreading throughout his team, players like Scottie Pippen, Horace Grant, and BJ Armstrong all made significant strides in their skills. Jordan was pushing them along the leverage spectrum, and it worked.

It's also important to note this process wasn't easy or smooth. Many players complained about the way Jordan tried to elevate his team. Leverage, like learning, is a process of its own; although Jordan had learned how to be the best player in the league, he had to start over at zero percent in the leverage dimension and get better at it over time. It was easy to criticize Jordan during that process. Most people never make the jump from learn to leverage because they don't want the criticism or ego hit, but there is no way to turn a job into a business without it.

Lead

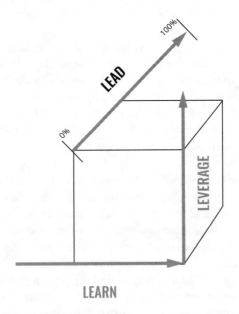

After learning and leverage are mastered, there is no place to go but to lead. At this stage, you move beyond learning the task yourself and using leverage to teach others how to do it. You're now making decisions about the direction of the company; you stop working *in* the business and start working *on* the business. This happened for Joe when he became a licensed contractor and began creating more opportunities for his teams and apprentices under his care.

This stage can resemble a franchise business model, like starting expansion projects or moving into new territories. Few people are willing to take their success this far, but those who do receive the greatest rewards. This dimension proves the ability to lead is the most valuable skill one can have. Leaders make decisions regarding the direction of the company, which standards to uphold, and how to read market conditions. Their choices—good and bad—affect all their employees. Without a strong spirit of leadership, cultivated over a long time and strengthened through acts of leadership, it's impossible to be a successful leader.

Jordan retired as the best basketball player of all time, having won multiple championships and earned millions of dollars. He could have sat back and enjoyed retirement, but he didn't. He became the owner of the Charlotte Bobcats (now the Charlotte Hornets), an NBA franchise team in need of help. In an unprecedented move, Jordan suited up with the players, joining them both in practice and in games. Jordan hoped to inspire the team to do better. This reveals a truth about leadership: When you are in this third dimension, you can move back into the other two dimensions as needed.

Those in the first dimension have the least freedom with two choices: move forward or stay where they are.

Those in the second dimension have more responsibility but also more freedom. This is the reward for embracing the leverage dimension. Jordan could still play the game and teach his teammates to be better.

Those in the third dimension have more freedom. Jordan's position as leader of the Bobcats afforded him a cornucopia of choices to improve his team's chance of success. Jordan could trade for different players, look for ways to increase team revenue, change coaches, or train the players himself. For a man who loved the game of basketball, Jordan's position as leader was perfect for him.

This is why it's so important to have a passion for winning and for becoming great. Otherwise, there isn't enough incentive to push you along the three dimensions of success. Accepting additional responsibility, rather than avoiding it, is required to move along the dimensions. Plus, using extreme ownership will give you the greatest chance to make the biggest changes.

KEY TAKEAWAYS
- Leaders always believe they can do something, even if they aren't in charge.
- The position of leader refers to the person who is in charge and responsible for an outcome. The spirit of a leader is the drive or compulsion to improve a team through right action. You act like a leader when you take initiative without being asked to do so.
- Increases in responsibility usually come with promotions and additional pay, benefits, and perks.

- Promotion opportunities exist when you work for someone else. In your own business, you get a "promotion" when you hire someone to do the things you used to, freeing yourself up to do other things for the business.
- Strong acts of leadership add fuel to the fire in others, improving their performance.
- In the journey toward financial freedom, you may find old wounds that need healing. These wounds can only be faced by stepping outside your comfort zone.
- A lack of faith in yourself or the mission will cause you to avoid leadership.
- What we feel and what we believe is reflected in our internal thoughts and external words.
- While discipline is the price you pay to win at defense, extreme ownership is the price you pay to win at offense. Practicing EO guarantees you will keep improving.
- The three dimensions of leadership are learn, leverage, and lead.

Chapter 10
A WINNING MINDSET

*There are no limitations to the mind except
those we acknowledge. Both poverty and riches are
the offspring of thought.*
—NAPOLEON HILL

The Oxford Languages dictionary defines mindset as "the established set of attitudes held by someone." In my youth, I put very little emphasis on the importance of attitude. I believed attitude was overrated because it couldn't be measured objectively. Being happy, sad, angry, or mad didn't affect how many tables I could handle at one time or how many days in the week I worked—or so I thought.

An incident with unhappy guests was my baptism into the power of attitude. I was serving an older couple who had terrible attitudes; I picked up on their cold demeanor and withdrew emotionally. However, I made sure everything was perfect: The food came out on time, they had everything they needed, and I was prompt in responding to their requests. I did everything by the book, but they left a horrible tip and then wrote a letter to complain about the service.

I was called into my boss's office for an explanation. I shared my perspective and expected to be commended for responding with grace under pressure—at least I did my job well. I was jolted when my boss explained that even though nothing was technically wrong with my service, I was still responsible for the experience of the customers, and their experience was poor. I had believed it was my job to conduct a series of objective tasks—take orders, serve food and drinks, fill requests. My boss had a different opinion: It was also my job to make the guests happy.

I was told to take the weekend off and think about if I really wanted to work in the service industry. I went through the emotional gamut of thoughts, from "this is unfair" to "I hate these guests for getting me in trouble" to "I'll show them, I'll start my own restaurant and make them all pay for how they treated me." When my parents asked why I wasn't working that weekend, they took my boss's side after I explained the situation. It seemed like everyone thought I was wrong. I realized my perspective was narrow and self-serving: I *wanted* to believe how the guests felt was not my responsibility, but that didn't mean I was right.

I went back to the restaurant and apologized to my boss. I wrote a letter of apology to the guests, which was incredibly humbling. Making people happy was now a part of my job. A new skill was beginning to form.

Predictability offers a certain level of comfort. That's why personal finance books focus on teaching a system that is predictable, simple, and repeatable. Save five dollars a day on coffee, put that money in your savings. This approach is easy to understand. Objective measures, like an annualized rate of return, systematic raises, or overtime pay, can be predicted. I covered creating money habits earlier in this book because they are indeed helpful—but they are not nearly as important as the mindset you bring with you to the market every day.

Looking back on my career's progression, I can see how attitude has played a larger role in my success than the objective measures I initially focused on. In hindsight, it's clear that my objective wins in the business world were directly related to my improved attitude. I received larger parties in the restaurant because my boss saw how hard I was trying to do the best job possible. I got the first call for overtime because my sergeants knew I'd say yes, and they liked having me around. I sold more homes because those people in my sphere of influence could see how passionate I was about helping them get the best deal possible. While business leaders will often advise you to measure your KPIs (and you should), it was my attitude that greased the wheels and made these actions possible.

This chapter focuses on having the attitude of a winner. Attitudes are not emotions. They are not a state of being or a feeling. They are beliefs. If you want to be the best, you must have a good attitude. Relying on willpower alone will leave you, and those around you, disappointed.

Willpower is required for jump-starting action, but willpower alone won't sustain you. The right attitude will keep you running when your willpower inevitably runs dry. Having a strong, never-ending power source of a positive attitude will do wonders for your productivity and skill development. If you were to do a quick analysis of your current attitude, what would you report?

Set Your Goals

Unexamined goals still live in your subconscious mind and drive your decisions. Those subconscious goals are affected by what you experienced and how you were treated in your upbringing. Those raised with purposeful planning, optimism, and intention are more likely to create intentional goals. For those who weren't, this chapter is your initiation into setting positive goals.

Those who want to work as little as possible but earn as much as possible frequently struggle with their finances in the same way someone who hates watching what they eat and exercising struggles with their health. In human nature, it's better to develop an attitude that is centered on others, or service before self. Learning to give others what they want increases reciprocity. With this understanding in place, you must focus on becoming the best version of yourself.

We have control over our attitudes. Like an angel on one shoulder and a devil on the other, there are always at least two competing ways we can interpret the same piece of information. The devil points out the ways you are a victim; this perspective is based on the expectation that you are entitled to good things, regardless of what you do or who you are. It is self-centered and hollow. You can't improve your performance if you think this way. What's worse, you aren't truly happy in life. Constantly seeing what you don't have and blaming others is a formula for resentment and bitterness.

The angel knows that you are not *entitled* to anything. The angel points out the ways you could improve yourself and reminds you that with responsibility comes blessings. This is an others-centered perspective. The angel empowers you to take control of the direction of your life and career and keeps you encouraged and hopeful that things are improving. The angel reminds you how far you've come, how much worse it could be, and what the best next step is for you to focus on.

Wrong Attitude	Right Attitude
I'll work harder when they finally give me that raise I'm owed.	I will do my best every day until someone notices me, whether it's at this job or a better one.
My boss dumps everything on me and I'm tired of it.	My boss trusts me, and that makes me feel good.
It doesn't matter what I do, they are going to do whatever they want.	This company wants to grow, and I can show how I can help make that happen.
That's not my job, ask someone else.	I have some free time; I'd love to help!
Why are they asking me to do this?	This is awesome. I get to learn something new.
I did my job. Why does it matter what my attitude is?	Part of my job is how my attitude affects our clients and customers.
I'm such a small cog in the wheel; what I do doesn't matter.	I am immensely powerful and can make or break someone's day.

Mentorship

Finding a mentor is one of the most effective ways you can improve your mindset and train to be a winner. Mentors are people who take a personal interest in your development and may even provide emotional support (but this isn't always the case). A mentor may even be someone you respect but whom you never meet; someone who has set an example for you to follow. An excellent way to shorten your learning curve and develop the right attitude toward the hurdles of your vocation is to follow the behaviors of the most successful people in your industry. Find the people who are good at their job and associate as closely with them as possible.

Researchers from the University of Toronto Faculty of Medicine and the University of California, San Francisco, School of Medicine studied the mentor-mentee relationship to determine what factors influenced successful and failed mentoring relationships. Findings showed that successful mentoring relationships were characterized by reciprocity, mutual respect, clear expectations, personal connection, and shared values. Failed mentoring relationships were characterized by poor communication, lack of commitment, personality differences, perceived (or real) competition, conflicts of interest, and the mentor's lack of experience. Furthermore, the researchers found successful mentorship to be vital to career success for both mentors and mentees.[64]

This study makes two things clear: Mentorship is crucial for career development, and productive mentorship isn't always possible. There's a clear need to analyze what a mentee needs and what a mentor can teach.

It starts with mutual respect and the mentor seeing something in you that shows promise. They also need to feel like you are both on the same team. The best mentors are successful in their field and already know how to think like a winner. This means you need to think that way too. Successful people have the right mindset, and they want to be around people like them.

Three of the wisest philosophers who ever lived formed a lineage of mentorship: Socrates mentored Plato, and Plato in turn mentored Aristotle. These relationships were not created by luck; the students showed promise and a commitment to the ideals the mentors valued.

We all remember a person who mentored us in some way. Whether it was your parent teaching you how to ride a bike or a senior staff member showing you how to do a job better, those impressions last. For mentors, it feels good to take that energetic person and show them the ropes. Being likable is an important factor in being a mentee, as

---

64 Sharon E. Straus et al., "Characteristics of Successful and Failed Mentoring Relationships." *Academic Medicine* 88, no. 1 (January 1, 2013): 82–89, https://doi.org/10.1097/acm.0b013e31827647a0.

is showing you have a winning mindset and are just as committed to learning as your mentor is committed to teaching.

To find a mentor, observe those around you or in your industry who are the most successful at what you want to learn. Reach out to them; it can be as simple as starting with a compliment on their work, or as complex as asking to shadow them for a day and help with simple tasks they don't enjoy or have time for. The key is to show them you want to win and you want to help *them* win.

Take Responsibility for Your Attitude

Extreme ownership in the workplace includes taking responsibility for the attitude you bring to it. It is too easy to let others determine your attitude. I was forced to learn this with that older couple at the restaurant, and I started using humor to diffuse tense situations. I learned to be charismatic when introducing myself to a table; setting a strong first impression made it much easier to maintain the rapport built in those few minutes.

I found patterns in communication that helped, such as leaving the table with a joke or smile and guessing what customers were thinking before they could ask it. "You're trying to figure out the difference between a porterhouse and a T-bone steak since they are the same price, right? Don't worry. Nobody who comes in here is an expert on bovines. Let me share some of my knowledge that is useless anywhere else!"

Most importantly, I learned a cardinal rule about relationships: When something feels wrong or tense, or you feel like you may have offended someone, don't disengage. That only grows the distance. Do the opposite of what you want to and engage. Dive into the problem, take responsibility (even if you can see the mistake was on their part), and show that you care more about fixing the problem than being right.

I never would have developed extreme ownership if I had not been called into my boss's office. I first needed to blame the customers, my boss, and even my parents. Then I realized I needed to change my perspective, not theirs. Had I not, how much different would my future have been? How about my level of maturity? How different of a person would I be today?

Learning how to engage in uncomfortable situations helped me immensely in other phases of my life. It has helped me earn millions of dollars in my real estate career. It's helped me develop solid, authentic relationships. It's helped make me a much better leader. Embracing a mindset where everything is my fault—and I have the ability to improve anything—changed everything.

Develop Urgency

Urgency is an undervalued trait, and it is often confused with being in a hurry or being anxious. That's not always correct. Operating with a sense of urgency can be a sign of respect for reaching a goal. Basketball players who jump on a loose ball show they values its possession, and soldiers who move quickly through duties show respect for the success of the mission. We operate with urgency in the areas we value. Consider the way you work at your job the week before a vacation: You're highly focused, completing tasks quickly and thinking ahead to what might go wrong while taking steps to prevent them from occurring. This increased work performance, this urgency, is because you value enjoying your vacation. It's amazing how well we perform when we're correctly motivated!

Working with urgency increases productivity. It turns your focus from a light bulb spread over space into a laser pointed on one area. To improve your offense, you need to always operate with urgency. Winners know every second counts. They know their competition is coming behind them. However, a sense of urgency doesn't come naturally. It's easier to operate at a comfortable pace and only go as quickly as we like.

Atlassian, a company that provides collaboration, development, and software for teams, published an article that explains this well:

> Parkinson's Law is the adage that work expands to fill the time allotted for its completion. The term was first coined by Cyril Northcote Parkinson in a humorous essay [about] a woman whose only task in a day is to send a postcard—a task which would take a busy person approximately three minutes. But the woman spends an hour finding the card, another half hour looking for her glasses, ninety minutes writing the card, twenty

minutes deciding whether or not to take an umbrella along on her walk to the mailbox ... and on and on until her day is filled. Let's look at an updated example. You and your team have two weeks to complete a relatively simple bug fix. Realistically, it should only take a few hours. But *because* you know you have more than enough time at your disposal, the project grows in scope. While you're looking into that bug, you decide to check into a few related issues as well. This prompts questions about what's causing the issues in the first place. While those diversions may ultimately prove to be useful, they don't get you any closer to achieving your object of handling the bug fix. Ultimately, the thing that should've really been a simple undertaking becomes something that actually *requires* the two weeks to complete. That's Parkinson's Law in action.[65]

An extreme example of avoiding Parkinson's Law is from Ed Mylett, an entrepreneur, best-selling author, performance coach, and speaker who has been on the *Forbes* "50 Wealthiest Under 50" list. Mylett splits each 24-hour period into three parts, or three "days," that are each six hours long. By compressing a "day" into six hours, Mylett creates a sense of urgency that compels him to be as productive as possible.[66]

It may seem ridiculous to value every single moment of the day, but what if you're trying to be a winner at work? How would your boss compare you to your coworkers if you valued your productivity and time so much that you didn't lose focus and slack off, not even for five minutes? Your skills would improve exponentially faster. Those who come from competitive environments learn this faster than those who don't. Their required sense of urgency to win is a big reason why.

Imagine if you approached your skill-building with the same urgency and importance you now place on earning compound interest. An earlier chapter showed the difference in investing $1,000 rather than borrowing it and paying it off over nine years. If money

---

65 Kat Boogaard, "What Is Parkinson's Law and Why Is It Sabotaging Your Productivity?" Work Life by Atlassian, February 12, 2022, https://www.atlassian.com/blog/productivity/what-is-parkinsons-law.

66 Ed Mylett, "One Day Is Not 24 Hours," The Outcome, YouTube video, September 22, 2022, https://www.youtube.com/watch?v=Y8B_1uZTLws.

can be compounded that much, why can't skills? How much would your time invested into skill-building turn into dollars over a year? Ten years? A thirty-year career?

Most people do not retire with large savings accounts because they do not place an urgency on creating momentum through compounding skills or earnings. Urgency is how we value and respect time and opportunity.

Ways to Increase Urgency

Urgency can be used to accomplish things by not wasting time. It can also be accomplished through increasing productivity by removing inefficiencies such as:

- Listening to podcasts while driving, exercising, cleaning, or cooking.
- Practicing how quickly you can complete tasks without making mistakes.
- Memorizing the screens and inputs needed to complete daily tasks, so you move through each step faster.
- Taking classes to learn faster ways to use computer software.
- Phrasing communication to receive a yes or no, rather than having to go back and forth to get an answer.
- Preparing mentally for your workday while driving to work, rather than waiting until you arrive.

Do It Faster, Better, and with Fewer Mistakes

Whenever you are unsure of what to do to improve your skills, remember three simple directives: Do it faster, better, and with fewer mistakes.

Do It Faster

Make it a game to see how quickly you can correctly finish a task. As a cop, I'd imagine clicking through the screens of the report-writing system. Then, when I was using the computer, I could click through the screens faster as I moved the mouse to the next appropriate spot. I took typing classes to improve my typing speed. I'd secretly race to see if I could do something faster.

Do It Better

It's easy to say the job is done, but is it done well? Can I get the restaurant guest to compliment me by name on the way out? Can I learn how to be a stronger writer by reading other officers' reports and learning verbiage, structure, and details they included? Can I close a loan so well that I get a five-star review from the client? The average do their job; the wealthy look to do it with excellence.

Do It with Fewer Mistakes

The fewer mistakes you make, the more trust you build with your coworkers, your supervisor, and your customers. To avoid mistakes, develop a deep understanding of what you want to accomplish. Those who go through the motions without focusing intently are prone to make mistakes. My law enforcement career taught me that others could die from my mistakes. My athletic career taught me that the entire team could lose from my mistakes. Avoiding mistakes will help your reputation for accuracy grow.

KEY TAKEAWAYS

- Business leaders will advise you to measure your KPIs (which you should do), but your attitude matters more.
- In a quick analysis of your current attitude, what would you report?
- It's better to have an attitude that is centered on others, not yourself.
- We have control over our attitudes.
- Having a mentor will help you improve your mindset and your career development.
- Parkinson's Law is the adage that work expands to fill the time allotted for its completion; it destroys productivity.
- If money can be compounded, so can your skills.
- The average do their job; the wealthy look to do it with excellence.

Chapter 11
PERFORMANCE IMPROVEMENT HACKS

Hacking Your Performance

Once you make the decision to improve your performance and think like a winner, there are several steps you can take to ensure each day is better than the last. Embracing these changes can be difficult at first—as all change is—but with time they'll become habits.

Schedule Your Day

When there isn't a lot to do, or you don't have your priorities in order, scheduling your day can seem unimportant. The fewer responsibilities you have, the more you can live in a reactive state. The employee at an auto parts store has the luxury of waiting for customers who need help to arrive; the owner cannot work the same way. They need to prioritize ordering inventory, creating a work schedule for the employees, and making sure payroll is completed. The more responsibility you take on, the less reactive you can afford to be.

Creating a calendar that blocks off time to complete your most important tasks and priorities will prepare you for the weight of responsibility. If you are currently struggling to make deadlines or complete important tasks, this may be why. My daily calendar includes meetings I need to attend and time blocked for book-writing, lead generation, content creation, and podcast recordings. When I find myself with unscheduled time, I use it to catch up on emails, check in on staff members, or follow up on real estate offers. By scheduling my most important tasks on a calendar, I rarely miss deadlines or important timelines.

Work from Your Calendar

This is a great habit to get into if you plan on starting your own business someday. Putting your responsibilities for the day into a calendar will reduce your anxiety because it releases your subconscious from having to remember when things need to be done. For example, my assistant, Krista, saves all my upcoming travel information in my calendar, including flight numbers, reservation codes, flight times, and rental car information. This method is so efficient that I can have no idea where I'm going or what I'm doing when I get there, but I have zero anxiety because all I need to do is open the calendar on my phone.

The key is preparation. By putting all your scheduled events in your phone's calendar, you'll save yourself time by not having to search through emails or other databases to find the information you need. Use the notes section liberally and include all important details for a meeting, presentation, or event. This will free up your subconscious mind, and you'll be better prepared for success.

Visualize Success

Visualizing success has been a tool used for years by high performers. In their study *Imagining Success: Multiple Achievement Goals and the Effectiveness of Imagery*, researchers Tim Blankert and Melvyn R. W. Hamstra studied whether visualizing outcomes had an effect on athletes' performance. Tennis players were given instructions on how to serve and the results were measured. Then, the players were led through a visualization to imagine their serve, and results were measured a second time. The study found that service performance was better after visualization."[67]

---

67 Tim Blankert and Melvyn R. W. Hamstra, "Imagining Success: Multiple Achievement Goals and the Effectiveness of Imagery," *Basic and Applied Social Psychology* 39, no. 1 (December 7, 2016): 60–67, https://doi.org/10.1080/01973533.2016.1255947.

This principle can work for you as well. As you shower or brush your teeth, imagine the challenges you might face at work that day and how you will deal with them. Visualize yourself handling frustrating problems or irritating people with class, grace, and calm. Many of us live with subconscious anxiety; this is your body's way of telling you that you are not prepared for some event. Overcome this anxiety by preparing your plans to face what you fear. Visualize yourself overcoming obstacles, ready for whatever challenges may hit you that day.

Prepare for Tomorrow, Tonight

As a police officer working a lot of overtime, I was frequently required to report to different locations in the San Francisco Bay Area. I made it a habit to check where I would be working the next day before leaving that day's shift; this helped me to know if I needed to bring spare batteries, uniform apparel, or other pieces of equipment home with me to be ready for the next day's work.

On my journey to become a top-producing Realtor, I would frequently have more things to complete in a day than I had time for. Before leaving the office, I would review both my calendar and the to-do list I kept to see what I had to be prepared for the next day. If possible, I would move necessary files into a Google Drive folder, or I'd leave my computer on with the browser tabs I needed open. Many times, I realized I needed to bring my iPad to the next day's listing presentation or needed to look up comparable properties before leaving that night. This habit of checking tomorrow's tasks at the end of the day was invaluable to my success.

Regardless of how much is on your calendar, it can be beneficial to check tomorrow's commitments the night before, so you can mentally prepare for them while you sleep. Reviewing information before a meeting, rehearsing difficult conversations, or preparing for objections you're likely to encounter can make a big difference in your confidence when those moments arise.

Internally Prepare for Conversations

A powerful trick I developed over the years has helped me to appear more articulate and confident than I naturally am: I hold conversations—usually difficult ones I know I'm not prepared for—internally. I imagine myself making a statement, then decide if the statement sounds accurate or unclear. Once I can articulate the statement well, I practice it over and over to commit it to memory. Next, I imagine how the person might respond. It's surprising how accurately I can anticipate the responses of people I know. This allows me either to tweak the way I planned to deliver the original message or prepare a response to their objection.

You can do this too. Consider how well you know your significant other. Many times friends or family advise us, "Just tell her…," to which our immediate response is, "Oh, she would…" You also know the personalities of many of your coworkers, and certainly of your friends. The better you know someone, the more tools you have to imagine and internally prepare for conversations with them.

Communicate Concisely

Getting to the point without using a lot of words shows respect for the person receiving the information because you are placing a high value on their time. Lengthy, unspecific, or unnecessary communication shows that you value what *you* have to say more than you value *their* time. If you don't make a conscious effort to be concise, you're gratifying your own needs at the expense of another.

Be concise when writing emails and texts. The first draft of an email is often something that can be whittled down; ask yourself, "What decision does the person reading this information need to make?" You don't know how busy they are or, if it's a stressful topic like buying or selling their home, what emotional state they'll be in when they read your correspondence. Get to what you need to communicate quickly.

A well-organized communication will go a long way too. In addition to being concise, using bullet points, headings, or grouping the relevant pieces of information into categories makes it easier for the recipient to make sense of what you're sharing. This shows them you are capable, smart, and considerate—which will make them want to work with you.

Here's an example of the wrong way to write an email.

Hey George, Lisa here.

So, I know you wanted an update on the project we have going on and I thought I would send you an email to let you know how it's going so you can know before the meeting. Basically, it's going really well and I've been working super hard on it and you'd be lost without me lol. Anyway, I've been on the phone all day long with XYZ Management and oh my gosh they are so stubborn but I just wouldn't take no for an answer (you know how I can be!) and so I told them they better lower their price or else. I was able to get them down to 8% because I'm awesome like that, but oh man was it a huge pain in my butt. I also asked them if they would go visit the job site to give us some feedback, but the guy I was talking to didn't get back to me so I left a couple of stern voicemails and finally someone got back to me and they are going to send someone else. They should have known I always get my way! Anyway, we also need to make a decision sometime about the loan. Let me know if you want a 30-year fixed or an adjustable rate mortgage. Also, the Personal Financial Statement you sent me isn't completed. I'm not sure if you knew that, but Roxanne says we can't submit it the way it is so it needs to be done. Oh I almost forgot that XYZ gave us an estimate on yearly revenue I just forgot what it was. I was on hold for so long with them! So Phase 2 is almost done and there's just some things they need your approval on before they finish so ask John with the construction crew and he'll tell you what they need. [You get it … more and more sentences].

—Lisa

Here's a better way to write an email.

George,

Here are updates to prepare you for tomorrow's meeting.

Rehab
- *Phase 2 is nearing completion and should be done by the end of the week.*

- *See updated photos of the construction here* [link].
- *We are currently 5% under budget.*
- *Items that need your approval include paint color, tile pattern, and light fixtures. See options here* [link].

Funding
- *Two loan options remain as our best bet with similar closing costs. A decision is not needed for another 30 days. Will check in with you later to get your thoughts on:*
- *30-year fixed rate at 6.5% with 20% down*
- *5-year ARM at 5% with 25% down*
- *Need a complete Personal Financial Statement for the company. Currently working with Roxanne to finish it. Will let you know if anything is needed from your end.*

Management
- *XYZ Management has dropped their rate from 10% to 8%, they are our best choice.*
- *Preliminary estimates show a conservative yearly revenue of $180,000.*
- *I've scheduled a rep from XYZ to visit the construction site upon completion of Phase 2 to give us any additional feedback on design or layout improvements.*

Let me know if you want to visit the site with the rep or just have them make a video of the site and send it to you with their thoughts.

Most important priority is your approval of the paint, tile, and light fixtures. If the boss asks, be sure to let them know you've got the project at 5% under budget and plan to keep it that way to completion.

I've also included these details in the calendar entry for your meeting.

—Lisa

The first email rambled, included information George did not need, and was written to make Lisa feel better about herself and her contributions. The second, better email was clearly written to give George only the information he needed, and it was much more concise and organized. With the better email, George is more likely to win in his meeting and recognize Lisa as being a part of that win.

Prepare for Meetings

Most people don't enjoy meetings. When facing a meeting you know you won't enjoy, you have two options: Give less effort and wait for it to be over or accept that it's happening, prepare for it, and get yourself through it.

You can approach other workplace events in the same two ways. You can show up uninterested, unfocused, and lazy, or you can prepare for them and arrive engaged, optimistic, and helpful. As the owner of a company who schedules a lot of meetings, I admit I don't enjoy them either. My goal is to be as productive as possible, as clear as possible, and convey a topic's importance as well as possible. Also, as the one who normally leads the meetings, I notice the big gap between those who show up prepared and those who do not.

You don't want to have to look up information when asked about a project you are in charge of, or "um" and "ah" your way through questions because you don't remember the answers. You'll look much more trustworthy if you can give clear, quick, and concise answers. Anticipate what you may be asked, and review the information the night before or the morning of the meeting. An employee who is clearly not prepared for a meeting sends a strong message that they cannot be trusted with their work and definitely should not be trusted with more responsibility.

Start the Day with Exercise

Exercise is easily one of the first things to fall to the bottom of the priority list, especially when we're busy. You can stay on top of it by doing it early in your day. Starting your day with exercise:

- Encourages you to eat healthier.
- Boosts your energy throughout the day.
- Improves your focus and cognition.
- Puts you in a better mood.
- Lowers your risk for diabetes and other health issues.
- Helps you sleep better.

I eat better throughout the day if I exercise first. The endorphins released through exercise help me avoid indulging in office snacks because I don't want to kill the good high with a crashing low. When I don't exercise, I am more tempted to snack because I'm looking for that buzz. Having more energy and being in a better mood allows me to put more effort into all aspects of my job, including appropriately handling the stresses or challenges of the day. This one simple shift can lead to massive improvements in how you do your job and, subsequently, your income. This really isn't an exaggeration!

Monitor Your Energy Levels

I spent much of my career oblivious to my energy levels, with no understanding of how important they were. Only when I became a business owner did I realize how important it was to monitor my energy. When I'm tired, distracted, or unmotivated, I cannot see solutions to complex problems, and my interactions with staff members are significantly less positive and productive. Several things affect your energy levels; to be a high performer with a winning mindset, you'll need to monitor all of them.

Food

What we eat throughout the day has a big impact on how much energy we bring to our work, especially as we get older. I don't know anyone who functions in a peak state while they're drowsy. The Harvard Medical School conducted research and found that big lunches affect the body's circadian rhythm (your sleep/wake cycle), and that those who eat smaller midday meals have more energy. [68]

This might sound counterintuitive. After all, food is fuel, right? Sort of. Meals that are high in carbohydrates trigger a spike in insulin, which leads to a whole host of scientific reactions. The bottom line is that a large lunch sets off a train of falling dominoes within our body that makes us feel drowsy. I could list each simple sugar, digestive juice, and cell response that plays a role, but I fear that would have the same effect as a big lunch and put you to sleep! Instead, I'll leave you with this: If you find your energy level is waning later in

---

68 "Eating to Boost Energy," Harvard Health, July 26, 2011, www.health.harvard.edu/healthbeat/eating-to-boost-energy. (commas replace periods in notes)

the workday, try eating smaller meals instead of a big lunch so you can skip the midday food coma. I prefer salads, vegetables, and fish for lunch. (But don't be the colleague who reheats their fish in the breakroom microwave!) I save the big meals that cause sleepiness for dinner, when it won't hurt my productivity.

By the same token, don't be the person who brings in donuts or other energy-draining foods that will kill your entire office's productivity. Protein bars, vegetables trays, or mounds of fruits are much safer options to keep everyone functioning at high capacity. Keeping healthy snacks at your desk will reduce your temptation to go to the vending machine or office kitchen. I keep protein bars, nuts, and bananas at my desk so that I always have something on hand that won't put me into naptime.

Thoughts

Though difficult to objectively measure, our thoughts—both positive and negative—play a huge role in the mindset we bring to work each day. The website Rethink Mental Illness discusses this:

> Negative thinking refers to a pattern of thinking negatively about yourself and your surroundings. While everyone experiences negative thoughts now and again, negative thinking that seriously affects the way you think about yourself and the world and even interferes with work/study and everyday functioning could be a symptom of a mental illness, including depression, anxiety disorders, personality disorders and schizophrenia.[69]

Of course, not everyone who has negative thoughts has a mental illness, but negative thinking is detrimental to your mental health and quality of life.

Negative thinking is harmful in proportion to how much you experience it. Common forms of negative self-talk include:

- **Filtering.** You magnify the negative aspects of a situation and filter out all the positive ones. For example, at work you completed a task ahead of time and were complimented on a job well

---

69 "Negative Thinking Overview," Rethink Mental Illness, https://www.rethink.org/advice-and-information/about-mental-illness/learn-more-about-symptoms/negative-thinking/.

done. Then you're given constructive criticism about another task. That evening, you focus only on what you did wrong and forget about the compliment you received.

- **Personalizing.** When something bad occurs, you automatically blame yourself. For example, you hear that an evening out with friends is canceled, and you assume that the change in plans is because no one wanted to be around you.
- **Catastrophizing.** You automatically anticipate the worst. The drive-through coffee shop gets your order wrong, so that means that the rest of your day will be a disaster.
- **Shoulding.** You talk harshly to yourself about all the things that you *should* have done but didn't get to.
- **Perfecting.** You have negative self-talk because you can't perform to your impossible standards.
- **Polarizing.** You see things only as good or bad, and there is no middle ground. If you're on the "bad" end, it must be your fault.

People can live their entire lives engaging in one or more of these harmful forms of negative self-talk without realizing the effect it has on them, especially when they accumulate over time. According to Norman Vincent Peale, the author of *The Power of Positive Thinking*, having low energy is often the result of negative thinking. He asserts that what's going on in your mind manifests physically. For example, if you think, "I am tired," your body will follow suit. However, if you are actively engaged and interested in a task and sleepy thoughts are far away, your brain will go to great lengths to ignore physical feelings of exhaustion and push on.[70] Ever gotten so wrapped up in a task that time slips away? Everyone from ultramarathoner David Goggins to Buddha agrees that the mind is a powerful thing. Use your thoughts to fuel and direct your energy, and you'll be amazed at the results.

To maximize your personal store of energy, you must learn to control both your thoughts and your emotions. Revered University of Notre Dame football coach Knute Rockne believed that hate blocked energy. It was important to him that every member of his team had positive feelings about their fellow players and held each other in high

---

70 Norman Vincent Peale, *The Power of Positive Thinking* (New York: Touchstone, 2003).

regard. In his mind, his players wouldn't play their best until they released all their negative emotions.

High performers throughout history, from engineers to athletes to entrepreneurs, have discovered the connection between controlling their thoughts and their emotional responses. To protect our energy levels, we must do the same.

Distractions

A controversial topic in the world of high performance is multi-tasking. Those who practice it love it. However, multitasking can be exceptionally inefficient, and constantly switching between tasks drains your mind's energy levels.

When we attempt to multitask, we don't actually do more than one activity at once. Instead, we switch rapidly between them. This switching exhausts the brain! Toggling between tasks uses the same energy reserve that the mind uses to focus on a task. When we go back and forth, we drain that tank faster than if we'd stayed focused on one task at a time.[71]

Taking fifteen-minute breaks or using the popular Pomodoro method can make you more productive. But remember, these breaks must allow the mind to actually rest and relax. Try going for a walk, staring out a window, or listening to music. Avoid social media at all costs! I know phone breaks feel fun, but the deluge of information online doesn't actually give your mind a rest. Falling into a scroll-hole on social media defeats the purpose of taking a break. Similarly, emails and office drama can drain our energy levels to the detriment of our ability to participate in "deep work." Putting up healthy boundaries, like keeping your office door closed or taking your breaks outside, can protect your energy and improve your performance.

Other People

Energy vampires are people who destroy positive energy. They prey on sensitive, empathetic, and happy people, drawing from their kindness until their victim is left feeling drained, lethargic, and defeated.

---

71 Olivia Goldhill, "Neuroscientists Say Multitasking Literally Drains the Energy Reserves of Your Brain," Quartz, July 3, 2016, https://qz.com/722661/neuroscientists-say-multitasking-literally-drains-the-energy-reserves-of-your-brain.

While "energy vampire" sounds a bit Hollywood (and even snarky), it accurately portrays the peril these kinds of people can have on your productivity.

To protect yourself from the productivity-suck of an energy vampire, you need to first identify them. If you know anyone in your workplace or life who takes advantage of your kindness to drain your time and energy, it's important to set boundaries that will keep your energy safe from their behaviors. Better yet, do your best to surround yourself with people who energize and inspire you!

Work Different Muscles

Some jobs require you to use the same muscle all day. This could include reviewing files for errors, compliance-related tasks, or analyzing spreadsheets. It becomes increasingly difficult to maintain focus when you're doing the exact same activity for eight hours.

Just like working out the same physical muscles can lead to problems like injuries, using the same mental muscles leads to problems like mistakes, slow performance, and weak productivity. We can avoid these problems by giving our muscles more breaks.

Selling houses as a Realtor required frequent conversations with clients in which they needed a high level of emotional support from me. This was not my strong suit. I got burned out during the day and found it hard to maintain a positive attitude with my clients; in turn, they did not feel heard. This diminished my passion for real estate and made lead generation for future clients harder to do. Ultimately, it cost my business money.

When I wasn't talking to clients, I was solving problems in my real estate portfolio. This required creative thinking and a chess-like approach—real estate problems are rarely solved in one move. This work required a different kind of energy than what was required in my client interactions. So did writing books, where a singular focus is required, or holding meetings, where I needed to read a room and make on-the-fly decisions.

I noticed a pattern about myself: If I was forced to do any one thing all day—meet with clients or solve problems in my portfolio or write for twelve hours—my mood soured, and I became mentally exhausted. It felt like a grind. When I moved from book writing to meetings to client conversations to portfolio problems, the workload felt much more manageable, and my mood was better.

I compared this to my gym workout: If I worked only my biceps, I'd run out of strength within a short period of time. If I switched muscle groups, I could (theoretically) stay in the gym hours longer. Each individual muscle group can be taxed only for a certain period of time, but moving from group to group extends the workout.

You improve your work performance significantly by learning to use different muscle groups throughout the day. I incorporate this principle by balancing my day with getting into a groove, or deep work, and taking breaks to switch to a new task. I leave myself prompts for when I return to the more complex task. For example, if I'm writing, I'll leave several bullet points or lines with ideas I was moving toward when I took the break. That way I can easily pick up where I left off when I return.

When I take a break from writing, I'll move to a task like a meeting where I'm solving problems, or a training where I'm speaking to a group. This allows me to spread my focus and energy across multiple areas. After a couple hours of this other task, I'm likely fatigued again. At this point, I'll end the task, use the bathroom, eat a quick bite, and visualize what I'll work on next and what a successful outcome looks like. I'm always mentally preparing for the next opportunity.

I may choose to answer emails, post to my Discord channel (DG's World), make a training video, or go live on social media. Sometimes I'll take a run or go to the gym in the middle of the day and listen to real estate, business, or economic podcasts while I work out, giving my brain a rest and my body a challenge. (This is different from multitasking difficult tasks; my brain can passively listen while my body works out.) After the workout, my mind is ready to jump into the next area of productivity. When people ask how I can work sixteen-to-eighteen hour days, this is a big reason why: *I'm never working the same work muscles the entire day.*

I realize that not all jobs will afford this opportunity to switch things up during the day. Some people do one thing, like move boxes in a warehouse, wash dishes in one restaurant, or dig ditches for eight hours. If this is you, I challenge you to look for opportunities to switch things up however you can. For example, can you alternate bussing tables with washing the dishes? If you can't, see if it's possible to use the information from previous chapters to find a job that gives you more opportunities to use your brain, skills, and abilities in new ways.

KEY TAKEAWAYS

- Working with urgency increases productivity. Use your focus like a laser, not a light bulb.
- Turn a 24-hour period into three separate six-hour days to increase urgency and improve productivity.
- As you prepare for work in the morning, imagine the challenges you may face and how you will deal with them.
- Reviewing information before a meeting, rehearsing difficult conversations, and preparing for possible objections can help you have confidence when those moments arise.
- Be concise when writing emails and texts.
- Our thoughts—both positive and negative—play a huge role in the mindset we bring to work each day.
- You improve your work performance significantly by learning to use different muscle groups throughout the day.

PILLAR III
INVESTING

$

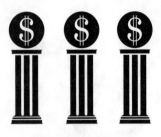

Chapter 12

BUILDING WEALTH THROUGH REAL ESTATE

Real estate cannot be lost or stolen, nor can it be carried away. Purchased with common sense, paid for in full, and managed with reasonable care, it is about the safest investment in the world.
—FRANKLIN D. ROOSEVELT

Let's recap a few of the lessons picked up so far on the journey.

1. You Can't Get Rich from Saving

Everything gets more expensive with time, from movie theater tickets and food to cars and college education. Those who only put money in a savings account to work toward financial independence are not factoring in inflation. Trying to save your way to wealth is like trying to run up the down escalator. It's certainly possible if you stick with it long enough, but everything is working against you.

Inflation can be measured several ways. One is from the U.S. Bureau of Labor Statistics; its Consumer Price Index (CPI) measures the average change over time in the prices paid by consumers for goods and services (everything from groceries to cars to rent). While this is the most widely used method to measure inflation, the CPI has its flaws. The biggest is that it is reported by the federal government, and that it does not include the price for all goods and services. As an example, the CPI does not include the complexity of real estate prices fully in its basket. Home prices rose 18.8 percent in 2021,[72] yet the CPI reported consumer prices rose only 7 percent.[73] Going from losing 7 percent of your purchasing power (through inflation) to gaining 19 percent is a 26-point swing. Over a four-year period, this would have nearly doubled your purchasing power—in essence, doubling the "energy" of your money purely by investing wisely in real estate. While this is a powerful example of why it's important to invest for your future, it's not even remotely close to showing the power of investing wisely when we consider the other way to measure inflation.

While the CPI focuses on a "market basket" of goods, the M2 is the U.S. Federal Reserve's estimate of the total money supply, including all of the cash people have on hand plus all of the money deposited in checking accounts, savings accounts, and other short-term saving vehicles such as certificates of deposit (CDs).[74] According-ing to Edmund C. Moy, a former director of the United States Mint, the M2 "soared a historic record 27 percent in 2020 to 2021. To put that in perspective, that is the biggest jump in the money supply in America's history."[75]

---

72 "S&P CoreLogic Case-Shiller Index Reports 18.8% Annual Home Price Gain for Calendar 2021," S&P Dow Jones Indices, February 22, 2022, https://www.spglobal.com/spdji/en/index-announcements/article/sp-corelogic-case-shiller-index-reports-188-annual-home-price-gain-for-calendar-2021/.

73 "Consumer Price Index: 2021 in Review," The Economics Daily: U.S. Bureau of Labor Statistics, January 14, 2022, https://www.bls.gov/opub/ted/2022/consumer-price-index-2021-in-review.htm.

74 "M2 Definition and Meaning in the Money Supply," Investopedia, May 27, 2023, https://www.investopedia.com/terms/m/m2.asp.

75 Edmund C. Moy, "Understanding the Money Supply," Wheaton Center for Faith, Politics & Economics, 2021, https://www.wheaton.edu/academics/academic-centers/wheaton-center-for-faith-politics-and-economics/resource-center/articles/2021/understanding-the-money-supply/.

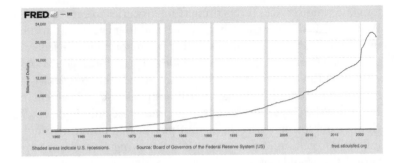

Shaded areas indicate U.S. recessions.   Source: Board of Governors of the Federal Reserve System (US)   fred.stlouisfed.org

This graph from the Federal Reserve Bank of St. Louis reflects the amount of money in circulation from 1960 to 2022. Measured in billions of dollars, the graph reveals that the supply has increased from $8.4 billion in January of 2010 to $21.3 billion in late 2022.[76] This increase in money supply is responsible for the inflation we see reflected in higher prices today.

If we look at the change in the number of dollars in circulation, inflation is much higher than what the CPI reflects. This information reveals the harsh truth about saving money as a wealth-building strategy: It can't work. Very few people can earn and save enough to overcome inflation at the grocery store, let alone build a nest egg large enough to quit their job. If you're going to achieve financial freedom, you need all three pillars: defense, offense, and *investing*.

2. You Won't Get Rich from Earnings

Spending more money each time your income increases, also known as lifestyle creep, prevents financial freedom. When you don't have a plan for each dollar you earn, especially for what you are going to save, lifestyle creep is natural. If buying new, better, and more is always a temptation, it becomes even more difficult to save. Constantly telling yourself no isn't fun, but having a plan to buy assets with your savings makes it easier to save and not spend.

For those not yet making much money, taxes are relatively insignificant and not a cause for concern. Since most of us start at a lower tax burden, it is easy to be unaware of how much money we're giving away to the government. Any increase in your income means an

---

76 "FRED Economic Data," St. Louis Fed, https://fred.stlouisfed.org/series/M2SL.

increase in taxes, especially when you don't know or understand strategies to protect your income from the IRS.

Particularly dangerous are taxes for those who move into the 1099 workforce. When you are a W-2 earner, taxes are taken from your salary before you receive your paycheck. This gives the impression that it was never your money in the first place. Those who move into the 1099 workforce are hit with a shock when tax time comes, and they learn for the first time that they are responsible for forking over big chunks of cash they didn't expect to pay. Those who are self-employed pay their share *and* what would be the employer's share of Social Security and Medicare obligations.

The following table is a breakdown of the current federal government tax brackets as of the writing of this book.[77] It does not include state taxes, but those are owed as well in most states (only a handful don't collect income tax), and it also doesn't include any deductions you may be eligible for. A certified public accountant or enrolled agent can help you with your taxes.

Tax rate	Taxable Income Bracket	Tax Owed
10%	$0 to $10,275	10% of taxable income
12%	$10,276 to $41,775	$1,027.50 plus 12% of the amount over $10,275
22%	$41,776 to $89,075	$4,807.50 plus 22% of the amount over $41,775
24%	$89,076 to $170,050	$15,213.50 plus 24% of the amount over $89,075
32%	$170,051 to $215,950	$34,647.50 plus 32% of the amount over $170,050
35%	$215,951 to $539,900	$49,335.50 plus 35% of the amount over $215,950
37%	$539,901 or more	$162,718 plus 37% of the amount over $539,900

---

77 Sabrina Parys and Tina Orem, "2022–2023 Tax Brackets and Federal Income Tax Rates," NerdWallet, July 7, 2023, https://www.nerdwallet.com/article/taxes/federal-income-tax-brackets.

As this table shows, taxes are tiered. It's a common misconception that when you move to a new tax bracket, you are taxed the higher amount on your *whole* income. You're actually only taxed the higher percentage on the income you make above the new threshold. Still, these numbers quickly add up. For example, someone earning more than $170,051 has every additional dollar taxed at 32 percent, which is basically a third of what you make! This means a dentist previously earning $171,000 a year who increases her business by $40,000 gross must pay *an additional* $12,800 in taxes, reducing her actual income increase to $27,200 net—a far cry from the extra $40,000 she thought she had made and could spend.

As earnings increase, and taxes increase, and spending increases, you need to continually work more hours, which puts you in the position of trying to run up the down escalator. Working longer and harder is an effective strategy for the period in your career when you are building your capital, but it's not a reasonably healthy—or effective—strategy to hit financial freedom. You'll need to earn additional investment income for that.

3. The Point of Earning and Saving Is to Invest

Once you understand that you've been running up the down escalator, it starts to make sense why you haven't made the financial progress you expected. You can work very hard for a long time and *still* make minimal progress when the forces of financial growth are working against you. The strategies in this book will help you turn the escalator in the right direction. When you combine that with running at top speed, you'll hit financial freedom exponentially faster than those using only one or two pillars—but not all three—to build wealth.

Next, we'll discuss the ingredients that lead to wealth accumulation. Use them to see your progress begin to snowball.

Wealth-Building Ingredients

If you want the perfect cake, you need the perfect recipe. A cake is just the right ingredients, in the right amount, in the right order, cooked at the right temperature, for the right amount of time. Recipes are instructions on how to do everything correctly to produce the intended result. Success in health and fitness follows the same formula: The right nutrition, combined with the right workout plan and the right sleep schedule, will produce a desired result. Wealth is no different. Understanding the ingredients that go into creating wealth will put you in the position to start accumulating them and mixing them together to build your wealth cake.

Capital

The Oxford Languages dictionary defines capital as "wealth in the form of money or other assets owned by a person or organization, or available or contributed for a particular purpose such as starting a company or investing." Capital will be the first—and possibly most important—ingredient in your recipe. This opinion is unpopular to some real estate investors because it *is* possible to invest without capital of your own. Real estate strategies like the Buy, Rehab, Rent, Refinance, Repeat (BRRRR) method, or other creative partnerships, can allow you to buy deals without your own money, but that doesn't mean they don't involve *someone's* money. Deals require capital, but as a new investor without a proven track record, it can be nearly impossible to get access to this capital. This is a source of frustration for many people attempting to build wealth through real estate.

Rather than share ways to build wealth that require using someone else's money, it's better for me to teach you the process of acquiring your own capital. Those investing their own money will usually take greater caution than those investing someone else's; after all, your money has value to you because of the time it took and work you did to accumulate it. To complete your first deal safely and successfully, you'll need enough capital for a down payment, rehab, closing costs, capital expenditures, and reserves. Real estate builds huge wealth over time, but it doesn't create it from thin air. You need capital to start and maintain this growth.

Those without sufficient capital can't take advantage of the best opportunities, which are usually real estate deals that involve solving a problem others are unwilling or unable to solve. Much like how working through obstacles will build up your offense pillar, acquiring properties others don't want will build up your equity. Not having access to capital will put these deals out of reach for you. Additionally, buying assets can be nerve-racking when you don't have sufficient reserves to protect you during down times.

Knowledge

The best investors don't just have the most money; they are continually seeking knowledge and new ways to grow, manage, and protect their wealth. Knowledge is required in several areas if you want to grow your wealth through real estate investing; this includes knowledge of different asset classes, tax strategies, psychology, communication skills, and analysis. Investing is not just a goal but a skill that can be grown. Just like you need to continue to acquire capital to keep investing, you also need to continue to acquire knowledge to be a better investor.

Knowledge comes in many forms. Some of my favorite sources are podcasts, books, and investor meetups. Immersing yourself in the world of investing will give you strategies and ideas to try; it will rewire your brain to look at the world through the lens of wealthy people, to understand what they see. Different angles, opportunities, and methods for growing your capital become clear when you gather improved perspectives and knowledge.

Results

It's not enough to just buy a cookbook and hope for the best; you have to study how bakers make their cakes. It's the same for understanding assets; you have to know how to analyze if they are performing optimally. The results of your investments will play a huge role in the quality of the wealth cake you bake. Building wealth means both acquiring it and maintaining it so you are able to invest it. It also means ensuring that those investments are performing and growing your wealth, not losing it. Assets don't come risk-free. Like burning a cake because you didn't check the oven, you can burn up your assets by not checking on them.

We combat this problem with regularly tracking, measuring, and analyzing our portfolio—I review mine weekly. I have a goal for each property I own, and I monitor whether it is hitting that goal. Before buying properties, you must have a good understanding of how you expect them to perform, what potential problems you might encounter, and what your game plan will be in response. It's hard work to earn and save money; you want to preserve what you've accumulated and ensure it's working hard for you in return.

Understanding the fundamentals of analyzing real estate means feeling confident in how you make decisions. Investors typically analyze three metrics: cash flow, equity, and return on investment (ROI).

Cash flow is determined by taking the income a property produces and subtracting the expenses. The number left over is the monthly cash flow. For example, if your rental income is $2,000 per month and your expenses (including mortgage, taxes, insurance, and maintenance—see the chart in the Cash Flow section of Chapter 1) add up to $1,300, your monthly cash flow is $700.

Equity is determined by taking the value of a property after it's been fixed up and is ready to rent and then subtracting the loan amount plus any money the investor put into the rehab. Investors look for large "spreads" when buying properties; a spread is determined by the difference between how much a buyer offers for a property and the initial amount asked for by the seller. Buyers want to pay as little as possible for an investment property, knowing they will likely have to improve its condition before renting it.

ROI is a metric used to measure how hard your capital is working for you. This simple formula involves measuring how much income your investment made in a year (profit) and dividing it by the total amount of money you invested (capital). This number indicates what percentage of your investment you receive back each year. From our earlier example, let's take the $700 monthly cash flow and multiply it by 12 (for each month in a year). If you invested $100,000 and your annual profit is $8,400 ($700 times 12 equals $8,400), your ROI is 8.4 percent. When we analyze investment opportunities, we are looking for a combination of the highest and safest returns possible.

Time

Time is the most powerful of the ingredients when it comes to real estate, largely because of compounding. Good things tend to get better over time. The longer we save money and control our spending, the easier it becomes to do so. Debt is paid off faster as payments snowball or avalanche. Doing well at work leads to promotions and more opportunities; more opportunities lead to more promotions and responsibility; and so on. The power of compounding works in all areas of your life, and especially for accumulating wealth.

It takes time to increase our skills in the workplace, our experience in our profession, our abilities as an investor, and the depth of our relationships. We must combine the powers of compound interest, loan paydown, and professional development, and that all takes time.

Leverage

Leverage is an amplification of our natural skills, abilities, and resources, and it makes a task easier. When used properly, it allows you to do much more with it than you could without it. In your wealth-building journey, you'll learn to leverage the power of money, people, knowledge, resources, and more. We leverage money when we borrow from others. For example, a $350,000 home costs $350,000. If you borrow 80 percent of the money required to buy the home, you are leveraging the bank to make your own capital investment go further. In this case, you pay only $70,000 (20 percent of the cost) up front, but you get ownership of an asset worth much more.

You also leverage people. In this home purchase, you don't need to be a lawyer, loan officer, expert in title chains, or home inspector. Rather than learn all these skills yourself, you leverage the expertise and skills of others. Your real estate agent handles the transaction, the loan officer secures the financing, and the home inspector lets you know what, if anything, is wrong with the house. You leverage the knowledge of CPAs, bookkeepers, and property managers to help you grow and protect your capital better than you could on your own.

You can leverage your own knowledge too. A wise person learns from their mistakes, and an even wiser person also learns from the mistakes of others. When we read books of others' experiences or learn from those who have spent years obtaining their knowledge, we are using leverage. When we seek counsel, ask questions, or obtain guidance, we are leveraging knowledge. The employee who looks to their supervisor for sales training is improving their feedback cycle by leveraging knowledge. The same is true for those who seek mentors. There is absolutely no reason to learn everything by ourselves. Leverage works better.

We also leverage resources. I am a real estate broker with Keller Williams Realty. Rather than lease a building to house my team and spend $10,000 a month on rent, utilities, and taxes, I use the same office building as other Keller Williams agents. I also leverage their errors and omissions insurance, attorneys, marketing consultants, file coordinator, and more. By sharing these resources, all of us in the office avoid having to hire our own individuals to complete each required task. I frequently leverage the knowledge of my friends, contractors, property managers, and repair people for various problems I encounter in my portfolio.

As you learn more about how to invest, pay careful attention to building capital, gaining knowledge, analyzing results, and leveraging multiple sources. These are the main ingredients in your wealth-building recipe.

Buy Assets

The goal in accumulating capital through earning and saving is to invest as much as possible into income-generating assets. To use another food analogy, the idea here is to look at your savings as seeds. Rather than spending (eating) these seeds or putting them away (expecting they'll multiply on their own), it's better to plant them. Planting your money seeds is the process of putting as much of your savings into assets that will grow in value over time. Investing is the art of doing this well.

A seed can't grow if it's not planted in the right soil, under the right conditions, and cared for the right way. If the seed has the right soil, conditions, and care, it will grow into a money tree. It will then produce more seeds, which can in turn be planted, thus harnessing the power of compound interest in your orchard. This type of growth creates multimillionaires—but it does come with a catch: *Seeds only grow when planted properly.*

Compound Interest in Action

We invest our money, earn a return on it, and then reinvest that principal along with the new interest. Those are the steps to get our returns to grow larger with each cycle. Similar to the feedback cycle associated with learning, and the snowball or avalanche method of debt paydown, each new cycle of reinvesting creates a larger profit base. Over a short period of time, compounding interest isn't particularly exciting. An initial investment of $50,000 at 10 percent annual interest will grow to $80,525 in five years. That's not bad, but over forty years it will grow to $2,262,962. And that's without principal being added. If you add another $25,000 a year to the initial $50,000, forty years of compound interest at 10 percent will give you $13,326,006!

Compound interest on its own is amazing, but it gets even sweeter when you add appreciating assets like real estate. The median home price in 1980 was $47,200. In 2020, it was $336,900.[78] That forty-year period saw home values increase by more than 600 percent! This does not take into account the cash flow you would have received from increasing rents or by paying down the loan leveraged to buy the property. Real estate over time does incredibly well, largely because inflation drives up both the value of the asset and the income it produces.

Additionally, home mortgages are designed to become increasingly beneficial to the investor over time. Home loans are typically amortized, meaning a portion of the payment goes toward the principal (the amount you borrowed) and another portion goes toward the interest (money you pay the lender for the right to use their capital). The majority of home loans are structured so that in the beginning of the loan, most of the monthly payments go toward the interest, but each subsequent payment has a slightly higher portion going toward the principal and a slightly lower portion toward the interest.

A $350,000 loan at 6 percent, repaid over thirty years, will have a monthly recurring payment of $2,098. The first payment will have only $348 going toward the principal and the rest toward interest. However, by the twentieth year, $1,146.22 will be paid toward the principal and $951.78 for interest. It takes a long time before big chunks of principal are paid off with each payment, meaning the longer you own a property, the more wealth you create for yourself through the loan paydown.

---

78 Nicole Johnson, "Here's How Much Home Prices Have Risen since 1950," Better, October 19, 2021, https://better.com/content/how-much-home-prices-have-risen-since-1950.

As you've now learned, capital left in your savings account can't take advantage of the power of leverage, and it won't grow enough to keep pace with inflation. However, money invested into income-producing assets benefits from inflation. There's no middle ground here: Your hard-earned money, the store of energy you gained through your labor, time, and sacrifice, will slowly lose value until converted into assets that appreciate with time. You're either losing value or gaining it. Fence-sitting is not an option.

Learning to save money was relatively simple (defense pillar), and earning more of it is something I improved on over time (offense pillar). Neither of those two pillars made me a millionaire; it was only when I started investing that my money tree sprouted from the seeds I had planted. That tree began to produce more seeds, and the cash flow from each property increased with time. I developed a maniacal focus on acquiring assets after buying my first property, and committed nearly 100 percent of my savings toward acquiring new assets (keeping only enough financial reserves to protect me during downtimes).

As you purchase more assets and start to experience better returns from your seeds, you'll be in the five-step process outlined below.

The Five Steps to Freedom

With freedom as the goal, you'll want to eventually replace the money you earn at work (active income) with money that comes in from your investments (passive income). I want to point out that no income is truly passive; there will always be some form of work that needs to be done or decisions that need to be made. Passive income is valuable because there is *less* work involved. There is also more freedom with it, as you can usually manage your investment portfolio from anywhere.

Step 1: Put 100 Percent of Your Savings Commitment into Savings

Your first challenge is sticking to your budget and consistently putting 100 percent of the money you promised yourself you would into your savings account. If you can't do this, you'll never have the discipline to follow the next steps.

Step 2: Put 100 Percent of Additional Income into Savings

As your offense improves and you make more money, it will be tempting to spend the extra income and put away only your originally budgeted savings amount. Don't. As your income increases, save all the additional income and keep your expenses the same.

Step 3: Put 100 Percent of Savings into Assets

Once you have a small bundle of savings, resist the temptation to spend it! You worked incredibly hard for those savings, and you should be proud of that. Honor yourself by putting this money into assets so the money pile can grow even larger. Buying stuff will only deplete the bundle.

Step 4: Replace 100 Percent of Active Income with Passive Income

Once your assets start producing cash flow, you should be in a more financially comfortable position. When you're no longer living paycheck to paycheck, it can be tempting to take your eye off the goal. At this step, you'll be seeing the fruits of your saving habits, and you'll be earning more income—without adding more j-o-b work. It's at this phase where it may seem easy to coast.

Upgrading your car, house, clothes, or children's school are all possible options at this step. If you take that bait, you'll never reach true financial freedom. Continue to reinvest all your passive income into new assets rather than spending it. This will create even more passive income until 100 percent of your budget is covered purely by passive income.

Step 5: Put 100 Percent of Non-Budgeted Passive Income into Assets

Once you have completely replaced your active income with passive income, you can officially say you've reached financial freedom! If you choose, you can stop here. My advice, though, is don't stop. Continue to reinvest the difference between what your investments earn and what you spend (yes, it's still important to stick to a budget here). This will grow the amount of discretionary income you can save and improve the quality of your life as you age. Picking up momentum in this area will pay dividends in your future.

At each of these steps, money represents something different. At Step 1, money represents time. At Step 2, it represents time and discipline. In Step 3, it represents respect for yourself and your hard-won accomplishments. By Step 4, money represents freedom, meaning that you have earned your time back. At Step 5, money represents opportunities and an amazing quality of life. Your relationship with money will change as you walk through your own financial journey; at least it should, if you're doing it right.

The Top Ten Ways to Make Money in Real Estate

There are numerous ways to make money in real estate, but most strategies fit into one of the following ten categories. Learning how to harness the power of each and, more importantly, why they work and what factors influence them will make real estate investing much easier to learn and master.

Category 1: Buying Equity

Buying equity means you are purchasing properties below their market value. Also known as "buying right," real estate investing is one of the few asset classes that allows you to make money when you buy it. Other asset classes, like stocks and bonds, have set prices determined by the market. You cannot buy Apple stock for less than what it is trading for that day, and bonds cost what they cost. Real estate allows for flexibility in the purchase price: It is possible to buy a property for $400,000 that appraises for $500,000 and then later resell it for $500,000. This creates $100,000 of equity from Day 1, even before other equity-building strategies are implemented, like rehabbing the property to sell for even more than the initial appraisal.

Investors buy equity by focusing on finding good deals; usually, they're from motivated sellers who can no longer afford or no longer want their property. Being able to offer a desperate seller a quick sale with limited restrictions can often provide them the incentive to sell a property for less than it could get on the open market, especially if the seller doesn't have to make any improvements, repairs, or upgrades.

Buying properties under less-than-favorable market conditions occurs too. Many sellers will sell for less than market value if they can't wait any longer for a better buyer (say they already bought a new home), or they believe the market may collapse even further.

Category 2: Forcing Equity

Forcing equity, also known as forcing appreciation, happens when an investor buys a property and improves its condition, size, or both to increase its value. This can be as simple as removing carpet and painting the interior in the latest Pantone Color of the Year, or as complex as adding square footage. Many investors buy run-down properties in need of new finishes and upgrades, then they gut and rehab kitchens and bathrooms to add immediate value and create quick equity. Buying properties at fair market value that are already upgraded prevents you from adding easy equity. In general, investors should avoid these properties and instead look for properties that standard home buyers would pass over due to neglect or other reasons.

In addition to cosmetic rehabs, equity can be created by adding living space: converting garages, basements, or utility rooms to be part of the main house. You can add walls to a covered porch or drywall to a sunroom to convert it into a four-season room. Clever investors will see ways to add square footage that are cheaper than building from the ground up. You will earn above-average returns by adding square footage to smaller homes. For example, adding 500 square feet to an 1,100-square-foot property will net a higher dollar-per-square-foot increase than adding 500 square feet to a property that already has 3,000 square feet.

Category 3: Natural Equity (or Inflation)

Think of inflation like a rising tide of prices; everything goes up. Food prices go up. Clothing prices go up. And home prices go up. The more homes that you have, the more you benefit from this tide. My real estate portfolio functions better with inflation. Groceries, gas, and other goods become more expensive, but the effect is far less serious on me because my investments are now worth more too. That means my equity is growing, which gives me more chances to buy more investment vehicles that will also rise with the tide.

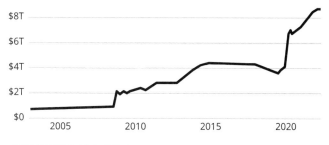

Federal Reserve Assets

Source: Federal Reserve Bank of St. Louis

Quantitative easing is the federal government's policy to introduce more money into the existing supply during periods of recessionary pressure. The graph indicates how much the federal reserves have grown since the early 2000s.[79] Those unfamiliar with macroeconomic strategy can understand this to mean that new money was introduced into our economy in proportion to the amount of debt the federal reserve took on during this time period. According to Bankrate, the U.S. balance sheet has ballooned to above $8.9 trillion since COVID-19, which is the largest amount in U.S. history.[80] Again, inflation makes saving your way to prosperity impossible. Buying real estate will allow you to take advantage of natural equity and have your money invested in assets that will also go up when inflation rises.

Category 4: Market Appreciation/Equity

Similar to natural equity, market appreciation/equity involves the value of assets rising over time. The difference is that market appreciation occurs from buying in markets where this can reasonably be expected, meaning areas expected to have both low supply and high demand at some point.

You can capitalize on market appreciation by doing research to choose an emerging market wisely. For example, these are areas,

---

79 "What Is the Money Supply, and How Does It Relate to Inflation and the Federal Reserve?" USAFacts, July 21, 2022, https://usafacts.org/articles/what-is-the-money-supply-and-how-does-it-relate-to-inflation-and-the-federal-reserve/.

80 Sarah Foster, "What Is Quantitative Easing?" Bankrate, March 8, 2022, https://www.bankrate.com/banking/federal-reserve/what-is-quantitative-easing/.

neighborhoods, and asset classes most likely to experience a population swell. Many areas have natural barriers to their expansion; it could be geographic—like rivers or mountains—or it may simply be that there is no more land for new construction. Look for places where the overflow of people will go, and that could be a good market to invest in. In many cases, this will be the nearest city or area where future tenants will want to live.

Examples of markets with limited supply and high demand are Austin, Seattle, San Francisco, Manhattan, and Southern California. Rising wages accompanied the tech industry boom, and areas with already limited supply had masses of new workers, which forced construction projects. Those investing in these cities from 2012 to 2022 did remarkably well and experienced above-average returns— much better than those who invested in the Midwest or markets with lower price points but also lower wages, lower population growth, and lower overall development.

This principle also works for properties with rare and valuable attributes or amenities. Properties zoned to allow certain activities that are uncommon—like horse properties, agricultural growth, and short-term rental permits—appreciate in value faster than properties in traditional zones. Beachfront properties or homes with unique views appreciate faster too. Not all real estate is created equal. Learn how to identify these types of locations, then plant your seeds and watch them grow.

Category 5: Natural Cash Flow
Natural cash flow is a measure of the money made through real estate after expenses are subtracted from income. Natural cash flow is the best known method of making money in real estate and is the result of inflation weakening the U.S. dollar, then rents rising as a response to that.

Category 6: Market-Appreciating Cash Flow
Much like market appreciation/equity, market-appreciating cash flow occurs when you own properties in an area where rents increase faster than the national average. Rent increases are a function of two components: higher demand than supply—which happens when there are more tenants looking to rent than there are units

available—and increased wages that can sustain higher rents.

Investors of multifamily apartment buildings or mixed-use properties use market-appreciating cash flow as a key profit driver. They target locations, for example, where tech jobs will move. They then build or buy in downtown locations or areas with high walking scores. Proximity to restaurants, shops, parks, jogging trails, and other amenities are key ingredients to market-appreciating cash flow.

Category 7: Forced Cash Flow

Forced cash flow, similar to forced equity, occurs when you buy a property and make immediate changes that decrease the expenses incurred by the previous owner. This can happen when you buy an apartment building and increase the efficiency of the management team, reduce vacancy rates, or hire an in-person superintendent rather than contracting out the work. Taking advantage of economies of scale reduces expenses to force cash flow higher.

Forced cash flow also occurs when you find ways to raise rents or create additional revenue streams. The easiest way to accomplish this is to buy property with below-market rents and immediately raise them to market value (this is common practice if the previous owner hadn't raised rents in several years). You can also increase revenue streams by adding additional units to a rental property, such as finishing a basement or converting a garage into livable space, then renting them out as separate units. Adding accessory dwelling units, also known as in-law units, granny flats, or Ohana units, is a relatively simple strategy to increase a property's revenue potential.

Cosmetic upgrades can also increase the demand for rental units, which will improve their cash flow. Upgrading kitchens and bathrooms is a quick and easy way to increase the current rent. More complex methods include converting asset type, meaning turning a traditional rental into something like a vacation or short-term rental. It can be lucrative to purchase a traditional property and turn it into a high-grossing vacation rental in areas with a significant amount of interest for travelers.

Category 8: Tax Savings

Real estate investments offer tax savings superior to any alternative asset class I know of. The main source of tax savings is depreciation.

Though this word looks like the opposite of appreciation, it's not. Depreciation is an accounting term that refers to the fact that real estate, just like other business assets (vehicles, equipment, etc.) get old over time. This wear and tear results in a loss for the business owner. The government compensates business owners, which real estate investors certainly are, by allowing us to write off these losses. This is depreciation.

At its most basic level, residential properties are considered to wear down over 27.5 years, or approximately 3.636 percent a year (100 percent divided by 27.5 years is 3.636 percent). Commercial properties are depreciated over thirty-nine years because they tend to have fewer moving parts that wear down faster and take less abuse than residential homes. Only the structure itself—not the land on which it lives—is eligible for depreciation. For example, someone with a $600,000 residential property with a structure determined to be worth $400,000 would be eligible to take $14,545 of losses a year ($400,000 structure divided by 27.5 years). This means if the property cash flowed $15,000 a year, taxes would only be owed on the difference of $455, which is a meager amount.

Profit earned through real estate is worth more than business ventures without similar tax savings because depreciation shields how much of that profit is taxed.

Category 9: Loan Paydown

As explained earlier, with each mortgage payment you make, you pay off a slightly larger amount of the principal you borrowed to buy the property. With your loan balance steadily decreasing, the difference between what you owe and what the property is worth decreases. Over the years, you create significant equity by doing nothing more than paying off the loan balance. Holding loans for longer periods, such as thirty years, is more advantageous to the borrower because a higher percentage of the loan payment goes toward paying off the principal portion of the loan with each payment. If you do nothing else, consider implementing the easiest strategy in the world to become a millionaire: buy $1 million worth of real estate and let the bank loan you most of the money while your tenants pay off the loan for you.

Category 10: Working in the Industry

This final method isn't exactly investing in real estate, but it still works to create additional income. While it takes capital to buy property, it won't always take capital—or not nearly as much of it—to work in a real estate business or to start your own. The options to make money are numerous for every personality type, skill set, and temperament. If you find yourself loving real estate and still need to earn capital, this option might be the perfect fit for you. As a bonus, the defense and offense pillars covered in the first two parts of the book are applicable here. Defense strategies include, for example, hiring someone to do your bookkeeping, while offense principles can be applied to create additional revenue streams. Let's look at the possibilities for jobs in real estate.

- Real Estate Agent
- Loan Officer
- Electrician
- Bookkeeper
- Property Manager
- CPA
- Stager
- Real Estate Advisor
- Consultant
- Admin in Office
- Assistant Agent
- Interior Designer
- Cold Caller
- Loan Processor
- Photographer
- Demolition Worker
- Landscaper
- Roofer
- Architect
- Engineer
- Pool Cleaner
- Pest Inspector
- Home Inspector
- Title Representative
- Title Officer

- File Coordinator
- Database Manager
- Sales and Marketing Manager
- SEO Lead Generator
- Inside Sales Agent
- Transaction Coordinator
- Asset Manager
- Underwriter
- Office Broker
- Private Money Lender
- House Flipper
- Wholesaler

These represent just some of the positions in the field. The three dimensions of success discussed earlier in the book (learn, leverage, and lead) could work to grow any of these opportunities into a business, since most of these positions are either jobs in a company or done by independent contractors. Creating income in these ways will help your investing as well because you'll get exposure to others in the industry, get paid to network, and find it easier to make deals with others. Don't neglect opportunities to make money and connections in real estate that aren't directly tied to owning property.

Resources to Get Started in Real Estate

I've mentioned throughout this book the importance of gaining knowledge. The following are some resources to help you get started. Keep using the format that speaks to your preferred style of learning; it will help you as you continue on this journey.

Podcasts

Listening to podcasts is one of the most helpful things you can do. Bar none, the *BiggerPockets Real Estate Podcast* (www.biggerpockets.com/podcast) is the best, highest-rated, and easiest real estate podcast. Subscribe to this show and you'll find several episodes a week in which successful investors describe how they invest, what works, and what doesn't. You can also catch topical shows on specific asset classes, investment strategies, and markets to pursue. Researching podcasts and subscribing to the ones you like most will keep real estate top of mind and help keep you motivated, even during the more difficult parts of the journey.

Meetups

Meetups are events at which investors get together to talk, learn, and socialize about real estate. Meetups are a great way to hear about new ideas, meet key players, and get exposed to strategies you may not hear elsewhere. They can also make real estate more fun and remind you that you're not alone in the journey.

Books

Many great books have been written about real estate investing, with the best being available at www.biggerpockets.com/store. (For example, you'll find my *Buy, Rehab, Rent, Refinance, Repeat* and *Long-Distance Real Estate Investing* best-sellers there). You should also check out noteworthy authors including Brandon Turner, Ken McElroy, Gary Keller, and Jay Papasan at your local bookstore or library.

YouTube

There's plenty on YouTube too, if you search on the topic. Real estate investors from every level of success—the smallest to the largest—make free content to view on YouTube. Content is made for commercial properties, trailer parks, residential properties, flipping, and more. YouTube videos also have the benefit of giving you visual information on top of the educational value. Seeing how a property looks, what to look out for, or how a rehabilitation project develops can give you confidence in knowing what to look for in your next project.

Forums

Engaging in forums is a terrific way to learn more about real estate investing, get exposed to new concepts, learn what others are doing, and get specific questions answered. The BiggerPockets forums (www.biggerpockets.com/forums) offer phenomenal access to a tremendous catalog of questions and answers. You can also ask your own questions and connect with those who reply to you to develop new relationships.

KEY TAKEAWAYS

- Inflation can be measured several ways; the most popular is the Consumer Price Index (CPI). However, inflation is often much higher than what the CPI reflects.
- As earnings increase, so do taxes.
- Working longer and harder is an effective strategy for the period in your career when you are building your capital, but it's not a reasonably healthy—or effective—strategy to hit financial freedom.
- Wealth-building ingredients are capital, knowledge, results, time, and leverage. Harnessing their power will yield huge returns.
- Money left in your savings account is eaten away by inflation, but money invested into income-producing assets *benefits* from inflation.
- Buying equity is purchasing properties below their market value.
- Forcing equity happens when an investor buys a property and improves its condition, size, or both to increase its value.
- Think of inflation like a rising tide of prices; everything goes up, including real estate prices. The more homes that you have, the more you benefit from this tide.
- Market appreciation involves the value of assets increasing with time in areas where this can reasonably be expected to occur.
- Natural cash flow is a measure of the money made through real estate after expenses are subtracted.
- Market-appreciating cash flow occurs when you own properties where rents increase faster than the market as a whole.
- Forced cash flow occurs when you buy a property and make immediate changes that increase the rent or decrease the expenses in place from previous ownership.
- The main source of tax savings through real estate is from depreciation.
- With each mortgage payment, you pay off a slightly larger amount of the principal you borrowed.

Chapter 13
WAYS TO INVEST IN REAL ESTATE

*Landlords grow rich in their sleep without
working, risking, or economizing.*
—JOHN STUART MILL

Real estate investors have developed many creative and fun ways to profit from owning real estate—I'm not sure there could be enough books written to cover them all. There are also new strategies developed every year that take advantage of changes in the economy, workplace restrictions, and lifestyle changes of Americans. This chapter will cover some of the most popular and easiest strategies of real estate ownership; I recommend you read this one with your creative thinking cap on. Real estate investing is not about following a specific blueprint, it's about finding a strategy that works for your personality and financial situation, while taking advantage of the simple and powerful ways that real estate builds wealth.

Remember the five ingredients, capital, knowledge, results, time, and leverage? Most of the investing strategies in this chapter involve all of them in some way. Mastering a strategy is nothing more than mixing the five ingredients in different ways and repeating at volume. Some strategies work better when you're getting started, while others make more sense when you have larger amounts of capital to spend.

This chapter will list the different real estate asset classes available to invest in. I'll lay out strategies to use that maximize efficiency and success when investing in those classes. I'll also lay out some tools you can use that will help you execute these strategies and improve your profits.

Asset Classes

Asset classes are the different types of real estate you can invest in to build your wealth. While most real estate will be some form of land and a structure on it, those structures can come in many forms. Many investors start with one asset class, and then realize they prefer another. There is nothing wrong with switching your preferred asset class. Different asset classes will require different sets of knowledge, analysis, and skills to acquire and manage.

1. Primary Residence

The simplest way to invest in real estate is to buy the home you live in rather than rent from someone else. Over time, your home builds equity, gains value, and saves you on housing expenses. The common argument against this strategy is that renting is usually cheaper than buying—at least at first. Buying, however, works much better over time. Consider a $400,000 property with a 6 percent interest loan, and 3.5 percent of the purchase price ($14,000) as a down payment. With taxes, insurance, and your mortgage, the total monthly payment is approximately $2,700, depending on the cost of the mortgage insurance. A comparable property could be rented for $2,400, making renting appear to be the smarter financial option.

Over time, however, 4 percent annual rent increases mean the monthly rental payment turns into $2,900 after five years, while a monthly mortgage payment stays the same—making ownership cheaper. Over a fifteen-year period, if rent continues to have 4 percent annual increases, it will grow to more than $4,320 a month; that $2,700 housing payment looks like a steal. While there are other costs associated with homeownership, like maintenance and repairs, that same 4 percent annual growth means the property becomes worth more than $720,000 over that fifteen-year period. Also, the loan balance gets paid down by more than $111,000, creating an equity total of $445,000—without including the rent savings. Homeownership is a greater investment over a long period of time.

2. Single-Family Rentals
Single-family rentals (SFRs) are homes purchased and rented to a family or single occupant. Classified as single-family residences, they are typically between two and five bedrooms and one and four bathrooms, with some form of parking (garage, carport, etc.). These homes usually have a private backyard and don't share common areas with other homes. This asset class appreciates faster than others and is the easiest to find tenants for. The downside of SFRs is the challenge of making them cash flow. SFRs typically only have one source of rental income and, in many cases, they make less money than they cost each month when you first buy them. Many investors who look for properties in this asset class evaluate options based on the 1 percent rule, which means the monthly rent should be equal to or greater than 1 percent of the purchase price. For example, a $100,000 property would need to rent for $1,000 a month to pass the 1 percent rule.

3. Small Multifamily Housing
Small multifamily housing (MFH) is classified as a property with two, three, or four units. They can be purchased with conventional financing at a fixed rate, thirty-year loan, making them an attractive option for both beginner investors and those looking to buy a home they can also live in. Small MFH is known for its stronger cash flows—more units means more revenue streams—and superior lending options. The downside is that these properties are often located in less desirable parts of town where zoning codes allow for more than one unit per property, which can have an impact on elements like appreciation and local crime rates.

4. Large Multifamily Housing
A large MFH property has five or more units and is often an apartment building. These properties are not eligible for conventional financing and usually involve an interest rate that is fixed for a period of time—three, five, or seven years, for example—and then adjusts

each year after that, known as balloon payments. This balloon payment means that after the fixed period elapses, the remaining balance of the loan is due in full unless the property is refinanced or sold. This makes financing much less desirable for large MFH.

Large MFH is also valued differently than small MFH or SFR properties. While the latter are valued based on comparable sales, large MFH is typically valued by taking its yearly profit (net operating income, or NOI) and dividing that number by a capitalization (cap) rate. (I cover these in more detail later in this chapter.) Cap rates vary, and they reflect how much demand there is for assets of a particular type in a particular market. Because of the variables involved in large MFH—the larger purchase price and the more difficult financing—this asset class is mainly invested in by those with more experience and a high net worth.

5. Short-Term Rentals

Short-term rentals (STRs) can increase the revenue a property brings in without necessarily having to add additional units. In areas where travel is common or there is a high demand for temporary housing, the STR strategy can be wildly lucrative. STRs are typically advertised as vacation rentals on websites like Airbnb or VRBO, with the owner-operators often functioning as the property manager, concierge, and booking agent. It easily replaces W-2 income, but it is notoriously difficult to scale. To maximize revenue comes at the cost of time and effort, so this strategy can feel more like a job than an investment.

This strategy is also unpopular with the hospitality industry, city municipalities, and angry neighbors. Mounting opposition to STRs has created zoning changes, permit hurdles, and cities issuing STR licenses through a lottery. Even so, this strategy continues to explode in popularity because it allows investors to buy more expensive properties—in much better locations—that they would not be able to cash flow as a long-term rental. Investors in the STR space need to stay abreast of what their competition is doing, how prices are adjusting, how much supply is available, and what amenities other properties are offering. Upgraded insurance is required for these properties, and it takes more work to make them profitable than traditional investment strategies.

6. Medium-Term Rentals

Like STRs, medium- or mid-term rentals (MTRs) are properties with rental leases shorter than the traditional twelve months. MTRs differ from STRs in that they are usually rented by traveling professionals or family members who want to visit nearby relatives. Popular with traveling nurses, many MTRs are in areas near hospitals or other large corporate locations. Investors often secure leases with insurance companies that need to place clients who have lost their homes in temporary housing; hospitals that need to secure housing for traveling medical staff; or corporations that need to house their new hires.

7. Syndications/Funds

Syndications are opportunities to invest in real estate with other people. Funds work in a similar fashion. Both provide investors the opportunity to do several things they could not do on their own, such as investing in larger deals, accessing more capital, and leveraging the knowledge and resources of other investors. They are also a truly passive real estate investment. In syndications, there is a group, or sometimes only one individual, referred to as general partners (GPs). This group provides most of the work, such as sourcing the deal, structuring it, and overseeing its execution. GPs typically get 20 to 30 percent of the profits. Another group, the limited partners (LPs), provide the bulk of the capital and split the remaining 70 to 80 percent of the profit. GPs also make money collecting acquisition fees, management fees, and other fees from money the LPs invest.

A typical syndication involves a GP finding a large property, like an apartment building or commercial property, securing the financing, analyzing the numbers, and raising the funds from LPs to close. Most syndications require the LPs to be accredited investors, according to SEC regulations, because these investments are not regulated by the federal government. At the end of an agreed-upon timeframe, usually five years or so, the property is either sold or refinanced and the LPs have their capital returned with a profit. Syndication ROI is typically evaluated based on the internal rate of return, a more complicated formula than the basic ROI formula described earlier.

8. Commercial

Commercial assets are properties built for the purpose of conducting business or commerce. They can be shopping centers, downtown skyscrapers, company headquarters, or apartment complexes. Commercial properties are analyzed differently than residential properties; while residential properties are valued based on what comparable properties sold for, commercial properties are valued on their profitability—the net operating income (NOI) mentioned above. The NOI does not normally include the loan repayment or mortgage.

Cap rates are reflections of the desirability of an asset class in a specific area. They can be understood as the ROI you could expect buying the property with no loan. A property purchased for $1 million in cash that is expected to make $50,000 in profit would have a cap rate of 5 percent ($1 million divided by $50,000 equals .05, or 5 percent). The lower the cap rate, the more desirable the property and the more money an investor is willing to pay for it.

Commercial investors add value to their property with a triple net lease (NNN), an agreement in which the tenants are responsible for the rent plus maintenance costs, operating expenses, and insurance on the property. This lease structure is common in office buildings and shopping centers. NNN leases benefit landlords because all monthly operating expenses belong to the tenants, but these properties also carry more risk for the landlords if the tenant stops meeting the agreements in their lease.

9. Flipping

Flipping homes, also called fix-and-flip, is a straightforward strategy that involves buying properties below market value, increasing their value in whatever way possible, then reselling them at a higher price. Easier to execute during periods of rising prices, this attracts real estate investors looking to make a quick turnaround on their investment or who want to supercharge how quickly they can accumulate capital to invest later into buy-and-hold properties. Flipping is a good strategy for making money, but it is not the same as investing capital in real estate. It falls more under the offense pillar than the investing pillar. Flippers typically pay short-term (and higher) capital gains taxes and don't experience cash flow.

10. Wholesaling

Similar to flipping (which I'll discuss next), wholesaling is more of a business than an investment strategy. Also similar to flipping, wholesalers look for motivated sellers so they can put properties under contract for below-market value, using negotiation strategies and local market knowledge. Once the property is under contract, the wholesaler then "assigns," or sells, the contract to a different real estate investor. For example, Wholesaler William puts a property under contract for $200,000 with Seller Sally who needs a quick sale to pay off bills. The property could be resold for $300,000. William assigns the contract (that is, the right to buy the property under the negotiated terms) to Buyer Betty for $50,000. Betty pays $200,000 to Sally and $50,000 to William (a fee for finding the property), getting a $300,000 property for $250,000. The wholesaler earns $50,000 without needing to do any work to fix up the property for resale, and Sally gets out of her house quickly.

11. Mobile Home/Recreational Vehicle Parks

Buying mobile home or recreational vehicle (RV) parks allows investors to use commercial financing without requiring the same level of operational commitment. While apartment owners are required to maintain, upgrade, and fix problems in their properties, mobile home park owners have little of that work. Tenants lease spaces for *their own* mobile homes or RVs, releasing the landlords from responsibility for the structure maintenance. Most mobile home parks provide the space for the home, electrical hookups, sewer hookups, and nothing else. These investments avoid the operational commitments and complexities of commercial real estate, but they tend to miss out on the appreciation and value-added components many commercial and MFH investors realize. MFH investors can improve their properties through cosmetic upgrades where mobile home parks cannot.

12. Notes

Some investors lend their money to other investors to be used for buying properties and are repaid over time. A note is a promise to repay that loan; this word can be used interchangeably with loan, as they both refer to a lender's right to collect payments from a borrower. Notes dictate the loan amount, loan period, repayment terms, the property securing the note, and more. It is also possible to sell the note (the right to collect the payment) to someone else. Investors who buy notes from other investors or note holders typically pay less than the loan balance; however, the original note holder then has more capital to invest elsewhere. When the borrower pays the note off in full, the new note holder receives more money than they paid to buy the note, turning a profit.

Investment Strategies

When it comes to buying different asset classes (and properties within them), there are different strategies. Most of these strategies involve some form of equity creation, low down payment, equity withdrawal, or value-add component. While many investment strategies will work on more than one type of asset class, some of them are asset class specific. If you're interested in a particular strategy and want to dive deeper, there are usually books, courses, or content devoted to these areas of interest.

1. House Hacking

House hacking is a strategy that involves "hacking into" your home's potential to generate income while you live in it. House hacking strategies are broad and often creative, and all have the same goal—reduce or eliminate your biggest expense—your housing costs—by renting out parts of the property.

The simplest method of house hacking is to buy a small MFH property, such as a triplex (three units), live in one unit, and rent out the other two. The rent collected from the two units often significantly reduces the out-of-pocket expenses for the homeowner. This strategy can also work with SFRs by renting out individual rooms or converting parts of the home into separate units. Spaces like basements, utility rooms, attics, ADUs, or even an RV parked in the backyard can generate income and reduce housing costs for the owner-investor.

House hacking allows real estate investors to take many of the best elements of real estate and incorporate them all into one property. House hackers can take advantage of lower down payments associated with purchasing a primary residence. Most investment properties (that is, you won't be living there) require a minimum of 20 percent down, while primary residences have options from 3.5 percent down. Primary residence mortgages also have lower interest rates and are easier to qualify for.

2. Second Home/Vacation Home
Most lenders will allow buyers to purchase a second home, or vacation home, with 10 percent down as opposed to the traditional minimum of 25 percent for investment properties. These loans have more stringent requirements, though, such as the property must be within a certain mile radius of where the borrower lives.

3. 15 Percent Down Loans
At various times in economic cycles, lenders will offer investment property loans for less than 20 percent down. These typically occur in seller's markets when values are rising rapidly, reducing risk to lenders because the equity in the property is growing and it's not as important for buyers to provide that equity with their down payment. Buying homes during these markets can provide investors an advantage because there's a lower down payment required, and you can save your capital.

4. Buy, Rehab, Rent, Refinance, Repeat (BRRRR)
The BRRRR is a strategy popular with investors who want to recover more of the capital they put into investment properties than they would with traditional rentals. When done correctly, the investor buys a property—often a fixer-upper—for a below-market price (buying equity), rehabs it (forcing equity), and rents it out (market-appreciating cash flow). The investor's work to create equity creates a significant gap between the loan amount and the property value; the investor then refinances the property, allowing them to recover some of their capital. The investor then repeats the process again.

Consider an investor who buys a fixer-upper in such bad condition that it sits on the market for months because no one makes an offer. The investor uses a hard-money loan (a short-term loan with higher rates than the long-term loan industry standard) to purchase the property for $120,000. They spend $80,000 rehabbing it, bringing the total amount put into the property to $200,000. After it's remodeled, the property appraises for $250,000, and the investor rents it for $2,200 a month. The investor then refinances the property with a $200,000 loan, which is 80 percent of the appraised value ($250,000). The loan amount of $200,000 is enough to pay off the original hard-money loan ($120,000) and pay themselves back for the money spent on the rehab ($80,000). This essentially returns 100 percent of their capital, gives them a completely remodeled property, and allows them to repeat the process again with another property without needing to save for the next down payment.

5. The Sneaky Rental

The sneaky rental strategy involves buying a property as a primary residence, living in it for a year, then moving out and making it a rental property. It's referred to as "sneaky" because purchasers can use a low down payment option, like 5 percent down, and purchase a property that will later be used as a rental property (which normally requires at least 20 percent down). Those using this strategy can reduce their housing expenses for the first year of ownership by renting out rooms in the house or units on the property. After they've lived in the property for one year, they can move out to make the entire home a rental property, further increasing their cash flow. This method can be repeated—buy a home, live in it for a year, make it a rental property, buy a new home, etc.—to build a portfolio of cash-flowing rental properties purchased with 5 percent down loans.

6. Buy an SFR and Add ADUs to Create an MFH

Those wanting to invest in SFRs who can't meet the 1 percent rule (where the monthly rent should be equal to or greater than 1 percent of the purchase price) often consider this strategy. Depending on the market, an SFR that costs $400,000 might need to rent for close to $3,500 a month to cash flow positively, eliminating most of the SFRs on the market as a viable option. Investors just need to be creative. You can buy an SFR and convert the garage and/or basement and/or another structure on the property into ADUs. These extra rentals can provide enough income to close the gap between rent and expenses. For a $400,000 SFR that could rent one unit for $2,800 a month, plus one ADU that can be rented for $1,250 a month, the total income becomes $4,050, which is more than enough to meet the 1 percent rule and make an SFR a cash-flowing option.

It's important to know zoning laws, but many neighborhoods do allow for more than one door (a.k.a. more than one rental unit) per property. In California, it is illegal for the state to stop investors from adding ADUs to their properties; the state allows for one full ADU and one junior ADU (a junior ADU is smaller and must be attached to the main property), regardless of a city's zoning laws.

7. The Stack

The stack is an investment strategy coined by Brandon Turner, author of BiggerPockets' best-seller *The Book on Rental Property Investing* and former host of the *BiggerPockets Real Estate Podcast*. This strategy encourages investors to double their portfolio each year but at a manageable level. It involves buying one SFR in the first year and learning to manage it yourself. The next year, you buy a duplex with two units (a small MFH), and the following year, a four-unit property. Each year, you are doubling your unit count: from one to two to four to eight units, and so on. By buying twice as many units each year, you'll continue to improve your real estate skills and abilities while not growing so big so fast that you collapse under the weight of learning how to manage the properties.

8. 15/15/15

This method involves buying fifteen homes over fifteen years with fifteen-year mortgages. At the end of fifteen years, the first property will be paid off and can be refinanced for tax-free wealth (refinances aren't considered income and cannot be taxed). The next year, the second house will be paid off, which you will again refinance for another year of tax-free money.

Let's look at an example. In Year 1, you buy a $450,000 triplex on a fifteen-year note at 6 percent interest. Each unit rents for $1,200, giving you an income of $3,600, and your expenses are roughly the same. You repeat this for fifteen years. By Year 15, the original property is paid off and rents have grown at 3 percent annually (let's say to $5,600 per month), netting you a cash flow of approximately $2,000 a month assuming insurance and taxes haven't risen disproportionately. The property has appreciated at 3 percent annually and is now worth $701,085. You refinance the property on another fifteen-year note, pulling out 75 percent of the equity, which nets you $525,813 of tax-free income for that year.

The new loan amount—the cash you pulled out to live on—of approximately $500,000 (let's say you pulled out money for the closing costs too) bumps your expenses up to around $4,700 a month, leaving you with a monthly cash flow of $520 and a lump sum of $489,375. In Year 16, you repeat this process with the property you bought in Year 2, now paid off as well, and net another $489,375 and an additional $500 or more in cash flow. For the next fifteen years, you repeat the same process, never paying taxes on this income, and maintaining a healthy cash flow across your portfolio. With the 15/15/15 method, you will work hard for fifteen years and then never work again.

The challenge with this strategy is finding properties that will cash flow on fifteen-year notes, which have higher monthly payments in exchange for less of it going toward interest. The alternative is to be in a strong enough financial position that you can support the payments should the properties not cash flow for the first several years. However, the payoff is there after fifteen years of *hard* work: You'll live the rest of your life on passive and *tax-free* income.

9. Classes A and B at Peak, Classes C and D at Crash

While real estate markets tend to gain or lose value as a group, they don't do so in proportionate amounts. In other words, the homes in the best locations (Classes A and B) don't lose value at the same rate as homes in less desirable locations (Classes C and D). Experienced investors buy properties in nicer locations (Classes A and B) when the market is closer to the top because they know these homes are less likely to lose value. They buy in less desirable locations (Classes C and D) after the market has tanked because these home values have nowhere to go but up.

Not understanding this strategy can lead to catastrophic results. Inexperienced investors often take the exact opposite approach: They buy properties in Class C and D locations when the market is at its peak because it feels safer to spend less money when the market is hot. Remember: Buy properties in Class A and B locations at the height of the market and properties in Class C and D locations after a crash.

10. Worst House in Best Neighborhood

A time-tested and proven strategy is the simple act of buying the ugliest home in the nicest neighborhood. Because ugly homes tend to attract fewer buyers, it's possible to buy these properties for less than what they would normally be worth; then you do cosmetic upgrades. When this is done to an ugly property in a great location, the value of that home is disproportionately higher than if it's done to an ugly property in an inferior location. This is as straightforward and easy as it gets for beginner investors, and experienced investors can easily combine this with other strategies to add big returns to their established portfolios.

11. Ride the Elevator

Riding the elevator is a strategy that involves buying large amounts of lower-priced properties during economic downturns (the ride down), then selling these homes as the economy improves and housing prices rise (the ride up). This is different from trying to time the market. It is impossible to know exactly when a market has reached its peak or when it is at its lowest, but investors can clearly tell when a market is *near* the peak or *near* the bottom. I buy real estate in every economic environment, but I definitely buy more when I believe properties are undervalued and have room to rise, and less when I feel the market is close to peaking.

In this strategy, you don't immediately reinvest the money from a sale into new real estate. Some investors buy low, wait, sell high, pay the capital gains taxes, then hold the remaining capital until the market crashes again, effectively only buying during the ride down and only selling on the ride up.

12. Section 8

The Section 8 housing program of the U.S. Department of Housing and Urban Development provides rental assistance to families and individuals who are eligible under specific guidelines. Some investors purchase properties with the intention of renting through the Section 8 program because their risk is lower when all or part of the rent is paid for by the government, as is the chance that tenants will fall behind or default on the terms of their rental agreement. However, the program also removes some flexibility for investors, as rent prices are determined by the government according to bedroom size and location of the property.

Here's an example of one person who uses this strategy. Joe Asamoah, a prominent investor in the Section 8 space, discovered that where he lives, larger homes—typically five or more bedrooms—have much higher rents compared to the price the homes could be purchased for. He also found there is high demand for these properties from rental tenants. Leveraging this knowledge, he created a system in which he buys fixer-upper properties for below-market prices, fixes them up, adds bedrooms and square footage (ADUs), then refinances them (the BRRRR method). He then rents these properties through the Section 8 government program.

This approach reduces his expenses, and each purchase adds significant equity to his portfolio. (Section 8 tenants reduce vacancy, and fixing properties up before placing tenants in them reduces capital expenditures.) He also sees yearly rent increases through the Section 8 program, improving his cash flow in another way.

13. Houses to Hotels

This strategy involves buying smaller asset types (SFRs or small MFHs), building equity in them, then trading them for larger asset types, like large MFHs or commercial buildings. Like in the game of Monopoly, where four small houses can be traded for one hotel, this strategy uses tools like the 1031 exchange (explained later in the Investment Tools section), buying equity, building equity, BRRRR, and forcing streams of cash flow.

You can start this strategy using a BRRRR approach; that is, buying a property under market value in high-demand areas and adding value to increase equity. You hold this property until the equity is larger than the cash flow can justify (analyzed for return on equity; discussed later in this chapter). A 1031 exchange is conducted; that is, you sell several of your smaller properties for one or more larger properties, essentially converting your Monopoly houses into a Monopoly hotel. These new, larger properties will produce more cash flow and will be easier to manage because there are fewer of them.

The strategy is especially effective when the cash flow from the larger properties is reinvested into more smaller properties, and then those are traded for larger properties—creating cash-flowing loops that never end.

14. Play the Coasts
Generally, coastal markets tend to see larger price fluctuations during economic shifts. It's common to see these markets both rise and fall in value faster than locations farther inland. An investor can use this information to ride an elevator on the coasts. Investor Irene saves her money during Economic Boom 1 (when prices are high), then buys California real estate during Economic Bust 1 (when prices are low). She holds these properties through Economic Boom 2 and watches her equity grow at an above-average pace as her properties quickly gain value.

Paying attention to macroeconomic factors influencing an impending Economic Bust 2, Irene trades her California properties using a 1031 exchange to defer her capital gains taxes. She protects her capital by investing in large MFHs in Wichita, Kansas, a Midwest market unlikely to be as affected by the coming market correction. Using leverage, Irene is able to buy four properties for each one she sold. When Economic Boom 3 is starting, Investor Irene once again uses a 1031 exchange to sell her Kansas MFHs, buy more coastal properties, and shelter her gains. The result is four coastal properties for every one she originally sold and a four times increase in equity as coastal markets once again increase in value.

Investment Tools
Investors use tools to save money, build energy, and operate their portfolios more efficiently. These tools help them make decisions on allocating capital efficiently, reinvesting energy from one asset class to another, or avoiding risk from market shifts. As you grow as an investor, you will learn to use more of these tools to help you in your journey. This section will introduce you to some of the more common ones and help you formulate plans for how you'll scale your portfolio in the future.

1. 1031 Exchange

According to NerdWallet:

> A 1031 exchange, named after section 1031 of the U.S. Internal Revenue Code, is a way to postpone capital gains tax on the sale of a business or investment property by using the proceeds to buy a similar property. It is also sometimes referred to as a "like-kind" exchange. A key rule about 1031 exchanges is that they're generally only for business or investment properties. Property for personal use—like your home, or a vacation house—typically doesn't count. Securities and financial instruments, such as stocks, bonds, debt instruments, partnership interests, inventory and certificates of trust aren't usually eligible for 1031 exchanges.[81]

Capital gains are the profits you make when you sell an investment. These are taxed differently than ordinary income, such as what you earn through W-2 or 1099 work, with the exception of capital gains made on investments held less than one year (which are taxed at the same rate as ordinary income). Gains made over a period longer than a year are usually taxed at a lower rate—between 15 percent and 20 percent, depending on your overall income. The 1031 exchange is a tool that allows investors to defer paying those capital gains taxes until a later date, essentially allowing them to snowball all the profits—without being taxed on them—into future investments. The government collects even more in taxes later while the investor grows their portfolio now, making this a win-win situation.

There are many rules with 1031 exchanges; a qualified intermediary should always be consulted first. Most 1031 exchanges require you to maintain the same loan balance on the new property as the old, invest 100 percent of the profit into the new property, identify potential new properties within 45 days of closing on the old property, close on the new property within 180 days, and more.

---

81 Tina Orem, "What Is a 1031 Exchange? A Guide to the Basics, Rules & What to Know," NerdWallet, February 2, 2023, https://www.nerdwallet.com/article/taxes/1031-exchange-like-kind.

2. ROE vs. ROI

Return on equity (ROE) can be measured in both cash flow or equity growth. The cash-flow measurement is the simpler of the two, accomplished by taking the yearly profit of a property and dividing it by the equity within the asset. When that number is lower than you could make by investing in new assets, you should consider selling and redeploying the equity into higher cash-flowing assets.

ROE measured as equity growth is more difficult, but it also provides a higher return on the time invested. Measuring equity can be tricky because it's more difficult to predict than future cash flows. Rent amounts are based on leases; while there is no guarantee your tenant will continue to pay, it's more predictable and measurable than if, and how much, a property will appreciate in the near future. Doing so requires an element of prediction. The investor has to look at demographic trends, population movements, and the future balance of supply and demand to determine if prices are likely to continue rising, stall out, or decrease in the future.

Return on investment (ROI) was discussed in Chapter 12, but it makes sense to go into more detail here. ROI is a measurement of the cash flow a property provides. It is based on the initial investment—usually the down payment plus rehab costs—and is initially calculated when the property is first purchased. It is calculated by dividing the yearly profit by the down payment amount. For example, a $400,000 property purchased with 20 percent down ($80,000) that makes $6,000 a year in cash flow has an ROI of 7.5 percent, a respectable number. ROI is an easy formula to understand and calculate: It reflects how well the property is performing—or rather, how well *your investment* in the property is performing.

Say the same property appreciates in value to $650,000, gaining $250,000 in equity in addition to your initial $80,000 investment. This brings your equity up to $330,000. On the other hand, the cash flow has only grown to $7,500 a year. In many cases, real estate investors see their equity grow faster than their cash flow. To reevaluate the performance of your portfolio, you'll need to track your return on equity, or ROE, not just your ROI.

With the cash flow up to $7,500, your new ROI is 9.3 percent, which is a solid improvement. If you take that same $7,500 and divide it by the *new equity of $330,000,* not your original down payment of $80,000, your ROE is less than 2.3 percent, a subpar return. If this happens, you can turn your equity into better cash flow by selling the property and exchanging the equity into a bigger and better property via a 1031 exchange, improving your return. That same $330,000 reinvested in a property that provides the original ROI of 7.5 percent would increase your yearly cash flow from $7,500 to $24,750. Experienced investors continually inspect the ROE of their portfolios to keep their capital performing optimally.

3. Trimming the Herd

Trimming the herd is the act of reviewing your portfolio each year to determine which properties performed well, which could be upgraded, and which should simply be sold. Markets change, strategies change, and investors grow in knowledge and skill over time, making it entirely possible to have properties in your portfolio that aren't serving you well. Some properties lose money, some take too much of your time, and some do both. When this happens, don't be afraid to get rid of poor-performing properties, even if it comes at a loss. Trimming the herd will force you to get rid of assets that are behaving more like liabilities.

4. Creative Financing

Real estate is traditionally purchased using conventional financing methods, such as loans sponsored by the federal government through Fannie Mae, Freddie Mac, the U.S. Department of Veterans Affairs, or the Federal Housing Administration. There are also non-qualified mortgage loans, which have increased in popularity and become safer over time. When someone purchases a property with financing outside of these methods, we refer to it as "creative financing." This term includes strategies like wraparound loans, subject-to, hard-money loans, lease options, private financing, and more. Many creative finance deals are structured so that the seller maintains their loan on the property while selling the title to the buyer. The buyer then pays off the seller's existing note for them. This can be advantageous for buyers when the seller's interest rate is better than current rates, or the buyer is unwilling to or can't secure their own financing.

5. Highest and Best Use

Changing a property's use to something more profitable is called highest and best use; it's a strategy investors use to maximize their returns and the performance of their portfolio. When determining how to get the most out of a property, investors ask what the highest and best use of the property should be. A beach home in a highly desirable location does have value as a primary residence, but it would make much more money as a high-end, short-term rental. Investors can use this to their advantage by applying for zoning changes to a property, adding ADUs, converting to STRs, renting out space on large lots, and other creative applications.

6. Long-Distance Real Estate Investing

Buying "outside of your own backyard" was considered risky for years, largely due to the lack of information available for review and the high potential for being the out-of-town "sucker" who didn't know what they were buying or where they were buying it. The internet changed this. As more information became available at our fingertips, long-distance investing decreased in risk. No longer relegated only to opportunities where they live, many investors now buy all across the country using a myriad of strategies, financing options, and resources.

I participated in long-distance investing when I lived in one area where I was paid a high wage but invested in markets with much lower price points. Police officers are not paid handsomely in any market, but working in the San Francisco Bay Area paid me better than law enforcement in any other market in the country. I made my investment dollar stretch further by investing in properties in southern states. Not living where I purchased meant not making lower wages or needing an advanced degree to make a high income. Nor did I need a high-paying job to save enough money to buy more expensive assets, allowing me to win twice. (I explain in my book *Long-Distance Real Estate Investing* helpful strategies to safely find the right market to invest in based on your specific situation.)

7. Portfolio Architecture

This strategy involves looking at your portfolio of properties as a single organism, rather than as a series of individual properties to be evaluated independently and separately. Investors can reduce their risk and increase their returns by combining the right asset types so the whole is greater than the sum of its parts. Many strategies work to increase equity faster than cash flow, and focusing on equity will usually provide a greater return—but not without risk. Having too much equity without enough cash flow can lead to foreclosure if you can't pay the mortgage due to financial hardship, unexpected repairs, or a sudden drop in market conditions.

To counterbalance this risk, consider the architecture of your portfolio as a whole, not just the merits of each individual property. For example, you can choose to build cash flow with reliable small MFHs before looking to create big equity in SFH fixer-uppers, or to build a solid foundation of income with large MFHs before investing in riskier short-term rentals. Balancing high-risk/high-return assets with low-risk/low-return assets can help reduce your exposure to sudden changes in the market or your personal finances, which can lead to the loss of properties. This is done by wisely diversifying your asset types, income streams, and locations.

Choose Your Asset Class, Strategy, and Tools

While far from exhaustive, this chapter has included many of the more popular assets, strategies, and tools used by real estate investors to grow the wealth they have created for themselves and provide the income necessary to escape the entrapment pattern. A basic understanding of these strategies can provide a solid jumping-off point for you to consider how your first investments could look and what direction you may take them in as your snowball and momentum build over time. Remember, it is not about simply *choosing* a strategy and using it—it's about *understanding* the principles that make a strategy work and how you can use that strategy to your advantage as you build wealth over time.

For general knowledge, the following classifications can help you determine where you might want to start, how to check your progress, and how to finish your real estate investing journey.

Beginner Investors

Beginner investors are usually best to start with single-family rentals and the strategies that employ it. House hacking should be every investor's first strategy (and repeated every year, if possible). SFRs are the simplest to finance, require the least money down, and are the easiest asset class to sell, should things go wrong. If you don't want to learn how to do your own property management, it's fairly easy to find property managers for SFRs. Plus, SFRs do not require complex analytical skills and are flexible enough to convert using various strategies.

Intermediate Investors

Investors with some experience often transition from SFRs into small MFHs of two to four units. These properties will usually cash flow better than SFR properties, but they may also be more expensive to purchase or be in less desirable neighborhoods. You need enough investment experience to avoid buying the wrong property and/or in the wrong location. MFHs are also more complicated to sell than single-family rental properties—in most situations, other investors usually buy MFHs, and investors want to make deals. Property management will be more extensive and expensive on a multiple-unit property, and the bookkeeping will be slightly more complex.

Advanced Investors

Most advanced investors are involved with large MFHs and commercial properties. These properties require a completely different underwriting standard and set of knowledge; they also use very different financing structures. Most larger properties will not be eligible for fixed-rate loans and will need to be continually refinanced or sold to keep cash flow. As economic markets shift, the value of these properties will shift as well. Cap (capitalization) rates are sensitive to local supply and demand, and fluctuating interest rates play a large role in the value of the property when it's time to exit. The property management of these assets is more intense and involved, as are the analytics.

Which Strategies to Select

Beginner Investors
My suggestion is house hacking, sneaky rental, worst house/best neighborhood, and Section 8 strategies. As noted above, beginners can reduce their risk, as well as the time it takes to save up their down payment, by investing in single-family rentals and using the strategies associated with them. House hacking, meanwhile, will reduce or eliminate your housing expense, making it the least risky strategy available. The sneaky rental takes advantage of low down payment options and can be combined with house hacking to reduce risk, and the worst house/best neighborhood is a strategy anyone can use. Section 8 investing is also solid for beginners as all, or a portion, of the rent is paid by the government, not the tenant.

Intermediate Investors
My suggestion here is BRRRR, SFRs with ADUs, 1031 exchanges, long-distance real estate investing, and houses to hotels. The BRRRR method can help slightly experienced investors scale their portfolio faster, but it requires a decent amount of knowledge on property values, rehab costs, financing rules, and value-add strategies. Investors can lose money just as quickly as they can make it by making mistakes with BRRRR, which is why I don't recommend this strategy for beginners. SFRs with ADUs is a solid strategy because it adds value in both cash flow and equity, and it stretches your vision of what is possible. Using the 1031 exchange to transfer the first round of single-family investments into larger multifamily investments (house to hotels) is another strategy available to intermediate investors, as is buying out of state.

Advanced Investors
Here I recommend the stack, 15/15/15, SFRs converted to MFHs, Classes A and B at peak and Classes C and D at crash, ride the elevator, and play the coasts. Advanced investors with a solid understanding of real estate fundamentals can take advantage of pushing the limits of portfolio growth using the stack method. The 15/15/15 method is simple, but it requires strong cash-flowing deals to make

the fifteen-year mortgages work. Converting SFRs into MFHs can be complicated and expensive, and buying Classes A and B at peaks and Classes C and D at crashes involves considerable knowledge and capital to buy properties at different points in the market cycle, something only advanced investors are likely to have. Advanced investors are far more likely to understand and have success with playing the coasts than beginner or intermediate investors.

Learning the various asset classes, strategies, and tools will become easier the more you use them. Some might even start to be boring. Immersing yourself in this education will take a seemingly overwhelming step and reduce it to very basic building blocks of wealth.

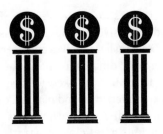

Chapter 14
GETTING BETTER REAL ESTATE DEALS

> *Successful negotiation is not about getting to 'yes';*
> *it's about mastering 'no' and understanding what*
> *the path to an agreement is.*
> —CHRISTOPHER VOSS

Supply and Demand

Getting better real estate deals starts with a firm understanding of supply and demand in a market and which side has the leverage, or upper hand. Supply and demand in real estate refers to buyer's markets and seller's markets. The former is where buyers have the upper hand (usually because there is more supply than demand), and the latter is when sellers have the upper hand (typically when there is less supply than demand).

It's important to understand that these are generalized descriptions. Not everyone in a seller's market will have leverage over what they make on a sale, nor will every buyer be able to name their price for a property. Ultimately, it is an asset's desirability that will determine its sale price; however, putting yourself in a position so you have the leverage *will* improve the quality of any deal you make. Once you're in that position, you need to know what to do with that advantage—having the leverage but not knowing how to use it is useless. Conversely, knowing all the negotiating tactics but not having an opportunity to use them is equally useless. Investors can make money in both markets when they understand the concepts in this chapter.

Market Equilibrium

Conceptually, market equilibrium refers to a market where there are an equal number of properties available (supply) and buyers who want them (demand). No market is ever in a state of true equilibrium, but some markets get close. These markets are recognized by stable pricing, predictable days on market (DOM), and list-to-sale price ratios that fall within a tight range. For a home to sell for more than its competition, it must be objectively superior: better condition, location, amenities. A home that is priced close to its competition but with inferior qualities will sit longer, forcing the sellers to eventually drop their price.

If real estate markets stayed in equilibrium, real estate investing would be boring. It is the undulations created by changing market conditions, economic environments, interest rates, and other factors affecting supply and demand that create exciting investing opportunities. Because learning about real estate through the lens of a perfectly balanced market is easier to understand, it's often taught this way. However, realizing that no market is completely balanced helps you understand why investing strategies will work better at some points and worse at others.

Buyer's Market

Days on market, or DOM, is a measure of how long a house sits for sale before a buyer puts it under contract. A buyer's market doesn't mean there are no interested buyers for properties in that market; many of the listings will sell with an appropriate DOM.

The chart below illustrates a market where demand for homes is lower than the supply—a buyer's market. In this market, 70 percent of available properties are within the same DOM (so there are buyers) and will not sell for a discount. The other 30 percent of these properties need to drop their price or improve their condition—or both.

They must improve their desirability one way or another so a buyer is interested; otherwise, the buyers have far better options.

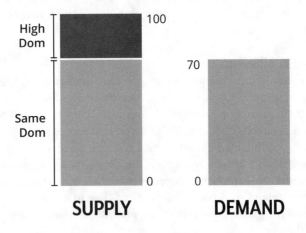

When there is more supply than demand, houses sit longer before selling; few, if any, receive multiple offers. Buyers always want to pay as little as possible and when they don't have to worry about multiple offers or competition, they won't offer above asking price. In buyer's markets, there are more sellers chasing fewer buyers, and when enough homes exceed the average DOM, the majority of sellers will drop their price. If this pattern continues for long enough, prices across the neighborhood will drop and the remaining inventory of homes for sale must follow suit or appear overpriced.

As prices drop, buyers have the leverage. They can be pickier about what they pay, which houses they pursue, and the terms they ask for in a contract. While this may seem like a good time to buy, buyer's markets come with a caveat: If the market continues to soften, the value of the assets themselves are likely to continue dropping. No buyer wants to buy an asset when its value is likely to drop. This causes the pool of buyers to collectively wait until they believe the market has "bottomed out," at which point they all jump in to buy. This contributes to the dynamic of markets changing direction quickly, moving from decreasing prices to increasing demand very suddenly. With enough demand and fewer houses for sale, this becomes a seller's market.

Seller's Market

A seller's market is defined as when there are more buyers than sell-ers. The scarcity of assets creates "bidding wars" and drives home prices higher. In a seller's market, a seller has the leverage: They are more likely to get the price and terms they want, and buyers are less likely to negotiate because another buyer is already in the wings.

This chart illustrates a market where demand for homes is higher than the supply—a seller's market. In this market, sellers have more negotiating power and can often command higher prices, because there is greater competition within the buyer pool for a constrained supply of properties.

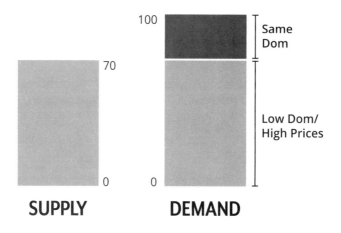

For home prices in an area to rise, there must be multiple offers and homes must sell higher than the previous market value. This sets a new baseline value and increases the value of the surrounding assets. In a seller's market, sellers often obtain multiple offers, with buyers paying much higher prices than they originally wanted to. This effect is compounded if buyers write several offers on consecu-tive properties and lose each time, eventually electing to give the next seller the price they want rather than lose out on another property. A seller's market makes it easier for buyers to make emotional decisions because they "just want a house." This is a dangerous attitude for a real estate investor.

Understanding supply and demand is crucial to understanding markets. However, the only measurable metric is the supply of available inventory in a market; that is, the number of homes available for sale on the Multiple Listing Service (MLS). There is no way to accurately measure how many potential buyers are in a market or their level of motivation.

I've learned to look at DOM as the best indicator for the condition of a market. A DOM of thirty to forty-five days is normal and indicates the market is close to equilibrium. A DOM of less than thirty days means it's a seller's market, and a DOM of more than forty-five days indicates a buyer's market. The more extreme these numbers become, the more intense the market will be, and the better leverage I have in the transaction, either as the buyer or seller.

Strategies for Investors

Buyer's Market Strategies	Seller's Market Strategies
Divert more capital into buying assets and less toward improving them or debt paydown; refinance existing assets to free up capital to buy new assets.	Put less emphasis on buying new assets and put more capital toward improving assets you've already purchased to increase their value.
Spend more time analyzing deals and writing offers.	Spend less time looking at deals and more time earning income, working OT, or starting a new business or improving an existing one.
Focus on equity growth for when markets recover.	Focus on reliable cash flow as continued growth is less likely to continue.
Write more aggressive (lower-priced) offers, and do it more frequently.	Write less aggressive (higher-priced) offers, and be pickier about which assets you pursue.
You are competing with the seller. Write offers with the intention of receiving a counteroffer, not having your offer accepted.	You are competing with other buyers. Write offers with the intention of having the strongest offer and being accepted immediately.

Include terms in your offers that give you flexibility to back out of the deal.	Do as much due diligence as possible before writing an offer, because you likely won't be able to easily back out of the deal if it's accepted.
Look for properties in the best locations you normally could not afford.	Look for properties in Class A or B locations less likely to lose value in a correction.
Revisit properties where your initial offer was rejected to see if they are still on the market; sellers often adjust expectations on price.	Revisit properties that are under contract and may be falling out; try to find them before they officially go back on the market and other buyers learn of their availability.
Move quickly on new homes hitting the market if they are priced well and highly desirable.	Ignore new homes hitting the market as your competition will be doing that; focus on homes with high DOMs or that have fallen out of escrow.
Ask for closing costs to be paid by the seller, or use seller contributions to "buy down" your interest rate.	Ask for as little as possible from the seller.

Pros and Cons of the Markets

A buyer's market makes it easier for buyers to go under contract. With less competition, you have more time to thoroughly consider, analyze, and weigh the decision to buy an asset. You can offer less capital to each deal, as sellers are more likely to pay your closing costs, title fees, escrow fees, transfer taxes, and more. Sellers are often open to creative strategies, like seller financing or leaving furniture behind to sweeten the deal for you. Buyers can be pickier and buy properties they love, not just settle for what they can get. And it's easier to "buy equity" by writing multiple offers significantly below list price and seeing which seller accepts them.

A seller's market makes it easier for sellers to get the price they want. A seller's market usually starts because demand is high, thus creating multiple-offer situations, and the surrounding assets get more expensive too.

Markets change quickly, though. A buyer who accepted a bidding war and "overpaid" in 2015 made a ridiculous amount of equity by 2021. The same cannot be said about buyers in 2009 who bought as prices were dropping. In most markets, they did not see an increase until 2013. Getting a good deal in either market can have a higher payoff, but we all face a market correction at some point.

How to Find Distress

Distress is measured in three ways—market, property, or personal—and is key to buyers getting better deals. When there is distress, the buyer holds the leverage.

Market Distress

This is when the entire market is in distress. Distressed markets are typically the result of decreased buyer demand, which is often a sign of a recession or depression, or where buyers have low confidence they will be able to make the payments associated with buying real estate. The housing collapse of 2010 is an example of a distressed market; that was the result of a severe economic recession. Most markets had heavily discounted properties, even in Class A and Class B locations, because of the low number of buyers willing or able to purchase more expensive properties. Waiting until there is market distress to buy assets offers investors the lowest risk to get great deals on solid assets; of course, you have no control over the market.

Property Distress

Properties that are in poor condition, are unsafe, or can't be occupied are difficult for sellers. Most buyers overlook or avoid homes with mold and mildew, fire damage, electrical problems, old roofs, foundation problems, or other serious structural issues. However, this creates opportunities for an investor willing to buy these properties, fix the problems, and then sell at a profit. Looking for properties that are outdated, have bad odors, are "hoarder houses," or other undesirable factors can be a great opportunity to have your low offer accepted. The goal is to find a property that no one else wants, where your low offer is better than no offer; then you make a profit after rehab or rezoning.

Personal Distress

Personal distress occurs when a person must sell their property because they need money quickly, or they don't want to deal with the hassle of preparing a home for the market. These are people who inherited a house and prefer a quick sale over a high price, or someone in debt who needs to liquidate a property to free up the equity. You can find people in personal distress by sharing within your sphere of influence that you buy real estate and asking them to notify you if they hear of anyone with financial difficulties. Many investors pay for online ads promoting that they pay cash to sellers in personal distress. While this sounds a little uncaring, it gets the person out of the house in a hurry, which is their goal. By offering a quick close, you can help people out of a tough situation.

Seller Behavior

As markets cool because the economy slows down, sellers don't immediately drop their home's asking price. Most sellers will wait sixty to ninety days on the market before they consider a price reduction. Even at that point, most will drop their asking price by a small amount, which is not enough to prompt offers from buyers. This approach leads to sellers "chasing the market on the way down." If not careful, it can lead to a spiral where the seller drops their price, but the market has already dropped further, leaving the house still priced too high. Buyers will write offers on the homes priced most competitively.

Target Price Reductions

Understanding the psychology behind why sellers make certain decisions will give buyers an advantage. Conversations between sellers and their listing agents typically involve how low the price needs to drop for the home to sell. Agents recommend a realistic price drop, but most sellers only agree to a less realistic number. You can benefit from this knowledge by writing aggressive offers on properties that have recently had a price drop.

For example, if a listing agent proposes a price drop of $75,000, but the seller wants to "see what happens" if they drop by $25,000, your offer at $100,000 less than what the home was listed for prior to the price drop may end up accepted. Why? When an offer like this comes in, the agent will present it to the seller and say, "We knew we needed to drop the price by $75,000. This offer is only an additional $25,000 off, it's not far off." Targeting homes with recent price drops increases the likelihood the seller is prepared to accept less for their property and is motivated to sell.

Target BOM

Properties come back on the market after a house falls out of contract and is marked as active in the MLS again. This can happen because the first buyer isn't able to obtain financing; there's a low appraisal and the parties don't reach an agreement; problems are found with an inspection report; or the buyer simply gets cold feet. Listing agents are usually not forthcoming about why their listing is available again, leaving back-on-market (BOM) properties with a bad reputation. Many buyers will pass over these properties and focus instead on new inventory.

BOM properties provide an advantage to a buyer for several reasons. One is the cumulative DOM has continued to increase while the property was in escrow. This means a property that sat on the market for twenty-one days, went under contract for thirty days, then went back on the market will show a cumulative DOM of fifty-one days, effectively making it a stale product. Then there's the emotional roller coaster that the seller's been on. Trying to sell a home is a stressful endeavor under any circumstances, and the stress is amplified during the escrow period when a seller does not know if the buyer may back out of the deal for any of the abovementioned reasons. At this point, a seller wants certainty with their next buyer.

I frequently search for BOM properties for myself and my clients. I bought my first two rental properties after they had just fallen out of contract with other buyers. I wrote offers for less than the home had recently been under contract for, but I provided better terms, including a larger earnest money deposit, a shorter home inspection period, and a shorter loan contingency period. Even though my offers were for less money, these sellers accepted them because they were more likely to get to close. I capitalized on the situation by negotiating certainty for the seller in exchange for a better purchase price for myself.

Target DOM

As previously stated, a seller loses leverage the longer their home sits on the market. A climbing DOM is directly related to a seller having to consider a price reduction. There is no metric on the MLS to track how a seller is feeling, but other metrics can tell you. You can target homes with high DOMs and write a low offer with the knowledge that you'll likely get a solid counteroffer from the seller, which is still significantly lower than their list price. Offer some carrots like I explained above (more earnest money, shorter contingency period, etc.) to make the sale much more appealing and reliable to them.

How to Retain Capital

Keeping as much of your capital as possible is an important part of real estate investing; you want this money available to buy new assets. Part of keeping your capital is learning how to write offers in which the seller covers the closing costs, helps with the down payment, or provides part of the rehab budget. These techniques are especially important when mortgage interest rates are low, making borrowing more money cheaper (the more capital you have, the more properties you can put a down payment on or the further your money can go).

Seller Pays the Closing Costs

Most markets have a traditional split related to closing costs, with both buyers and sellers each paying a portion. Closing costs are required in every transaction, independent of financing, and include city transfer taxes, title fees, escrow fees, home warranties, county taxes, and more. When buyers fill out a purchase contract, they can request that the sellers pay all the closing costs, and the sellers can accept or reject these terms. Your agent can explain why you are requesting the sellers to pay some or all of the closings costs: You need the extra money to make the down payment (to close the deal), you are offering a higher price in return, they are saving money from not having to make improvements to the property, and so on.

Seller Credits

In transactions in which the buyer is using financing to purchase a home, most lenders will allow buyers to request credits from the seller, in which the seller also contributes to recurring closing costs involved in the financing of the transaction. These closing costs differ from the closing costs mentioned in the previous paragraph in that they are related to the financing, not the transaction. These costs can include points on the loan, origination fees, appraisal fees, and more. Most lenders have a limit on how much the sellers can contribute, usually between 2 percent and 3 percent of the total loan amount. Getting seller credits will keep more money in your pocket.

Sellers agree to seller credit when they believe it will lead to a sale or believe they are a normal part of a transaction and frequently requested by a buyer.

Buying Down the Loan Rate

Something we implemented at The One Brokerage and The David Greene Team is to increase the amount sellers are allowed to contribute toward our buyers' closing costs by increasing the closing costs themselves. The scenario looks like this:

A buyer gets an offer accepted on a property with a $10,000 credit toward closing costs. The buyer uncovers additional negotiation leverage in the escrow via issues in an inspection report. The buyer wants to request additional closing costs but can't because the seller is already covering 100 percent of them. What to do? The buyer then gets additional closing costs, or points, on the loan, which is money a buyer pays to the lender in exchange for a lower interest rate. The buyer pays $10,000 to the lender in exchange for a rate drop, say from 6 percent to 5.25 percent. The seller accepts the buyer's request for $20,000 in closing costs instead of the original $10,000, effectively paying for this lower interest rate on behalf of the buyer and giving the buyer the money to fix the issues in the inspection report.

Low Down Payments

One simple way to increase the amount of money you keep is to put less down toward the financing of the property. While most investment properties require a minimum of 20 percent down, there are a few exceptions to this rule discussed in the last chapter: house hacking, sneaky rental, vacation homes, and 15 percent down loans.

Seller Financing

Seller financing occurs when a buyer purchases property from a seller but does not use outside capital to fund the deal. Traditionally, a person obtains a loan to purchase a property, and then uses that loan to pay the seller a portion of the agreed upon purchase price, with the buyer's down payment providing the rest. With seller financing, buyers usually contact a seller directly—outside of the MLS—and write an offer to buy the property without outside lender funds. The situation can look as follows.

Seller Sam has a property worth $600,000. Sam owes $100,000 on the mortgage and is open to selling his house, but not with a Realtor. Current interest rates are 8 percent. Buyer Billy meets Sam and writes an offer for $625,000, which is more than the fair market value. However, there's a stipulation: Billy will pay Sam $100,000 for a down payment (so Sam can pay off his remaining $100,000 mortgage note), and Sam will give Billy a note via seller financing for the remaining $525,000 at 1 percent interest amortized over thirty years.

Billy will make monthly payments to Sam of $1,689 for thirty years. Were Billy to buy the house traditionally for $600,000, borrowing 80 percent of the purchase price at 8 percent interest, his monthly payments would be $3,522. Seller financing allows Billy to pay Sam monthly payments that are less than half of what he would with traditional financing. In return, Sam will receive more than the fair market value for his house and does not have to pay commission to an agent. The caveat is Seller Sam does not receive a lump sum of money on the sale of his house as he would with a "normal" sale.

There are several ways to do seller financing, including wrap-around mortgages (where Billy pays Sam's remaining mortgage of $100,000 rather than have Sam pay it off) or second position loans (where Billy obtains traditional financing to pay off Sam's note, then obtains a loan from Sam for a portion of the purchase price, then pays Sam back each month on the loan). Both approaches help the seller keep more capital in their pocket—albeit over time and not in one lump sum—and the buyer has smaller monthly payments for the life of the loan.

More Negotiation Strategies

Online Dating

The world of online real estate sales has evolved to be like online dating. In the real world, before dating apps, a friend or family member introduced you to a single person you might like, or you'd have to meet someone by chance. The real estate world worked the same way: Buyers had to find interested sellers, and sellers had to put their listing in front of interested buyers. This was done through real estate agents who marketed their properties through word of mouth, print advertising, and so on. But the game has changed, and success is now found online.

Today, real estate sites like Zillow and Redfin blast out listings to interested parties. The key to success is to offer more amenities and have better photos of your listing—the equivalent of enticing someone to swipe left or right. At the showing, an emotional connection can be formed between a buyer and the property. This leads to offers being written (marriage proposals) that turn into escrows (engagements) and hopefully into closings (marriages).

Hidden Value

As a buyer, your goal is to look for mis-marketed listings; these are quality homes with unattractive photos because the seller didn't want to spend money on a professional photographer or a listing that includes too many photos because the Realtor uploaded fifteen photos of one bedroom. This strategy netted me deals on properties that appraised $100,000 over the purchase price, simply because the seller uploaded pictures sideways or used blurry photos. These photos gave the impression that the properties were in disrepair, and my competition passed on these properties—all because of bad photos.

Another hidden value situation was with sellers who were afraid no one would buy their house. They had reduced their price by $50,000, and I wrote an offer for $75,000 less than that. The offer was countered, as I fully expected, and we settled on a price that was still great for me. After closing, I learned they had received zero showing requests during my entire escrow process, yet the property was in turnkey condition with a third bedroom that wasn't even marketed.

Unlisted bedrooms, square footage, or amenities all provide opportunities for overlooked value deals.

A property I bought near the highly desirable Bay Area had top-rated schools and lower crime than surrounding areas. The property was marketed as a two-bedroom, 900-square-foot home in an area known for having three- or four-bedroom homes with 1,500 square feet. It was listed for $950,000, while other homes were selling between $1.2 and $1.4 million. I sent my assistant to investigate why it looked so much larger in the photos than the size in the listing. She found an unconverted basement space with 1,000 square feet, which meant it had space for two additional bedrooms not included in the listing. It also had an attached two-car garage with another 500 square feet, which could be converted into more living space or accommodate an ADU above the garage and an attached two-car garage with another 500 square feet. This property, in that neighborhood, with a total of four bedrooms and nearly 2,500 square feet, would be valued over $1.4 million.

I purchased this property for $825,000 with the seller paying for $25,000 of my closing costs. My rehab was estimated to be $150,000, bringing my potential instant equity to $425,000 on a fabulous property suffering only from poor marketing, which other buyers hadn't noticed.

Seller Buying Too Soon

A common mistake sellers make is to look for their next home before their current listing has sold, and assuming their own home will close quickly. They fall in love with their next home, don't want to lose it, and under the direction of their agent (who doesn't want to lose a potential sale), write an offer that is contingent on their current home selling. While this is convenient, it's not profitable. The seller has no leverage because they just need a buyer to close, or they risk losing their new home. While losing a buyer is a risk inherent in every transaction, the stakes here are much higher. When a seller has their next home under contract contingent on the sale of the first, losing the buyer of their first home means losing their next home too. This is obviously a weak position to negotiate from.

I always advise sellers I represent to avoid finding their replacement property until after the property we are selling has closed, just to avoid this exact scenario. For my buyer clients, it's different; when I discover the seller of a property already has put a new house under contract, I advise my clients to be more aggressive and ask for closing cost credits, repairs, or price reductions. How do I find out the seller has put themselves in this position? It's easy: through casual conversations with the seller's Realtor, or when the seller of the home has a friendly conversation with my buyer clients at a walk-through. When you learn this about the seller of a property you are investing in, ask your agent to negotiate more than normal because the leverage is in your favor.

Inspection Report Findings

Inspection reports are written by property inspectors on the findings of the condition of a property. These can include whole home inspections or inspections targeted to pests, roofs, septic systems, pool systems, water systems, and more. If these reports reflect issues with a property, especially if they were not previously disclosed by the seller, it creates an opportunity for buyers to request additional seller credits, price reductions, or improvements made to the property. The worse the reports reveal the condition of the property to be, the more leverage the buyer has to ask for more concessions. However, this changes if the buyer doesn't have an *inspection contingency* that allows them to back out of the deal and retain their deposit. That contingency is the foundation of the buyer's leverage.

As an investor, you always want inspections—even if you plan to buy the property regardless of the findings (perhaps you want the land and are willing to raze the structure, but the seller doesn't need to know that). The information might provide you with the leverage you need to ask the seller for credits, repairs, or a lower purchase price.

Low Appraisals

There are many methods to valuing real estate, from the cost of building a structure from the ground up to the income the asset is expected to provide, among others. The sales comparison method is based on how much nearby properties have sold for, and it is how most residential real estate is valued. While the value of a property is always going to be what someone is willing to pay for it, lenders like predictability and the ability to place an objective value on an asset. For this reason, they require appraisals on a property that will have financing to ensure the buyer is not paying more for an asset than other buyers have paid for similar properties.

When an appraised value is lower than the agreed upon price, lenders will lend on the appraised value, not the price a buyer contracted to pay. Say a property is under contract for $525,000 but appraises for $500,000; the lender will lend at 80 percent of $500,000, not $525,000. This means the buyer is responsible for covering the extra $25,000 with their own funds, on top of the 20 percent down payment of $105,000. If the buyer has an appraisal contingency in their contract, they can back out of the deal and recover their earnest money deposit. If they don't, they must pay the extra $25,000 out of pocket or risk losing their earnest money if they don't close.

Having an appraisal contingency gives buyers the leverage to negotiate in case of a low appraisal. A seller is not required to lower the selling price but would likely have to do so to prevent the buyer from walking away. A buyer can ask for a reduction down to the appraised value or an amount between the contracted price and the appraised value. It's worth noting that an appraisal *above* the purchase price does not give the seller an opportunity to request a higher purchase price. Appraisals only protect lenders and buyers.

Capitalizing on Bad News in the Media

As explained above, a seller's market gives sellers the leverage to wait for the best price and best terms possible. The reverse is true in a buyer's market. When there is a shift in the economy, specifically a shift from a seller's market to a buyer's market, some sellers overreact and accept below what they should. This is especially true if the news is particularly pessimistic.

Negative news in the media is reflective of a shifting economy, and buying early could be a bad idea. When market fundamentals appear strong but the news is saying otherwise, consider writing more aggressive offers than you normally would. Sellers may be worried and willing to accept offers they normally wouldn't.

Conversely, there will also be markets where the TV pundits are talking nonstop about rising prices and the hot economy—even when market fundamentals don't support this optimism. These are markets when it makes sense to sell, especially before everyone else jumps on board.

KEY TAKEAWAYS

- Supply and demand in real estate refers to buyer's markets and seller's markets. The former is where buyers have the upper hand, and the latter is when sellers have the upper hand.
- Those with the leverage control the negotiations.
- When there is more supply than demand, the average days on market (DOM) goes up.
- A buyer's market makes it easier for buyers to go under contract. A seller's market makes it easier for sellers to get the price they want.
- There are three kinds of distress: market, property, and personal.
- A real estate investor can watch market metrics—BOM, DOM, etc.—to get a feel for a particular asset and movement of the market.
- Look for mis-marketed listings to find a deal as a buyer. These are quality homes with unattractive photos because the seller didn't want to spend money on a professional photographer, or a listing that includes too many photos because the Realtor uploaded fifteen photos of one bedroom.

Chapter 15
CAPITAL CYCLES

*True wisdom is acquired by the person who sees patterns,
and comes to understand those patterns in their connection
to other patterns—and from these interconnected
patterns, learns the code of life.*
—HENDRITH VANLON SMITH JR.

As you learn and improve your ability to make, save, and invest capital, you'll start to observe patterns in your behavior. Money follows certain principles and is attracted to those who practice good habits. As these patterns emerge, take advantage of them to make your progress easier and to capitalize on your knowledge and momentum.

You'll notice similarities in each strategy discussed in this chapter. The key is to identify and amplify their strengths, so they take the capital you've saved and make it work as efficiently as possible. Understanding how capital moves through these various cycles will create momentum in building your wealth.

Cycle of Amplification
The pillar of investing in assets amplifies the capital of your defense and offense pillars. But capital becomes illiquid and harder to access and control once it's converted to equity. The solution is to add a step

and amplify (grow) your capital before investing it. This can create massive gains in the amount of money you invest and shorten your investment horizon significantly compared to simply making, saving, and investing it.

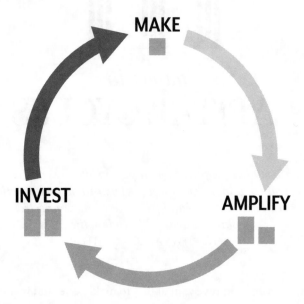

Traditional investment strategies skip the step of amplification. Investing money into a 401(k) account, mutual fund, or company-matched retirement account is simple and easy to understand, but the returns are weak and provide no way to amplify your capital. Traditional investment strategies like this are often practiced by those who pay taxes on their income before investing it, a fact that shouldn't go unnoticed. Earning, being taxed, then investing is actually amplifying *losing* money before investing it. This is avoided when you make your income through real estate and take additional depreciation as a full-time real estate professional. This means starting a real estate business and using write-offs and deductions for expenses such as travel, entertainment, vehicles, and more.

This strategy can amplify your returns, or it can work against you if you lose capital in the process. This means avoid investing big capital until you first develop competence in real estate.

As you gain experience, this chapter will help you grow your returns. The following amplification strategies offer creative approaches to increasing your capital as you gain competence.

House Flipping

Flipping a property is the simplest way to amplify your capital in real estate (along with your knowledge). Some investment strategies, like value-add or buying equity, don't work in some markets, such as a hot, appreciating market where the properties don't cash flow positively. When this happens, consider using an alternative strategy, like flipping. This can net you a short-term financial windfall.

Buyer Ben was looking for a small MFH that would net him a 10 percent return on the $100,000 he had saved over four years. A particularly ambitious agent instead proposed an SFR that needed a quick close. The property was worth $300,000 as is—but with a new kitchen, bathroom, and roof repairs, it could be valued at $400,000. The seller's agent told Ben that the property could be purchased for $220,000 in cash. Ben saw the potential in the deal, but he was committed to the 10 percent cash-on-cash return he needed on his investment. And then he considered the opportunity to amplify his capital.

The agent was familiar with the home-flipping process and connected Ben with a hard-money lender to secure the deal and a reputable contractor for the remodeling work. Ben offered below what the seller said they would take and was successful getting his offer of $200,000 accepted. The hard-money lender required 20 percent down ($40,000) and the seller covered the closing costs. The contractor gave a bid for the roof repairs, bathroom, and kitchen remodel at $25,000. Between the 20 percent down and the remodel costs, Ben invested $65,000. Two months later, the rehab was completed, and Ben sold the property for $400,000, netting himself a profit of $135,000 after Realtor fees and closing costs. Ben paid short-term capital gains taxes of $50,000, and now had $100,000 to invest again.

Equipped with his original $100,000 plus the $100,000 profit, Ben purchased an eight-unit property instead of the three-to-four-unit property he had been considering, doubling his original expected cash flow.

BRRRR Method

When executed correctly, the BRRRR method allows investors to buy properties, add value to them, and recover all or most of their capital to be reinvested. This is an ideal strategy for amplifying capital before purchasing additional units.

After closing on his eight-unit deal, Buyer Ben saved another $100,000 over the next three years by combining his work savings and the cash flow from his new apartment investment. While searching for another MFH, Ben was once again approached by the same agent, who had an opportunity on the horizon: a listing that was not selling because of its poor condition. The property would not qualify for conventional financing, and no buyers were creative enough to find ways to purchase it. The agent proposed using the same hard-money lender and contractor to flip the property. This time, Ben had a better idea.

Ben closed for $200,000 due to the property needing so much work. The same contractor quoted $120,000 for the rehab because the entire house needed upgrading. Ben borrowed not only 80 percent of the $120,000 construction bid from the hard-money lender but also 80 percent of the purchase price, requiring him to put only $64,000 into the deal. During the renovation, Ben had an additional unit added by combining the garage and a bonus room. This additional unit increased his cash flow and allowed the SFR to function as a buy-and-hold rental property. Ben decided to keep the property as a rental.

Ben refinanced the property for 80 percent of its after-repair value (ARV) and took out a loan for $320,000. This paid off his original hard-money loan of $160,000 and his construction loan of $96,000 (totaling $256,000), leaving Ben with $64,000—the same amount he had originally invested. With the return of 100 percent of his capital, and with a new SFR that he essentially acquired for free (and its new cash flow), Ben searched for his next MFH.

Private Lending

Private lending is the act of lending your money to someone in return for them paying you interest. Your investment is protected by securing it with an asset, essentially guaranteeing you will receive something of value (i.e., the property) should the borrower default on repayment. Private lending is a viable option to amplify capital before investing it in a long-term vehicle, provided you understand how to evaluate the value of the real estate and the borrower's ability to repay you.

Ben knew how much he had paid in lender fees to the hard-money lender on his last two deals and realized that, with his background in finance and his amplified capital, he could be a lender. Ben tells the agent to let him know the next time an experienced buyer needs money for their own flip project.

One month later, the agent calls and tells Ben a buyer has a property that could be valued at $400,000 and has it under contract for $200,000. The agent's buyer stands to lose their deposit—and the great deal—and is desperate for a solution. After doing due diligence on the buyer's real estate experience, Ben agrees to lend the buyer the $200,000 for the property and $50,000 for the rehab. The loan will be made at 15 percent and three points (3 percent of the loan balance). The buyer agrees, closes on the property, and after six months, finishes the remodeling and sells the property. With the sale of the upgraded property, Ben is paid his 15 percent interest and three points for that period of six months, netting him $18,750 and $7,500 (respectively) for a total profit of $26,250.

Ben adds this to the $100,000 he has saved over the last two and a half years to buy his next MFH.

Wholesaling

While wholesaling doesn't always require a financial investment, it is certainly improved with one. Many wholesalers spend money to send letters to distressed homeowners, offering to buy their properties for a discounted price. Others create online ads or websites seeking people who want to sell their homes quickly. For those who know how to evaluate a property and negotiate with a seller, this method can create new cash or amplify cash you've already saved.

Following the defense and offense pillars in this book, Ben was learning all about real estate investing while still working. He received a promotion with a 50 percent pay increase that was accompanied by more responsibility and oversight. Ben's desire to buy more real estate was growing, but he couldn't pass up this work opportunity to earn and save more money at a faster pace. Ben's new promotion required him to be in the office for eight hours a day, but he had become so proficient that he could finish a day's work in five hours.

Ben took $20,000 of his savings and invested in Google ads, SEO-equipped landing pages, and a direct mail campaign for an up-and-coming neighborhood. After six months of speaking with sellers, Ben was able to put four properties under contract for close to 60 percent of their market value. Wanting to flip them but realizing he didn't have enough capital, Ben assigned the contracts to other investors he met in online forums. Ben's four deals provided him with $100,000 in assignment fees, giving him a five times return on his initial $20,000 investment. Ben was able to do this real estate business from his workplace in those three spare hours every day, amplifying the capital he had to invest while also earning and saving money from his job.

Syndications

Though they tend to operate over a time frame of several years, syndications afford investors the opportunity to amplify their money before investing it. Their passive nature also makes it possible to allocate a portion of your available capital into them while keeping the rest for other investment opportunities. Incorporating syndications into your investment strategy can offer future profitable windfalls that can then be reinvested at your discretion.

Five years after his first investment, Buyer Ben was making more money at work, saving a higher portion of his income, and earning money through cash flow in real estate. Ben had saved another $300,000 from work and, after reviewing his portfolio to find areas where it could be improved, he sold two properties and used a 1031 exchange to improve his ROI. He also refinanced two properties, which put $200,000 into his bank account, for a total of $500,000 liquid capital. Ben saw his momentum and the snowball he was creating for himself.

Through his connections with other investors, Ben had met a talented commercial property investor. Wanting to leverage this person's knowledge, Ben invested $150,000 as a limited partner with this apartment syndicator for a four-year period. The deal was expected to produce an internal rate of return of 15 percent a year. During this period, Ben continued to save money, flip houses, and wholesale deals when he could. He accumulated a few additional BRRRR deals with no money of his own in the properties. This increased Ben's net worth substantially, all while he kept his expenses to a minimum and his income at a high rate.

At the end of four years, Ben had grown his net worth by $750,000 and his passive income to $5,000 a month. Ben bought several more MFH properties, draining him of most of his savings but increasing his monthly cash flow to nearly $9,000. When Ben's syndication investment period was over, he got his original $150,000 back, plus a profit of $112,500, for a total of $262,500 into his bank account.

Actively looking for ways to amplify your capital is a proactive approach to increasing your "seed count" without working more hours or cutting back on additional expenses. These strategies, and others like them, begin to feel natural in the progression of an investor. You're learning new strategies while pursuing investment opportunities. The wealthy don't ask themselves if they should do A or B; they ask themselves how they can do A *and* B. Always look for creative and efficient ways to amplify your capital before placing it in assets, where it can be hard to recover quickly.

Self-Sustaining Cycle

The self-sustaining cycle capitalizes on the power of combining rental income with leverage (or other people's money, known as OPM) to effectively create a system where you use limited or no amount of your own money to achieve big returns. This cycle is responsible for many regular people becoming millionaires and achieving financial freedom through real estate. Learning how to use OPM to own and control assets is key to buying enough of those assets to escape the entrapment pattern and enter the freedom pattern. It occurs in two phases.

Phase 1: Acquisition

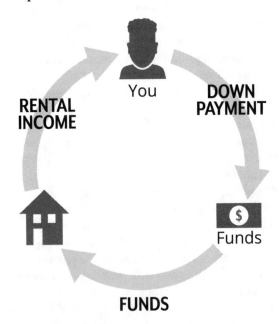

Let's say you purchase a rental property as an asset using little of your own money. The cycle starts with you, as the buyer, giving the lender (in this case the bank) your down payment—note that you aren't actually giving the bank your money. You're giving it to the seller, but it's easier to understand as if it goes to the bank first. The bank takes your down payment—anywhere from 3.5 percent to 25 percent of the asset's price—and funds the remainder of the money needed to purchase the asset. This allows you to own the asset using little of your own money. You gain title to the property and are eligible to receive the income it provides, even though you were responsible for only a small portion of the purchase price. Part 1 of the self-sustaining cycle is learning how real estate investors gain control of expensive assets without saving 100 percent of the money needed to buy them.

Phase 2: Debt Repayment

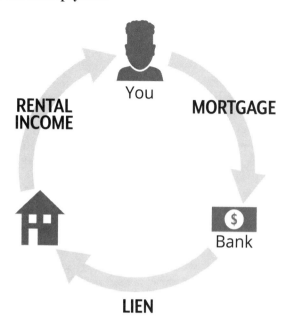

The second phase involves how you as an investor develop cash flow from owning assets purchased with OPM. The property owner (you) makes monthly mortgage payments to the bank to repay the money borrowed to buy the asset. The bank places a lien on the property, which allows them to foreclose should you stop making payments. A tenant who leases from you pays you rental income; you use that rental income to pay back the bank, keeping the difference between the rental income and the mortgage amount to pay your other expenses. You pocket the remaining cash.

With each lease's annual rent increase, you keep more money because your mortgage to the bank stays the same. By keeping your expenses lower than the income your assets produce, you slowly produce extra income for yourself. This money eventually replaces what you earn actively working and allows you to quit your job. The key to the self-sustaining cycle is understanding where the capital comes from. Borrowing money from a bank to buy an asset that a tenant rents from you, and then using the tenant's rent money to pay back the bank, removes your own money from being needed to own the asset. At the end of the cycle, the only money you contributed to this ever-growing machine is your down payment toward the property, which was a small percentage.

Velocity of Money

The velocity of money is an economic term used by the federal government to determine how fast dollars are circulating throughout the U.S. economy. The metric matters because each time a dollar changes hands, taxes should be paid. When your boss gives you a paycheck, they withhold income and retirement taxes that are paid to the government. With some exceptions, every time you buy something with the rest of your income, the government collects sales taxes. The businesses where you spend your money then pay taxes on that money, and the cycle never ends.

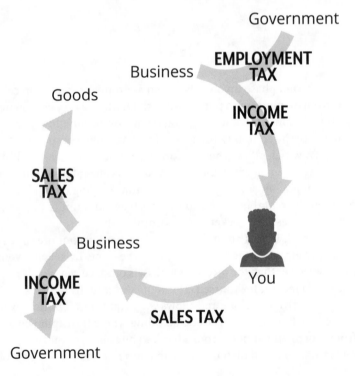

The government can increase its income, collected through taxes, by:

1. Increasing the amount of taxes collected.
2. Increasing the types of taxes collected.
3. Increasing the speed at which money moves through this tax system.

The first two methods are unpopular with citizens and require votes on whether to pass legislation. The third method is much easier, and sneakier. By increasing how fast dollars move between parties, the government collects more taxes without needing to pass legislation to raise them. As you can imagine, tracking how fast these dollars change hands, which is the velocity of money, is of the utmost importance to the government.

This book has taught you multiple ways to reduce the amount of taxes you pay. With the defense pillar, we spend less, decreasing what we pay in sales tax. With the offense pillar, we make more money and continually improve our earning potential. With the investing pillar, we have multiple real estate strategies to reduce taxes, such as depreciation. Understanding the velocity of money will help you save in taxes too, but it can do more than that: You'll learn how to replicate the government's formula to grow and collect more capital as your own money moves from one location to another.

Improving the velocity of your capital can lead to rapid and efficient equity growth. The following illustration shows how.

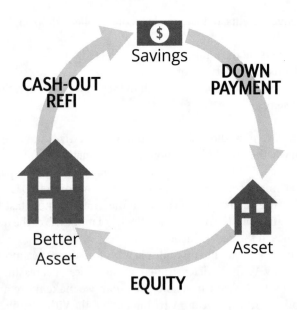

CASH-OUT REFI

DOWN PAYMENT

Savings

Better Asset

Asset

EQUITY

We start with the money we've saved, which is used as a down payment on an income-producing asset (see the self-sustaining cycle). The objective is to buy an asset below market value, in a high-growth area, that you can improve after purchase (the cycle of amplification). This increases your equity in the asset. A cash-out refinance or home equity line of credit (HELOC) allows the investor to pull their initial capital out of the asset and convert the equity into cash, which can be used to purchase additional assets so the cycle continues.

Adding value through equity is necessary to increase the velocity of your money. If you don't, your capital sits in the asset, where it grows slowly over time. While this is better than not growing at all, it certainly isn't as beneficial. Mastering velocity of money allows you to take advantage of both the amplification cycle and the self-sustaining cycle to increase your wealth with the very same dollars.

Like the federal government, you can supercharge this strategy by moving your capital through the cycle faster. Buying assets more often, at better prices, and in better locations all improve the velocity of your money. Improving them quickly and refinancing them afterward does so as well, freeing up the capital to be reinvested and continue the process. This can happen simultaneously by earning more money at work and saving a high percentage of your income, so all three pillars are now supporting your financial freedom goals.

The velocity of money also increases your momentum. As we head into our last section, keep in mind that the goal is to earn small wins at multiple steps in these cycles. Home runs are difficult to get, but continuous singles eventually score runs.

The Equity Cycle

Understanding money as a store of energy will change the way you view building wealth. Cash flow is the ultimate goal—it represents the energy in your bank account where it is most liquid, and liquid capital has the most utility in exchanging it for goods and services. The downside to this is that money in the bank does not grow efficiently. If you want to spend your energy, you want it in the bank. If you want to grow that energy, you want it in an investment vehicle. This pattern to maximize equity growth and convert it into cash flow is the *equity cycle*. It works as follows.

Step 1: Create Equity

- **Buy equity**: Buy distressed assets or buy from distressed owners at below-market value.
- **Force equity**: Add value to assets via cosmetic improvements, additional rental units, or increasing square footage.

The more of these you can work into each property you buy and the better you can accomplish them, the more equity—or energy— you'll create with each asset. Your energy increases when you add value to the properties you buy. Continuing to make more income and save more money also creates more energy when those savings are invested into real estate.

Creates Equity	Doesn't Create Equity
Buying more real estate using low down payment loans	Buying fewer appreciating assets because you put more down on each property
Writing aggressive offers below market value	Paying market value
Buying fixer-upper properties	Buying turnkey properties
Spending most of your savings buying assets	Putting your saving in markets like bonds or treasuries
Researching markets to determine where growth is most likely	Assuming all real estate is equal
Measuring your properties' ROI	Not analyzing the metrics
Buying properties where square footage can be added	Buying properties that cannot be altered
Continuing to use all the pillars (defense, offense, investing)	Using the first two pillars without using the third pillar

Step 2: Increase Equity

As your saved capital is converted into equity, shift your focus to increasing or improving it through market appreciation. For example, buying in areas more likely to see property values increase will increase your equity passively and over time, especially with inflation.

As discussed in an earlier chapter, you can buy a fixer-upper, move into it, and then slowly improve its condition over time. This also improves your financing options. While house flippers often use hard-money/high-interest, short-term loans to buy their properties, live-in flippers can use low down payments and get lower interest rate loans to secure the same property. And while traditional house flippers must pay their own rent or mortgage *and* fund the property they are flipping, live-in flippers make the same payment for both. The live-in flip is a simple way to increase your equity.

The BRRRR method also increases the equity in your portfolio. I did this when I sold a property in one state and reinvested the $90,000 of equity in another state. I added value to the second property and took the original $90,000 of equity back out of the property via a cash-out refinance. This allowed me to buy more properties and continue my snowball, earning $30,000 of equity with each additional property by using my same initial $90,000 and adding value to each one.

Step 3: Convert Equity

Converting equity is the act of moving it from a weaker asset to a stronger asset after the equity growth in the weaker asset stalls. For example, seeing price appreciation and cash flow growth stall after buying a small MFH property at a great price and fixing it up should trigger equity conversion. This property could be sold to an investor looking for a turnkey property, and you move the equity into a new or bigger project to grow that equity. Avoid winning on the buy, winning on the rehab, and losing on the equity by regularly reviewing your portfolio for opportunities to convert equity.

Taking advantage of market cycles is another way to do this. As we learned in an earlier chapter, market crashes come in cycles. These create opportunities for savvy, well-capitalized investors ready to take advantage of a buyer's market. Buying into a market early, when prices are discounted, and riding the increase in value until it stalls and a seller's market kicks in can be easy equity. Then you sell using the 1031 exchange and buy into a new, emerging market, increasing your equity through conversion without much additional work.

For example, real estate in California crashed in late 2009 as the foreclosure crisis swept the nation. Five years later, prices shot up— creating fast and easy equity. Selling these properties and moving your equity into the next hot market and letting your equity continue to grow there would have kept the party going. As prices stabilized in those new markets, moving again to the next hot market would continue your equity growth.

Step 4: Manage Equity

Managing your equity is the act of ensuring your properties are performing optimally. It's easy to demand the most of every dollar when you start investing and are focused on the deployment of your hard-saved capital. Akin to an employer who trains a new employee and then stops paying attention to their performance, we can forget to continually review our investments to ensure they are still working as hard as they did when we first bought them.

As detailed in Chapter 13, frequent reviews of return on equity will ensure you're managing your equity well. I suggest you reread that section every time you do a review.

Properties with a low ROE in cash flow, a low expectation of increased equity growth, or a combination of the two should be sold and reinvested into hotter, emerging markets and specific deals where new equity can be created. Again, Chapter 13 is filled with information on how you can accomplish this, such as using 1031 exchanges.

Step 5: Repeat

The equity cycle is not nearly as time-consuming as the act of making and saving new capital. Plus, you can simultaneously earn income, improve your skills, and create new capital while using your equity cycle to create, increase, convert, and manage your equity. As you amplify your initial capital, you are also investing new capital. Over time, these snowballs will explode the growth of your wealth.

Creative Capital Cycles

Many investors earn more income and improve their offense pillar through knowledge, experiences, and resources accumulated through their equity cycles. This occurs, say, when MFH investors who manage their own properties start a property management company. Or when an SFR investor gets their real estate license and starts representing clients. Or when house flippers start their own construction company and take over others' home renovations while saving money on their own rehabs. The wealth-building journey starts off slowly and builds steam over time as success with each pillar grows and they start to overlap.

You can see how powerful momentum is for creating wealth: building your discipline to save, developing your real estate plan, tracking your metrics, creating a system, and reviewing your portfolio. Your growing knowledge, leverage, confidence, and pattern recognition will improve your capabilities, income, and wealth.

KEY TAKEAWAYS

- Money follows certain principles and is attracted to certain behaviors.
- Capital becomes harder to access and control after it's converted to equity. The solution is to amplify your capital before investing, so you increase the amount available to invest.
- Traditional investments like 401(k)s, mutual funds, or company-matched retirement accounts skip the step of amplification.
- Private lending is the act of lending money to someone; in return, the lender is paid interest.
- The self-sustaining cycle is a system where limited amounts of your own money—or none—are needed to achieve big returns.
- The self-sustaining cycle is made up of two phases: acquisition and debt repayment.
- The velocity of money measures how quickly money moves through an economy. We use it to measure money moving through our portfolio.
- The equity cycle creates equity, increases equity, converts equity, manages equity, and repeats the cycle. It is not nearly as time intensive as the act of making and saving new capital.
- As you build skills in certain areas, income-producing opportunities appear.

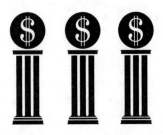

Chapter 16
BUILDING WEALTH THAT LASTS

Those born to wealth, and who have the means of gratifying every wish, know not what is the real happiness of life, just as those who have been tossed on the stormy waters of the ocean on a few frail planks can alone realize the blessings of fair weather.
—ALEXANDRE DUMAS, *THE COUNT OF MONTE CRISTO*

Financial freedom is the result of years of discipline, personal growth, and prudent decision-making. My goal is for you to jump into that journey and make as much progress as possible. While wealth is the goal, I'd be remiss if I didn't tell you that all wealth is not the same. Some wealth will stand the test of time, while other wealth will fall apart when markets shift, economies turn, or a run of bad luck occurs. In most cases, wealth follows the same pattern as other things in life: easy come, easy go.

Financial freedom does you no good if it only lasts for a short time, and you drop from the top of the mountain all the way to the base to start over again. Understanding how to build wealth that lasts is crucial to attaining and maintaining financial freedom. I've made many mistakes in my own journey; had I known then what I know now, I could have prevented most of them. This chapter includes information to help you prevent losing what you've built.

Equity vs. Cash Flow: The Great Debate

Within the world of real estate investing, there are two approaches to creating wealth: One is to pursue cash flow directly—buying assets that produce it and investing in stocks or bonds that provide a predictable return—and the other is to buy assets that increase in value. Both approaches work to create wealth. If you remember from the beginning of the book, we measure wealth in three ways.

1. Net worth
2. Passive income
3. Cash flow

Your net worth improves when your assets increase in value; your passive income improves when you acquire cash flow; and the goal is to win in both areas without any headaches. The debate comes down to which is the faster, safer method of building wealth: focusing on building cash flow or focusing on building equity?

The Cash Flow Path

Since financial freedom requires enough cash flow to replace your active income; most investors start on the path of cash flow. The problem is that, while cash flow is the ultimate goal, it's notoriously hard to achieve or control. To build up cash flow in real estate, you must keep your expenses low and keep pushing your rents higher. How much control you have over these expenses and rent prices affects how well you do with these goals.

Investment vehicles like stocks, bonds, CDs, and so on produce income without attached debt. With no debt, it's easy to determine the return. Debt and other expenses attached to the asset require you to subtract them from the income to determine how much money you made or lost. Keeping expenses low is an art form that good real estate investors learn. Large expenses like mortgages, property taxes, and homeowners insurance don't decrease, while others like property management fees, vacancy, and maintenance costs can only be reduced so much. Expenses can be controlled but not eliminated. This makes increasing cash flow difficult.

Cash flow improvement includes increasing your real estate income. This is done primarily by raising rents, but rents cannot be increased arbitrarily; they are controlled by the market. If you charge $1,500 for your apartment units while the similar complex across the street charges $1,000, no one will rent your units. Rents can only be increased when all comparable units raise their rents. The collection of these units in an area is the market, and the market determines rent prices.

Markets are dictated by supply and demand. If there are more units available than tenants to rent them, rents can't go up. Rents only increase when:

1. There is more demand than supply.
2. Wages support the higher rent amount.

Cash flow investors look at the demographics that influence these two. Locations where people are moving to will likely have increased demand. Rising wages or new industries likely allow workers to afford higher rents. Areas with limited housing options increase the likelihood of rent increases. Understanding the factors that lead to rising rents will increase your cash flow (as will keeping your expenses low).

Cash flow accumulates slowly. Rents increase over time, but that happens because of factors outside your control. This makes long-term cash flow unpredictable. Here, time is the only one of the five wealth-building ingredients working in your favor.

The Equity Path

The alternative approach of building equity allows you to use all five ingredients to make progress. Equity is the difference between what you owe on a property and what it is worth. A property worth $500,000 with a loan balance of $400,000 has approximately $100,000 of equity. Investors have more control over building equity because there are several methods to do it, and most of them are not dependent on factors outside of their control. The best investors combine methods into each deal to supercharge their returns.

Of the ten ways you make money in real estate (discussed in Chapter 12), five apply to equity. These are also the five most powerful methods.

- Buying equity
- Forcing equity
- Market equity
- Natural equity
- Loan paydown

Together, these methods produce big results that are amplified when leverage is used. Consider putting 20 percent down ($100,000) on a $500,000 property that appreciates to $600,000. While the asset has increased by 20 percent, your initial investment of $100,000 has doubled, which is an ROI of 100 percent. Leveraged capital can sky-rocket equitable returns.

A Clear Comparison

I didn't focus on building cash flow when growing my passive income; I focused on building equity to convert to cash flow. This solution makes sense when you view money as a store of energy. Cash flow from a property is stored in the bank, joining your savings as a store of energy. Equity in your properties is also a store of energy, but it grows faster. Let's compare the two methods over a five-year period.

Cash Flow Carl buys a triplex from a Midwest turnkey company for $300,000 at a 5 percent interest rate. Each unit produces $200 a month in profit after expenses, netting Carl $600 a month, or $7,200 a year. Carl put $60,000 down on the property, which means he has an ROI of 12 percent, a healthy return most investors would be happy with. After five years, Carl has earned $36,000 in cash flow, paid $20,000 off his loan, and seen appreciation of 2 percent per year, improving his property's value to $330,000. This gives Cash Flow Carl a total of $86,000 of energy.

Build Equity Barbara takes a different path. Barbara does her research on demographic trends and recognizes that business and atmospheric climates are favorable for population growth in South Florida. Barbara finds a large but ugly fixer-upper two blocks from the beach, with poor marketing photos and no mention of the unpermitted finished basement. The property is listed for $650,000, which is in line with more desirable properties in the area. Noticing it's been on the market for sixty days, Barbara writes an offer for $525,000; after several counteroffers, she goes under contract at $535,000.

During the inspection period, Barbara negotiates $10,000 off the purchase price when the inspector discovers the basement is up to code, but it was never permitted and disclosed to the city. Barbara puts $105,000 down and after closing, she spends $40,000 to improve the property with new paint and carpet, granite countertops, better cabinets, an additional bathroom, two bedrooms framed in the basement, and updated landscaping. With the work completed and new square footage added, Barbara gets a new appraisal at $700,000.

Barbara rents the main house and basement as separate units to two different tenants. In the first year of ownership, Barbara breaks even on cash flow. As South Florida begins to see rising demand, Barbara's rents increase asymmetrically faster than other U.S. cities, and so does the value of her property. After five years, South Florida real estate has appreciated 7 percent a year, so her property is worth approximately $945,000. Though she could have easily done so, Barbara chose not to increase the rents on either units, solely to prove the point that equity creates wealth faster than cash flow.

Five years later, Barbara has $0 from cash flow; $75,000 from buying equity; $10,000 from forcing equity; $35,000 from loan paydown; and $245,000 from market appreciation/equity, for a total of $365,000 and an ROI of 347 percent. By doing more leg work, making decisions based on financial growth, and focusing on a market where she has more control, Build Equity Barbara has made $279,000 more than Cash Flow Carl, even without increasing her rents.

At this stage in the analysis, cash flow apologists will argue that equity isn't cash in the bank—and they're right. Equity in your properties will stay in a form unusable to you unless and until you convert it into a different store of energy. Home equity lines of credit, cash-out refinances, sales, and 1031 like-kind exchanges are tools investors use to convert equity from one property into capital, cash flow, or additional opportunities to build more equity elsewhere.

As you build your own investment portfolio, it's easier to focus on building equity and converting it to cash flow later. Even if Build Equity Barbara only achieved half of Cash Flow Carl's 12 percent ROI, a return of 6 percent on Barbara's $365,000 profit would earn her $1,825 a month compared to Carl's $600.

Avoid "Easy Come, Easy Go" Investments

Investment opportunities are tempting, and money that comes easily is particularly tempting. This is especially true if we wait until we are in financial difficulty before learning about wealth or making a focused effort to acquire it. Being in financial—and thus emotional—turmoil does not lead to wise financial decisions. Even if someone knows get-rich-quick strategies are unwise, they still may pursue them if their situation is dire enough. This is why the first pillar of wealth is defense; it limits mistakes in your journey to financial freedom.

From 2017 to late 2022, cryptocurrencies were all the rage. Stories of instant millionaires were all over social media. Groups formed, online forums exploded, and money rushed into the space. As fears about inflation in the U.S. economy became more real, cryptocurrencies touted themselves as an alternative currency and a hedge against inflation. As their values skyrocketed in typical bubble fashion, people borrowed against the valuations of their crypto wallets with real U.S. money. These loans were then used to invest in more unstable currencies, bringing leverage into the already volatile market of crypto trading.

In November 2022, FTX, one of the largest cryptocurrency exchange platforms in the world, was exposed as having mismanaged customer funds and fraudulently increased both its valuation and its liquidity. As FTX fell from grace, it started a domino reaction that toppled the cryptocurrency house of cards. All crypto lost value, and most became nearly worthless. Reports of instant millionaires committing suicide because they could not pay back their very real debts began to circulate, and very real people felt very real pain because of very *unreal* asset class disaster. The crypto bubble had burst wide open.

Is this to say crypto trading is bad? "Bad" is a subjective term. When dabbled in correctly, there's a place for alternative investment platforms in *an already healthy* portfolio. The key is understanding the nature of the asset, the risk associated with it, and the percentage of your wealth and liquidity exposed to these platforms. Just about everyone who got into crypto early made money. Just about everyone who held it until 2022 lost money. For those interested in alternative vehicles, the key is understanding your portfolio architecture.

Reduce Risk with Portfolio Architecture

Most real estate investors learn how to invest successfully in specific asset classes like SFR, small MFH, large MFH, or commercial properties. In some cases, you can build a portfolio based on one asset class that will help you achieve financial freedom built to last, but this typically only happens with larger properties in more expensive asset classes. Even in these cases, you may have financial freedom, but you won't have financial flexibility. Portfolio architecture is the science of building a portfolio that is safe, contains flexibility, and will stand the test of time. It involves buying different asset classes in various amounts to cover any weaknesses of your other asset classes.

Portfolio architecture is the way you build a well-balanced portfolio. The best shape is a pyramid, as opposed to a skyscraper. At the base of your pyramid are boring, predictable, stable, and continually growing assets; in other words, assets that produce the most cash flow with the least risk, fewest headaches, and least amount of time required to manage them. Stabilized commercial properties with triple net (NNN) leases or small MFHs should make up the base—and the bulk—of your portfolio. These properties are unlikely to explode in value. They are also unlikely to crash, which is what makes them a stable base. 401(k) and company-matched retirement accounts fit in this category. They should represent the largest percentage of your portfolio.

The next tier up in your portfolio should be assets with slightly higher risk and a slightly higher upside. These could be SFRs that don't produce as much cash flow but appreciate faster, or properties in locations likely to experience above-average growth in the future but may not be top performers when you first buy them. Vacancies at this level are likely to be more expensive, and net operating income won't increase until time passes. The benefit of this tier is its flexibility: It's easier to force equity by upgrading appearance or adding square footage. Market appreciation equity plays a stronger role here. You can target your equity to a great deal, even if it doesn't cash flow as well as more basic options. These properties will grow wealth faster than your foundational pieces—but they also can lose money faster.

Your next tier continues to increase risk while increasing upside. This could be short-term rentals, medium-term rentals, or a live-in flip. These properties tend to produce more income but require more time to manage, and the effort makes scaling more difficult. It would be extremely hard to build the foundation of your portfolio on assets like this because they require far more time, energy, and attention, and they have increased risk. These asset classes are more sensitive to shifts in the economy, market trends, and competition from other investors. Highly desired for their income-producing potential, they represent a significant risk to your portfolio and thus make a weak base.

At the apex of your pyramid is your highest-risk, highest-reward assets. These should make up the smallest percentage of your portfolio. Opportunities like flipping homes, luxury properties, hospitality asset classes, speculative investing, cryptocurrencies, and series A financing (investing in other companies at early stages) are all in this category. The low percentage of your portfolio they represent provides you with the additional time they require to manage correctly, and the strong base of low-risk assets they are built on helps shield and protect you from the market shifts inherent in their nature. Constructing your portfolio in this fashion will provide you with the strongest opportunity to build your wealth safely.

Wealth built to last is not just about the right assets but also about the right *amount* of assets, accumulated in the right way, and in the right proportions.

One last factor: Your portfolio should consider the assets you buy *and* how you earn your income. In other words, those who have a solid, full-time, W-2 job are stepping into this scenario with a strong base to their pyramid already started. This is especially true of those working in solid industries like government, health, or local municipalities. Business owners, 1099 workers, or those in sales do have a form of consistent income, but while it is less stable than other positions, it also comes with more upside. Don't forget to include your current income streams in your portfolio. Before you can quit your job and live off the income of your assets, you'll need to build that strong foundation.

As you add assets into your portfolio that are cash flow strong rather than equity strong, make good cash flow your foundation and build equity asset on top of that. If you don't plan on quitting your job, it makes sense to focus on equity growth over cash flow (since that is more effective at building wealth) with the understanding that equity will be converted into cash flow later. If you want to quit your job at some point, focus on strong cash-flowing assets that will buy you back the time you need to leave your job. In both cases, portfolio architecture is the key to understanding what assets to buy, when to buy them, and when to leave your job.

Defense-Focused Strategies

Invest in What You Know

During the cryptocurrency and NFT crazes between 2017 and 2022, it was tempting to get involved. Virtual real estate, tied closely to the rise of cryptos, made some people a lot of money during the same time. It also made people lose a lot of money too. What kept me safe from investing in these bubbles was my commitment to invest only in what I know and understand.

Survivorship bias describes the bias that stems from the fact that survivors live to tell the tale (and so unsuccessful outcomes are ignored). When you hear about someone who made money investing in penny stocks, who got into Uber or Coinbase early, or who made millions in virtual real estate, it's important to remember you are hearing the story of only the few people who did well. The unknown who lost money don't announce their failures. Even in assets that are traditionally safe, like real estate, we tend to hear the stories of only those who did well—or stories that are exaggerated to make it sound like the investor did better than they really did.

Avoid FOMO

It is not possible to know if buying a celebrity's NFT will be a good decision ten years from now, but don't let the fear of missing out (FOMO) make your decisions for you, even if you hear stories of others who made good money. The tip of the iceberg is the only part we see, but it is a small overall percentage of the total object. Forgoing a potential opportunity in something you aren't familiar with to instead put your capital toward an asset class you *do* understand and can control is always the better decision.

As noted earlier in the book, pyramid schemes take advantage of the same FOMO weakness in people. The pyramid opportunity is often presented in a logical and can't-miss manner. The presenter discusses the information in a way your brain can understand. They bait you with equal parts excitement and FOMO and cause you to lose your common sense and make a decision that is clearly foolish (but only in hindsight). I've seen this happen to many smart, strong, and capable people. Avoid putting your money into anything you don't understand, especially if the opportunity is brought to you by someone else.

Avoid Foreclosure

Foreclosure occurs when the borrower cannot make payments on their loan. When this happens, the lender initiates a process to take the title from the borrower and then sells or operates the asset themselves to recoup the money they lent the borrower to buy the asset. This does not happen often in real estate, but it can during specific windows in the market when sales are down, prices are down, and vacancy is high. These windows are almost always tied to economic recessions.

For a foreclosure to occur, two things need to happen: The property must fail to cash flow, and the owner must have run out of reserves. If only one of these conditions is present, a foreclosure won't happen. This is why foreclosures tend to occur most frequently during recessions; borrowers have burned through their reserves and tenants have lost their jobs and are unable to pay their rent. The key to avoiding foreclosure is to break your reliance on tenant rent and your own reserves. Find alternative income sources that make you bulletproof, like starting additional businesses, working additional jobs, picking up overtime, or using the other strategies highlighted in the Offense section.

Don't Quit Too Soon

I recommend people do *not* retire as soon as they escape the entrapment pattern. These decisions are usually made during economic booms—times when tenants have no problem paying rent, values are increasing year over year, and money is easily pouring in. While it can be tempting to quit your job during these environments, think again. This is like the runner who sees no one behind him during the last half mile of a race and starts to enjoy the victory before it's achieved. This opens the opportunity for another runner to pass you before you cross the finish line.

Always prepare for worst-case scenarios. Make your decisions with a bad market in mind, not a strong one. This is especially difficult to do if you've had a decade of prosperous economic conditions. Whatever you think is enough to keep in reserves, keep more. Have more cash flow coming in each month than you can spend, so your savings continually increase. Keep your lifestyle inexpensive to increase your level of safety. Rather than living off tenants' rent alone, consider adding additional income streams through business endeavors, business ownership, or consulting gigs. Continually add to the base of your pyramid in any way you can.

Let Your Assets Buy Your Toys

Early in the book, I provided examples of celebrities and businesspeople who built big wealth and lost it all because they did not track their income. This happens when people are spending large amounts of money without knowing how much is coming or going, an unfortunate side effect of "easy come, easy go" money. Finding financial freedom and delaying gratification for years is only fun if, at some point, you get to enjoy that money. Since there will be a certain point where you want to buy toys and enjoy life, it's important to understand how to do so in a way that will keep you from going broke.

The key is to have your assets buy your toys. You can buy Ferraris, trips to the Bahamas, and multiple luxury homes—as long as they are paid for by the cash flow from your assets, not the income you are actively earning. Solid bookkeeping makes this easy to track: Keep separate books for the income your assets produce and what you produce. Each business I run has a separate profit and loss statement that tracks its monthly profit. The is the same manner that I use to I track each asset's monthly performance and how much income that asset made or lost. I base my lifestyle on the income generated by my assets, not my business income, so I'll never run out of money.

This can be accomplished in two ways: The first is to buy your toys with debt and use the income from your assets to pay the debt. This strategy is more effective when interest rates are low, making debt cheaper. For those who don't like taking on consumer debt to buy their toys, you can refinance your investment properties to pull money out of the portfolio, or the cash flow from the assets can be saved to pay cash for the toys. Both approaches make sure any "play" money you spend is not created by your time and effort, but from the performance of assets that will generate income long after the car, home, or vacation is paid off.

Zoom Out

Zooming out is taking a step back when you feel fear and avoiding an emotionally charged decision. It is my strategy for not taking the easy road when I feel the pressure, fear, or anxiety that inevitably occur in business and real estate investing. Some of our worst decisions are made when we are tired, weary, scared, or can't see an immediate way out of a bad situation. Our primordial instincts kick in, telling us to protect ourselves at all costs. In many situations, this means selling a property before we need to, backing out of a deal rather than negotiating, or quitting on a business when it could be reorganized. To avoid these disasters, practice zooming out.

We often zoom in on the source of danger. When mountain bikers see a boulder or tree root in their path, it's common for them to focus on the danger and subconsciously steer their bike right into it. When soldiers and police officers are faced with a threat, such as a firearm or knife wielded by a violent person, it is common to focus on the weapon rather than something they can use as cover and protection. People in scary situations do better when they actively slow down, breathe deeply, and zoom out from the situation, opening their mind and—literally—their peripheral vision to opportunities they miss when they're zoomed in.

I've seen this many times with first-time home buyers. Not well capitalized, unaware of real estate investing principles, and scared out of their mind, they teeter on the verge of wanting to move forward and wanting to back out. Sleepless nights and massive anxiety can be crippling and terrifying. Then the home inspection report enters the scenario. As an experienced agent, I see a report reflecting a home with very small, cosmetic issues like cracks in the plaster of old drywall. The inexperienced first-time home buyer fixates on the report and believes they are buying a crack with a house around it.

I've learned that helping buyers zoom out is the only way to bring perspective to the situation. The same is true for agents too; sharing our problems, worries, and concerns with other investors can be fruitful because they see your situation more clearly, can offer advice, and give you a perspective that helps you zoom out.

One situation that was especially embarrassing for me was when I was in the middle of several rehab-gone-wrong scenarios. Contractor budgets had skyrocketed at the same time my business income had all but ceased. Lumber shortages, labor shortages, and competition from other investors created havoc in the prices I had budgeted for the square footage I was adding to three separate properties.

I feared running out of money before the projects could be completed. The only option I could see was to sell other assets to convert the equity into cash to pay the contractors. As I shared my dilemma with another investor, they asked a simple question: "Don't you have any assets paid off in cash you can refinance?" As simple as this was, I had missed it. In my worry, fear, and worst-case scenario thinking, I had completely forgotten about three assets I owned free and clear that I could pull money out of within thirty days. This conversation led me to look at the rest of my portfolio, and I realized I had four additional properties with massive equity I could cash out as well.

Not only did I find the money for the contractors, but I bought five more cash-flowing properties with the money I had left over—being careful not to buy anything that would need labor or materials!

Offense-Focused Strategies

Time in the Market

Many investors make the mistake of trying to time the market: finding the best time to buy (the absolute bottom), purchasing assets, letting them increase in value, and selling at the perfect moment. Investors who are unfamiliar with the fundamentals of real estate will frequently take this time-the-market approach, unaware it isn't possible. This idea comes from stocks, where money is made by buying low and selling high.

Real estate is different from stocks. Values of real estate assets do not spike up and crash down based on news cycles, international events, or herd psychology. Assets are not bought and sold via computer programs designed to respond to particular real estate market behavior. Real estate values respond much more slowly, with more emotion involved from the buyers and sellers. Unlike stocks, residential real estate was not created to build wealth but to give someone a place to live. Creating wealth is a secondary purpose of real estate, largely possible because of inflation. Do not treat real estate like stocks, because the strategy and approach are different.

Trying to time the bottom of a real estate market is made particularly difficult because of interference by the federal government. The Fed's efforts to create economic stimulus through quantitative easing, increasing the money supply, and lowering or raising interest rates wreaks havoc on one's ability to make sound financial decisions based on the fundamental understandings of supply and demand. Many investors were thrown curveballs between 2013 and 2022 when they expected the market to slow down or crash, only to find prices rose with economic stimulus, preventing common sense results from occurring.

Rather than trying to time the market, it's better to increase your time *in* the market. This does not mean to foolishly buy property when a market correction is likely. It means to focus more on the things you can control in the deal—cash flow, forcing equity, buying equity, asset class, and location—than the things you cannot control, like timing in the market. Many investors have lost money passing on strong, fundamentally sound and solid opportunities—not because the deals were bad, but because they hoped they'd get an even better deal if they waited.

Three Rules of Real Estate

The three rules of real estate—location, location, location—stand the test of time. Buying in better neighborhoods will always be in your favor over the long run. Buying in states with increasing populations or cities with constricted supply makes you a highly disciplined, wealth-building journeyman. Mistakes are often made in real estate when we make something more complicated than it is. Tinkering with spreadsheets, agonizing over what color paint to select, or working hard to get positive reviews all pale in comparison to buying real estate in the best locations and just waiting.

While location should be the first thing to consider, it isn't the *only* thing to consider. When a property is sold, three things determine its sale price: location, condition, and price. However, of the three, location is the only one you can't improve. You can't throw enough money or adjust enough details to make up for a property being in a location where no one wants to live, whether it's related to crime, pollution, overhead aircraft, flood zones, or other conditions you have no control over. Buying in the right location is the best thing you can do to help prevent disaster in your purchase decision.

Location is the first condition considered by tenants in long-term rentals, guests in short-term rentals, traveling workers in mid-term rentals, or businesses in commercial property. If location is the first thing considered by your tenants, it should be the first thing considered by you. Location has the biggest impact on demand, and demand affects performance. Finding locations with high demand that also have limited supply is the magic formula in real estate investing. Playing the long game here is buying in the best locations and letting time and inflation do their work.

Learn to Pivot

Pivoting is an important part in building wealth that lasts. Much like professional sports franchises that build a team by drafting specific players who fit a mold or style that works for that team, your approach to business will have to change to fit the changing times. Those who pivot—that is, adjust quickly—will survive the longest. We've all heard the examples of Blockbuster taking too long to pivot, or Polaroid going from an industry titan to going out of business. Failing to pivot can destroy wealth you've already built.

The keys to pivoting successfully are to pivot faster than your competition and to be aware when it's necessary. "Stick to what works" is a great slogan, but when what works changes and you don't, you end up sticking to what *doesn't* work. For a long time, people would use search engines to find company sites and do their research that way. Businesses would pay big money to have professional websites with FAQs, contact forms, and lengthy "About Us" sections. This all changed when social media took over.

Within a few short years, people were searching Facebook, Instagram, and TikTok to determine what a business had to offer. Those who failed to integrate social media or use it regularly ended up losing business to those who were projecting the image they wanted others to see. Those who believed that social media was for personal use and websites were for business learned the hard way that this was no longer true. We are judged for everything, both business and personal, via our social media representation.

I made a pivoting mistake of my own when I bought too many properties at one time, assuming the permitting process was similar to what I had experienced the previous time I bought in bulk. I found out the hard way it wasn't. What I thought would take two to three weeks ended up taking four to five months, and that was only for the construction. Short-term rental permits doubled that timeline, ballooning my carrying costs and bleeding my reserves, all hitting me at the exact same time. Moving forward, I was sure to check on situations like that before buying in bulk.

Many investors move into an area when they hear other investors are buying there, only to find they are too late to the party and the returns they heard about are no longer available. Some investors jump into asset classes that were popular years ago, only to find the supply has increased and their competition is greater than they anticipated. This has been seen recently in the short-term rental space, for example, thanks to the popularity of platforms like Airbnb. As information becomes more readily available, strategies that work spread, and cycles complete much faster than when it took longer for successful strategies to spread.

KEY TAKEAWAYS

- Financial freedom is the result of years of discipline, personal growth, and prudent decision-making.
- Understanding how to build wealth that lasts and avoiding easy money is crucial to not just attaining but also maintaining financial freedom.
- In real estate investing, there are two approaches to creating wealth: Pursue cash flow or buy assets. Both approaches create wealth.
- Your net worth improves when your assets increase in value; your passive income improves when you acquire cash flow; and the goal is to win in both areas without any headaches.
- Of the ten ways you make money in real estate, five apply to equity: buying equity, forcing equity, market equity, natural equity, and loan paydown.
- Avoid get-rich-quick schemes. They never work.
- Portfolio architecture is the science of building a portfolio that is safe, contains flexibility, and will stand the test of time. It involves combining several different asset classes in various amounts that cover for the weaknesses of the other asset classes you own.
- Avoid putting your money into anything you don't understand, especially if the opportunity is brought to you by someone else.
- For a foreclosure to occur, the property must fail to cash flow and the owner must have run out of reserves.
- Make your decisions with a bad market in mind, not a strong one.
- Three things determine sale price: location, condition, and price. Only location cannot be improved.

CONCLUSION

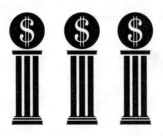

Chapter 17
THE SUMMIT

All you need is the plan, the road map, and the courage
to press on to your destination.
—EARL NIGHTINGALE

The Journey, the Climb, and the Grind

When I was in college and dedicated to saving $500 a week from restaurant tips, my peers made fun of me. When I turned down trips to Cancún, expensive dinners, or nights out and worked instead, they said I was working my life away. When I tracked every dollar I made and could tell people how much was budgeted for car insurance, gas, gym memberships, and more, they told me I overanalyzed things. When I stayed late to work at night, the other waiters told me to live a little.

These people were well-intentioned, but I'm glad I didn't listen. I had a small voice inside screaming at me to stay focused, stay on the path, and work even harder. This voice was possibly the biggest blessing I had in my youth. My guess is you have a form of the same voice.

It shows up as guilt every time you swipe your credit card to buy something you didn't really need, or when you order something online just because you're bored. It shows up as shame when you consider joining a group of people on the same path, knowing it will be good for you, but you're embarrassed for others to see your financial situation. That voice is trying to help you. To do so, it has to tell you the truth—and sometimes the truth is hard to hear.

It does feel great when you follow that voice, and it leads you on a journey to improve your situation. The guilt is replaced by pride when you say no to anything that isn't in your budget. The shame is replaced by excitement at belonging to something bigger and something worthwhile, and seeing your savings grow every month. The voice will lead you on, like it did for me, if you take the first few steps. Get honest about your situation, start tracking your spending, make a budget, then make changes in yourself to improve your defense potential. That voice is your friend, and our true friends tell us the truth, no matter what.

The money I saved from working in restaurants became the down payments for my first two houses. The appreciation in those houses grew to a total of over half-a-million dollars that I later pulled out to buy five more houses. The ingredients of capital, knowledge, results, time, and leverage turned those initial nights of staying late at work into seven properties with well over a million dollars in equity between them. More importantly, they functioned as the foundation for learning how real estate works, building a real estate business, hosting a podcast, and more. Meanwhile, the well-intentioned friends and coworkers who warned me about throwing my life away are still doing the exact same thing: waiting tables, working low-wage W-2 jobs, and struggling financially.

I didn't work my life away. I worked to build momentum that carried me to building successful businesses, and I designed a life that allows me much more freedom. I still work, but now I work on what I want to, on things that bring me joy, and from the locations where I want to be. I don't stress over the cost of a flat tire or grocery prices increasing. The advice I received was about living for the moment; I chose to live for the future.

I feel for those struggling financially. It's horrible. Each year it gets harder to buy the types of assets that provided me with financial freedom. That's why I'm so adamant about teaching you. I want to see you grow, see you thrive, see you win, and see you build momentum that will take you to an exciting life full of opportunities and freedom.

I've been honest about my story. I didn't buy crypto to build wealth. I worked long hours, pushed myself to uncomfortable places, and took on as much responsibility and as many challenges as I could. I treated opportunities like they were scarce and valuable and made the most of each of them. I wasn't perfect, often staying in a comfortable situation for too long before taking the jump or needing others to push me. I didn't value health like I should have and was slow to learn new things, instead choosing to stick with what I knew and just do it more frequently. I lacked vision at times, and it slowed my progress. What got me through was having the right people looking after me.

This book is my way of doing the same for you. Maybe you're stuck in a comfort zone and haven't realized it until now. Maybe you were really good at something like sports, school, or a hobby, then stopped. The voice inside has been reminding you of the greatness in you, but you haven't given it a chance to manifest. Is there an opportunity for you to get back to that place of greatness, in the marketplace or in your job, and start living in excellence again? Have you let your weight go, or stopped making and pursuing goals? My guess is a part of you has died, like it has in all of us, and it's waiting to be woken up and allowed to dream again.

Nights spent sleeping in my car or going to the gym alone at 2:00 a.m. to work out while everyone else partied wasn't fun. Being treated unfairly for chasing the vision I had hurt sometimes. What *is* fun and what *doesn't* hurt is the fruit of all that work. I don't sit in traffic on my way to a job. I wake up when I want to, not when I have to. I see money as a seed to plant, not as a means to survive. The journey—as hard, uphill, and full of setbacks at it was—was absolutely worth it.

What's one thing of value you have that you didn't work extremely hard to get? Every parent endures the sleepless nights and mental gymnastics of keeping a baby alive; the wealth-building journey is no different. It's going to be hard, but it has to be hard, because everything worth having is hard. Without the personal growth and discipline involved in building wealth the right way, you'd lose it. A fool and their money are soon parted.

Goals, Groups, and Accountability

When you reach the summit of the real estate mountain and you see the view below, the feeling of accomplishment and pride in yourself is incredible. It's the same for trading the entrapment cycle for the freedom cycle and experiencing financial freedom. There's nothing like it. The relationships you build along the way will be incredible. No journey this valuable and difficult can be accomplished alone. Whether it's online forums, meetups, or podcasts, there are many places where you can learn from others along the journey.

As I mentioned at the start of this book, you will increase your odds of success by surrounding yourself with others on a similar journey. Those budgeting their money, seeking promotions, or starting businesses can be huge assets to each other. If you're feeling the call to pursue the journey laid out in this book, I highly recommend you find one (or several) groups to join. The members of Gobundance helped me leave law enforcement and become an entrepreneur. My group Spartan League teaches our members to budget their money, protect their assets, and have a plan to invest in real estate. My Discord channel, DG's World, gives members access to my team of experts to review their deals, learn from, bounce ideas off, and be exposed to what successful people are doing. The goal is to create a community where both wins and losses are shared and encouragement is abundant. It's tough to know what greatness is inside you when it's not being fed, watered, and developed.

Having goals can be a form of accountability. If you don't have a goal, you can't fail—but you also can't succeed, and you won't change. I make goals every year for each business and each part of my life that's important to me. In the same way my dollars are given a plan, so are my businesses and goals. If you're not looking for that much intentional interaction, I still advise you to find at least one person you trust and tell them the following.

I am committed to making significant life changes with my money, and I'd like you to hold me accountable for five things.

1. I will make a budget and give every dollar a job.
2. I will track my money every month.
3. I will give my absolute best every day at work.
4. I will continually look for ways to earn more income and provide more value.
5. I will invest in real estate for my future.

You can copy and paste this information to send to them. It's important that while you're committed, while you're on fire, you take action that can't be reversed. Commit to your journey with someone. Ask for their help. Make allies of others and, by all means, look for groups where you can find support.

There is no elevator to the top of the mountain. The journey is full of obstacles and challenges, but this is the way to build real wealth that lasts. The journey *does* get easier over time. Many who build enough wealth to be able to retire choose not to. The joy and fun they find in taking on new challenges, starting new businesses, or buying new investments motivates them to continue. As you start on this journey, I hope the pieces come together and your motivation to be free to do as you wish with your life and your money grows. The first steps are always the hardest, but the view at the top is worth it.

Too many people have shared a false gospel of wealth-building: that it comes easy, without effort, and without change from you. This book instead paints a very clear picture of what it takes to get to the top of the mountain so we can share the view together, tell stories of what the hero's journey is like, and throw down ropes for those coming up behind us.

It's been my pleasure to share this part of the journey with you, and I'd love to continue to assist you on your path!

BIBLIOGRAPHY

Allen, David. *Getting Things Done: The Art of Stress-Free Productivity*. New York: Penguin, 2015.

Allen, Lark. "2022 Coffee Statistics: Consumption, Purchases, and Preferences." Drive Research. https://www.driveresearch.com/market-research-company-blog/coffee-survey.

Allen, Summer. "The Science of Generosity." Greater Good Science Center. https://ggsc.berkeley.edu/images/uploads/GGSC-JTF_White_Paper-Generosity-FINAL.pdf.

Arias, Elizabeth, Betzaida Tejada-Vera, Kenneth D. Kochanek, and Farida B. Ahmad. "Provisional Life Expectancy Estimates for 2021." CDC's National Center for Health Statistics. https://www.cdc.gov/nchs/data/vsrr/vsrr023.pdf.

"Barbara Corcoran's Wild Real Estate Tactics You'll Want to Repeat." Interview by David Greene and Rob Abasolo. *BiggerPockets Real Estate*. Podcast. May 9, 2023. www.biggerpockets.com/blog/real-estate-763

Blankert, Tim and Melvyn R. W. Hamstra, "Imagining Success: Multiple Achievement Goals and the Effectiveness of Imagery." *Basic and Applied Social Psychology* 39, no. 1 (December 7, 2016): 60–67. https://doi.org/10.1080/01973533.2016.1255947.

Boogaard, Kat. "What Is Parkinson's Law and Why Is It Sabotaging Your Productivity?" *Work Life* (blog). Atlassian. February 12, 2022. https://www.atlassian.com/blog/productivity/what-is-parkinsons-law.

Chartrand, Tanya L., and John A. Bargh. "The Chameleon Effect: The Perception–Behavior Link and Social Interaction." Journal of Personality and Social Psychology 76, no. 6 (January 1, 1999): 893–910. https://doi.org/10.1037/0022-3514.76.6.893.

Cialdini, Robert. "The Science of Persuasion: Seven Principles of Persuasion." Influence at Work. https://www.influenceatwork.com/7-principles-of-persuasion.

Clason, George S. *The Richest Man in Babylon*. Denver, CO: BiggerPockets Publishing, 2022.

Clear, James. *Atomic Habits: An Easy & Proven Way to Build Good Habits & Break Bad Ones*. New York: Penguin Publishing Group, 2018.

Clifford, Catherine. "Tony Robbins: This Is the Secret to Happiness in One Word." CNBC. October 6, 2017. https://www.cnbc.com/2017/10/06/tony-robbins-this-is-the-secret-to-happiness-in-one-word.html.

"Consumer Price Index: 2021 in Review." The Economics Daily: U.S. Bureau of Labor Statistics. January 14, 2022. https://www.bls.gov/opub/ted/2022/consumer-price-index-2021-in-review.htm.

Crouch, Michelle. "13 Things Lotto Winners Won't Tell You: Life After Winning the Lottery." *Reader's Digest*. April 27, 2023. https://www.rd.com/list/13-things-lottery-winners/.

Dieker, Nicole. "Guide to Credit Card Minimum Payments." Bankrate. May 25, 2022. https://www.bankrate.com/finance/credit-cards/guide-to-credit-card-minimum-payments/.

"Eating to Boost Energy." Harvard Health. July 26, 2011. https://www.health.harvard.edu/healthbeat/eating-to-boost-energy.

Egan, Matt. "Mike Tyson: I Didn't Think I'd Survive My 30s." CNN Business. May 24, 2017. https://money.cnn.com/2017/05/24/investing/mike-tyson-bankruptcy/index.html.

"83 Percent of Organizations Have Skills Gaps, according to ATD Research." Association for Talent Development. December 19, 2018. https://www.td.org/press-release/83-percent-of-organizations-have-skills-gaps-according-to-atd-research.

Elkins, Kathleen. "8 Ways Rich People View the World Differently than the Average Person." CNBC. October 11, 2016. https://www.cnbc.com/2016/10/11/8-ways-rich-people-view-the-world-differently-than-the-average-person.html.

Erb, Kelly Phillips. "IRS to Rapper: It's Hammertime!" Forbes. December 8, 2013. https://www.forbes.com/sites/kellyphillipserb/2013/12/08/irs-to-rapper-its-hammertime/.

Fay, Bill. "Debt in America: Statistics and Demographics." Debt.org. April 3, 2023. https://www.debt.org/faqs/americans-in-debt/demographics/.

Flynn, Jack. "Average American Income | 25 U.S. Salary Statistics." Zippia, Oct. 26, 2022, https://www.zippia.com/advice/average-american-income/.

Foster, Sarah. "What Is Quantitative Easing?" Bankrate, March 8, 2022, https://www.bankrate.com/banking/federal-reserve/what-is-quantitative-easing/.

"Fourth's Truth about Dining Out Survey Report." Fourth. May 15, 2019. https://www.fourth.com/wp-content/uploads/2023/01/US_White_Paper_Truth_About_Dining_Out_Survey_Report_110119.pdf.

"FRED Economic Data." St. Louis Fed. https://fred.stlouisfed.org/series/M2SL.

Gardner, Howard. Frames of Mind: The Theory of Multiple Intelligences. New York: Basic Books, 1983.

Goldhill, Olivia. "Neuroscientists Say Multitasking Literally Drains the Energy Reserves of Your Brain." Quartz. July 3, 2016. https://qz.com/722661/neuroscientists-say-multitasking-literally-drains-the-energy-reserves-of-your-brain.

Goleman, Daniel. Emotional Intelligence: Why It Can Matter More than IQ. New York: Random House, 2012.

Gottlieb, Jeff. "Michael Jackson Trial: Pop Star Was 'Tapped Out,' Millions in Debt." Los Angeles Times. August 12, 2013. https://www.latimes.com/local/lanow/la-xpm-2013-aug-12-la-me-ln-michael-jackson-debt-20130812-story.html.

Greenwood, Chelsea. "Firstborn Children Are More Likely to Be CEOs, and Other Things Your Birth Order Can Predict about Your Future." Business Insider. April 8, 2019. https://www.businessinsider.com/siblings-birth-order-2018-4.

Grover, Tim S., and Shari Wenk, Winning: The Unforgiving Race to Greatness. Simon and Schuster, 2021.

Hamermesh, Daniel S. Beauty Pays: Why Attractive People Are More Successful. Princeton University Press, 2011.

Harkin, Benjamin, Thomas Webb, Betty Chang, Yael Benn, Andrew Prestwich, Mark Connor, Ian Kellar, and Paschal Sheeran. "Frequently Monitoring Progress toward Goals Increases Chance of Success." American Psychological Association. October 28, 2015. https://www.apa.org/news/press/releases/2015/10/progress-goals.

Holiday, Ryan. The Obstacle Is the Way: The Timeless Art of Turning Trials into Triumph. New York: Portfolio/Penguin, 2014.

Johnson, Nicole. "Here's How Much Home Prices Have Risen since 1950." Better. October 19, 2021. https://better.com/content/how-much-home-prices-have-risen-since-1950.

Jordan, Michael, and Mark Vancil. I Can't Accept Not Trying: Michael Jordan on the Pursuit of Excellence. San Francisco: HarperSanFrancisco, 1994.

King, Jude. "The Science-Backed Secret to Rapidly Improving Any Skill." Medium. June 11, 2019. https://medium.com/swlh/the-science-backed-secret-to-rapidly-improving-any-skill-530e573aa546.

Kniffin, Kevin M., Brian Wansink, and Mitsuru Shimizu. "Sports at Work." Journal of Leadership & Organizational Studies 22, no. 2 (June 16, 2014): 217–230, https://doi.org/10.1177/1548051814538099.

Kolmar, Chris. "24 Powerful Cosmetics Industry Statistics [2023]: What's Trending in the Beauty Business?" Zippia. May 12, 2023. https://www.zippia.com/advice/cosmetics-industry-statistics/.

Maguire, Eleanor A, Katherine Woollett, and Hugo J Spiers. "London taxi drivers and bus drivers: A structural MRI and neuropsychological analysis." *Hippocampus 16*, no. 12 (2006): 1091–1101. https://doi.org/10.1002/hipo.20233.

McCormack, Kayla. "Examining the Price of Eating at Home vs Eating Out." SoFi Learn. April 27, 2023. https://www.sofi.com/learn/content/price-of-eating-at-home-vs-eating-out/.

Melore, Chris. "Want a Higher Salary? Acquiring New Skills Is More Important than Having Connections." Study Finds. August 24, 2022. https://studyfinds.org/higher-salary-acquiring-new-skills/.

"Michael Jackson Died Deeply in Debt." *Billboard*. June 26, 2009. https://www.billboard.com/music/music-news/michael-jackson-died-deeply-in-debt-268276/.

Moy, Edmund C. "Understanding the Money Supply." Wheaton Center for Faith, Politics & Economics. 2021. https://www.wheaton.edu/academics/academic-centers/wheaton-center-for-faith-politics-and-economics/resource-center/articles/2021/understanding-the-money-supply/.

"M2 Definition and Meaning in the Money Supply." Investopedia. May 27, 2023. https://www.investopedia.com/terms/m/m2.asp.

Mylett, Ed. "One Day Is Not 24 Hours." The Outcome. YouTube video. September 22, 2022. https://www.youtube.com/watch?v=Y8B_1uZTLws.

Nassauer, Sarah. "Using Scent as a Marketing Tool, Stores Hope It—and Shoppers—Will Linger." *The Wall Street Journal*. May 20, 2014. https://www.wsj.com/articles/using-scent-as-a-marketing-tool-stores-hope-it-and-shoppers-will-linger-1400627455.

"Negative Thinking Overview." Rethink Mental Illness. https://www.rethink.org/advice-and-information/about-mental-illness/learn-more-about-symptoms/negative-thinking/.

"Old Idea, New Economy: Rediscovering Apprenticeships." Interview by Sasha Aslanian. *The Educate Podcast*, APM Reports. September 3, 2018. https://www.apmreports.org/episode/2018/09/03/old-idea-new-economy-rediscovering-apprenticeships.

Olen, Helaine. "Buying Coffee Every Day Isn't Why You're in Debt." *Slate*. May 26, 2016. https://slate.com/business/2016/05/the-latte-is-a-lie-and-buying-coffee-has-nothing-to-do-with-debt-an-excerpt-from-helaine-olens-pound-foolish.html.

Oppong, Thomas. "Psychological Secrets to Hack Your Way to Better Life Habits." *Observer*. March 22, 2017. https://observer.com/2017/03/psychological-secrets-hack-better-life-habits-psychology-productivity/.

Orem, Tina. "What Is a 1031 Exchange? A Guide to the Basics, Rules & What to Know." NerdWallet. February 2, 2023. https://www.nerdwallet.com/article/taxes/1031-exchange-like-kind?trk_location=ssrp&trk_query=What%20Is%20a%201031%20Exchange&trk_page=1&trk_position=1.

The Oracles. "Real Estate Is Still the Best Investment You Can Make Today, Millionaires Say—Here's Why." CNBC. October 2, 2019. https://www.cnbc.com/2019/10/01/real-estate-is-still-the-best-investment-you-can-make-today-millionaires-say.html.

"The Origins of the Law of Supply and Demand." Investopedia. September 21, 2021. https://www.investopedia.com/ask/answers/030415/who-discovered-law-supply-and-demand.asp.

Parys, Sabrina, and Tina Orem. "2022–2023 Tax Brackets and Federal Income Tax Rates." NerdWallet. July 7, 2023. https://www.nerdwallet.com/article/taxes/federal-income-tax-brackets.

Peale, Norman Vincent. *The Power of Positive Thinking*. New York: Touchstone, 2003.

Perez, Dikla, Yael Steinhart, Amir Grinstein, and Meike Morren, "Consistency in Identity-Related Sequential Decisions." PLOS ONE 16, no. 12 (December 8, 2021): e0260048. https://doi.org/10.1371/journal.pone.0260048.

Pierson, Judith. "The Power of the Subconscious Mind." ResearchGate. November 9, 2022. https://www.researchgate.net/publication/365211107_The_Power_of_the_Subconscious_Mind.

Pressman, Sarah D., Karen A. Matthews, Sheldon Cohen, Lynn M. Martire, Michael Scheier, Andrew Baum, and Richard Schulz. "Association of Enjoyable Leisure Activities with Psychological and Physical Well-Being." *Psychosomatic Medicine* 71, no. 7 (2009): 725–32. https://doi.org/10.1097/psy.0b013e3181ad7978.

Sandberg, Erica. "Survey: More Americans Are Carrying Debt, and Many of Them Don't Know Their APRs." Bankrate. January 10, 2023. https://www.bankrate.com/finance/credit-cards/more-americans-carrying-debt-and-many-dont-know-apr/.

"S&P CoreLogic Case-Shiller Index Reports 18.8% Annual Home Price Gain for Calendar 2021." S&P Dow Jones Indices. February 22, 2022. https://www.spglobal.com/spdji/en/index-announcements/article/sp-corelogic-case-shiller-index-reports-188-annual-home-price-gain-for-calendar-2021/.

"69% of Americans in Urban Areas Are Living Paycheck to Paycheck; 14 Percentage Points Higher than Suburban Consumers." LendingClub. May 24, 2023. https://ir.lendingclub.com/news/news-details/2023/69-of-Americans-in-Urban-Areas-are-Living-Paycheck-to-Paycheck-14-Percentage-Points-Higher-than-Suburban-Consumers/default.aspx#:~:text=Sixty%2Dnine%20percent%20of%20consumers,reported%20living%20paycheck%20to%20paycheck.

Stevenson, Betsey. "Beyond the Classroom: Using Title IX to Measure the Return to High School Sports." National Bureau of Economic Research. February 1, 2010. https://doi.org/10.3386/w15728.

Straus, Sharon E, Mallory O. Johnson, Christine Marquez, and Mitchell D. Feldman. "Characteristics of Successful and Failed Mentoring Relationships." *Academic Medicine* 88, no. 1 (January 1, 2013): 82–89. https://doi.org/10.1097/acm.0b013e31827647a0.

"225 Years of Tar Heels: Dean Smith." The University of North Carolina at Chapel Hill. May 13, 2019. https://www.unc.edu/posts/2019/03/08/225-years-of-tar-heels-dean-smith/.

"25 Surprising Leadership Statistics to Take Note Of." Apollo Technical LLC. May 25, 2022. https://www.apollotechnical.com/leadership-statistics/.

Vásquez-Vera, Hugo, Laia Palència, Ingrid Magna, Carlos Mena, Jaime Martínez Neira, and Carme Borrell. "The Threat of Home Eviction and Its Effects on Health through the Equity Lens: A Systematic Review." *Social Science & Medicine* 175 (February 1, 2017): 199–208. https://doi.org/10.1016/j.socscimed.2017.01.010.

"What Is the Money Supply, and How Does It Relate to Inflation and the Federal Reserve?" USAFacts. July 21, 2022. https://usafacts.org/articles/what-is-the-money-supply-and-how-does-it-relate-to-inflation-and-the-federal-reserve/.

Williams, Geoff. "7 Tricks Advertisers Use to Make You Spend Money." U.S. News & World Report. September 10, 2015. https://money.usnews.com/money/personal-finance/articles/2015/09/10/7-tricks-advertisers-use-to-make-you-spend-money.

Willink, Jocko, and Leif Babin. *Extreme Ownership: How U.S. Navy SEALs Lead and Win*. New York: St. Martin's Press, 2015.

Yeung, Pokin, "Why You're a Startup Founder: Nature and Nurture." TechCrunch. April 7, 2012. https://techcrunch.com/2012/04/07/founder-nature-vs-nurture/.

Zeman, Ned. "Burt Reynolds Isn't Broke, but He's Got a Few Regrets." *Vanity Fair*. November 5, 2015. https://www.vanityfair.com/hollywood/2015/11/burt-reynolds-on-career-bankruptcy-regrets.

Zitelmann, Rainer. "Scientific Study: Luxury Is Not What Motivates Rich People to Become Rich." *Forbes*, June 8, 2020. https://www.forbes.com/sites/rainerzitelmann/2020/06/08/scientific-study-luxury-is-not-what-motivates-rich-people-to-become-rich/.

Acknowledgments

To **Tim Rhode**, who always praised my defense and encouraged me to be wise with money (but still smell the roses).

To **Dave Osborn**, who helped me learn to lead, start businesses, and step up my offense.

To **Brandon Turner**, who gave me the opportunity to influence and guide the BiggerPockets community in wise investing principles.

To **Josh Dorkin**, who built this platform.

To the **publishing team**, who breathed life into this book. Thank you to designers Wendy Dunning and Haley Montgomery; editors Lila Stromer, Mari Shirley, and Hayden Seder; reviewers and collaborators Ali Lupo and Josh Lupo; publishers Katie Miller, Kaylee Walterbach, and Peri Eryigit. And thanks to Savannah Wood, for absolutely slaying and being such a vivrant thing.

And lastly, to **my mom**, who helped support me throughout college so I could get a great financial start for the rest of my life!

More from
BiggerPockets Publishing

If you enjoyed this book, we hope you'll take a moment to check out some of the other great material BiggerPockets offers. Whether you crave freedom or stability, a backup plan, or passive income, **BiggerPockets** empowers you to live life on your own terms through real estate investing.

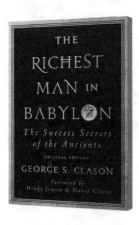

Richest Man in Babylon
Written after the stock market crash of 1929 and set in ancient Babylon, this collection of simple parables has made a huge impact on the way millions of people have approached wealth building. Though the stories are ancient, the wisdom is timeless—including principles of financial planning, frugal living, and wise investing. Including forewords by *BiggerPockets Podcast* and *BiggerPockets Money Podcast* hosts David Greene and Mindy Jensen, this unaltered version of the original text maintains its integrity as one of the greatest financial literacy books of all time.

Buy, Rehab, Rent, Refinance, Repeat
Invest in real estate and never run out of money! In *Buy, Rehab, Rent, Refinance, Repeat*, you'll discover the incredible strategy known as BRRRR—a long-hidden secret of the ultra-rich and those with decades of experience. Author and investor David Greene holds nothing back, sharing the exact systems and processes he used to scale his business from buying two houses per year to buying two houses per *month* using the BRRRR strategy.

Find the **information**, **inspiration**, and **tools** you need to dive right into the world of real estate investing with confidence.

 Sign up today—it's free! Visit **www.BiggerPockets.com**

 Find our books at **www.BiggerPockets.com/store**

Long-Distance Real Estate Investing

Don't let your location dictate your financial freedom: Live where you want, and invest anywhere it makes sense! The rules, technology, and markets have changed: No longer are you forced to invest only in your backyard. In *Long-Distance Real Estate Investing*, learn an in-depth strategy to build profitable rental portfolios through buying, managing, and flipping out-of-state properties from real estate investor and agent David Greene.

The Book on Rental Property Investing

With nearly 400 pages of in-depth advice for building wealth through rental properties, this evergreen best-seller imparts the practical and exciting strategies that investors across the world are using to build significant cash flow through real estate investing. Investor, best-selling author, and longtime co-host of *The BiggerPockets Podcast* Brandon Turner has one goal in mind: to give you every strategy, tool, tip, and technique you need to become a millionaire rental property investor!

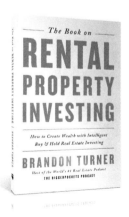

Looking for more?
Join the BiggerPockets Community

BiggerPockets brings together education, tools, and a community of more than 2+ million like-minded members—all in one place. Learn about investment strategies, analyze properties, connect with investor-friendly agents, and more.

Go to **biggerpockets.com** to learn more!

 Listen to a **BiggerPockets Podcast**

 Watch **BiggerPockets on YouTube**

 Join the **Community Forum**

 Learn more on **the Blog**

 Read more **BiggerPockets Books**

 Learn about our **Real Estate Investing Bootcamps**

 Connect with an **Investor-Friendly Real Estate Agent**

 Go Pro! Start, scale, and manage your portfolio with your **Pro Membership**

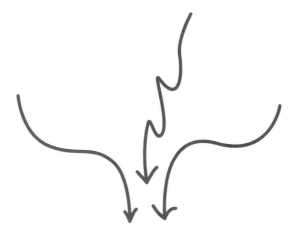

Follow us on social media!

Sign up for a Pro account and take **20 PERCENT OFF** with code **BOOKS20**.

 BiggerPockets®